✑ AN AGE OF ENORMITY

ISAAC ROSENFELD

An Age of Enormity

LIFE AND WRITING IN THE
FORTIES AND FIFTIES

EDITED AND INTRODUCED BY
Theodore Solotaroff

FOREWORD BY *Saul Bellow*

THE WORLD PUBLISHING COMPANY
Cleveland and New York

PUBLISHED BY The World Publishing Company
2231 WEST 110TH STREET, CLEVELAND 2, OHIO

PUBLISHED SIMULTANEOUSLY IN CANADA BY
NELSON, FOSTER & SCOTT LTD.

LIBRARY OF CONGRESS CATALOG CARD NUMBER: 62-10622

FIRST EDITION

CONTENTS

ACKNOWLEDGMENTS

IN SELECTING REVIEWS and articles for inclusion here, I have confined myself to Rosenfeld's published work. It has been easier to include than to exclude, for he had the Midas touch and sooner or later even the casual review of a third-rate book turns to gold. The pieces are arranged in roughly chronological order in keeping with the development of Rosenfeld's career as a critic and with the changing climate of the age and the culture which his writing records. I have exercised a good deal of editorial freedom—and I hope some discretion—in retitling about half of the pieces here to solve the problem of presenting reviews that were, often as not, given a title by an editor that was appropriate only to the page on which the review itself appeared. At the end of each selection, I have noted the periodical and date in which it first appeared. To the *New Republic, Partisan Review, Commentary,* the *Nation,* the *New Leader, Kenyon Review, Midstream,* and the *Jewish Frontier* I am indebted for permission to republish Rosenfeld's contributions. I am also especially indebted to Vasiliki Rosenfeld, Oscar Tarcov, Wallace Markfield, and Aaron Asher for their help in preparing the text and in writing the Introduction.

THEODORE SOLOTAROFF

FOREWORD

by Saul Bellow

ISAAC had a round face and yellowish-brown hair which he combed straight back. He was nearsighted, his eyes pale blue, and he wore round glasses. The space between his large teeth gave his smile an ingenuous charm. He had a belly laugh. It came on him abruptly and often doubled him up. His smiles, however, kindled slowly. He liked to look with avuncular owlishness over the tops of his specs. His wisecracks were often preceded by the pale blue glance. He began, he paused, a sort of mild slyness formed about his lips, and then he said something devastating. More seriously, developing an argument, he gestured like a Russian-Jewish intellectual, a cigarette between two fingers. When he was in real earnest, he put aside these mannerisms, too. A look of strength, sometimes of angry strength, came into his eyes.

He had a short broad figure. His chest was large. But he was round rather than burly, and he could move gracefully. His lazy lounging manner was deceptive. He was quick with his hands and played the flute well, and the recorder superbly. He was haunted, however, by an obscure sense of physical difficulty or deficiency, a biological torment, a disagreement with his own flesh. He seldom enjoyed good health. His color was generally poor, yellowish. At the University of Chicago during the thirties, this was the preferred intellectual complexion. In the winter Isaac was often down with the flu or with attacks of pleurisy. He was told that his skin couldn't bear much exposure to the sun. But during the war when he was Captain Isaac, the entire crew of a barge in the

New York harbor, he had good color. He read Shakespeare and Kierkegaard on the water and found it agreed
with him to be in the open air. He had friends on the
waterfront. In such circumstances Isaac would never be
the visiting intellectual. He never went slumming. It was
impossible not to be attracted by the good nature of his
face, and I assume his ineptitude with ropes touched
the hearts of the deckhands on the tugboats.

I am among his friends perhaps not the best qualified
to speak of him. I loved him, but we were rivals, and I
was peculiarly touchy, vulnerable, hard to deal with—
at times, as I can see now, insufferable, and not always a
constant friend. As for him, his power to attract people
might have made more difference to him than it did.
He wanted their affection, he wanted also to return it . . .
but then these matters we have learned to speak of so
simply have not thereby become simpler.

He had one of those ready, lively, clear minds that
see the relevant thing immediately. In logic and metaphysics he was a natural. He had a bent for theology,
too, which he did everything possible to discourage. His
talent for abstraction displeased him; he was afraid it
indicated a poverty of his feelings, an emotional sterility.
To the overcoming of this supposed sterility, a fault fed
by his talents themselves, exaggerated by them, he devoted his best efforts, his strength. He didn't like to be
praised for achievements he regarded as largely mental.
Heartless abstraction filled him with dread. Originally
his purpose in coming to New York was to study philosophy. During one of his bouts of pleurisy, he went
through Melville and he wrote me that after reading
Moby Dick he could no longer be a logical positivist.

There followed a period of exaggerated "feelings." But
whether he gave himself over to the Theory of Signs or
exclaimed sentimentally over the poor sprouting onions
in an impoverished grocery, Isaac never went very long
without laughing.

He was a playful man. He loved hoaxes, mimicry,
parody, and surrealist poems. He was a marvelous clown.

He imitated steam irons, clocks, airplanes, tugboats, big-game hunters, Russian commissars, Village poets and their girl friends. He tried on the faces of people in restaurants. He was great as Harry Baur in *Crime et Châtiment,* the inspector Porfiry Petrovitch, smoking cigarettes with an underhand Russian grip. He invented Yiddish proletarian poems, he did a translation of Eliot's *Prufrock,* a startling X ray of those hallowed bones which brings Anglo-Saxons and Jews together in a surrealistic Yiddish unity, a masterpiece of irreverence. With Isaac, the gravest, the most characteristic, the most perfect strokes took a comic slant. In his story *King Solomon,* the magnificence of Jerusalem mingles raggedly with the dinginess of the Lower East Side. The great king, also mortal and slovenly, sits in his undershirt. He fondles children in the park. They sit on his knees and smudge his glasses with their thumbprints.

He preferred to have things about him in a mess. I have an idea that he found good middle-class order de-vitalizing—a sign of meanness, stinginess, malice, and anality. The sight of one of his rooms with Isaac hard at work, smoking, capably and firmly writing on his yellow second-sheets, would have made Hogarth happy. On 76th Street there sometimes were cockroaches spring-ing from the toaster with the slices of bread. Smoky, the rakish little short-legged brown dog, was only partly housebroken and chewed books; the shades were always drawn (harmful sunlight!), the ashtrays spilled over. There was no sweeping, dusting, mopping, or laundering. The dirt here was liberating, exciting. Later, downtown, it was a little less gay. In the intricate warren of rooms called the Casbah and on Hudson Street it was simply grim. Toward the end of his life, on Woodlawn Avenue in Chicago, he settled in a hideous cellar room at Petof-sky's where he had lived as a student. The sympathetic glamour of the thirties was entirely gone; there was only a squalid stink of toilets and coal bins here. Isaac felt that this was the way he must live. The disorder had ended by becoming a discipline. It had acquired an ascetic significance for him which, at least to me, he never explained.

By now he had given up the Reichianism which for a time had absorbed us both. He no longer questioned people impulsively about their sexual habits or estimated the amount of character armor they wore. His homemade orgone box did not follow him in his later travels. He had at one time (in St. Albans) experimented with tomato seeds kept in the orgone accumulator; they produced better fruit, he claimed, than seeds which had not been exposed. Friends with headaches were urged to put on the tin crown or "shooter." He treated the neighbors' sick pets in his box. But during the last years of his life all his quaintness—incomparably charming and accompanied by brilliantly persuasive lectures and arguments—was laid aside. His wit was clearer and sharper, purged of crankiness. There had been a quality in him in earlier days, described by one of his friends as "hard-headed *Gemütlichkeit.*" For eight or ten years his mood was anything but *gemütlich.* He judged people harshly, he was not less harsh with himself.

I am convinced that in his view the struggle for survival, in the absence of certain qualities of life, was not worth making. Without heart and without truth there was only a dull dogged shuffle about things and amusements and successes. Singlemindedly, Isaac was out for the essential qualities. He believed that heart and truth were to be had. He tried to fix them within himself. He seemed occasionally to be trying to achieve by will, by fiat, the openness of heart and devotion to truth without which a human existence must be utterly senseless.

He was perfectly aware that in this America of ours he appeared to be doing something very odd. To appear odd did not bother him at all. Nor did he ever pursue eccentricity for its own sake, for its color. He followed an inner necessity which led him into difficulty and solitude. During the last years of his life he was solitary, and on Walton Place in one of his furnished rooms, he died alone.

INTRODUCTION

by Theodore Solotaroff

"THAT WHICH DIES acquires a life of its own." The statement, made by Isaac Rosenfeld himself in his story "The Colony," describes what has happened to him since July 12, 1956, when a heart attack suddenly ended his life at the age of thirty-eight. The figure that survives is less of an immensely gifted writer than of a man whose life and character have come to seem more remarkable than anything he wrote—or could have written. In Chicago, where he grew up and went to the University and where he returned to teach in the final two years of his life; in New York, where he began his literary career in 1941 and lived on for some ten years; in Minneapolis, where he sojourned and taught for another two years in the early 1950s—in these places and elsewhere he has become a legend: the wise and tender, the charming and fated "Isaac" of the various stories that are remembered far more vividly than those he wrote. There is the Greenwich Village sage who loved to sit for hours in the Waldorf Cafeteria on Sixth Avenue and slowly weave his elaborate conversation, naming the essences of things; the recondite critic who was followed around the campus at Minnesota by a band of freshman students, to whom he distributed A's as marks of affection; the representative of American learning at the Salzburg Seminar who during one of his formal lectures on pragmatism demonstrated a point by a fully executed hook slide. Even after five years his very name itself still seems to possess an incantatory power: some of his friends speak it as though "Isaac" were a magic word for joy and wit; others as though it were the most poignant word in the language.

Nor did one have to know him to be touched in this way or to make a legend of him. His work itself tended to be so permeated with the sense of a forthright and full humanity that one could read him—as I avidly began to do in college—less for the specific importance of what he had to say than for the pleasure and encouragement of that calm, intelligent, invariably warm voice. In fact, I soon erected my own legendary image of Isaac Rosenfeld simply from reading his stories and reviews and the little biographical notes attached to them. Many of my details turned out, I have since learned, to be pretty wide of the mark. However, the substance of my image was accurate, for it was spun from the reality of a genuine marriage of mind and heart, of a high intellectual style combined with a directness and naturalness of feeling; and in adopting him as my special mentor, I was behaving no differently than his students who trailed after him. Some years later I even followed him, I think, to Chicago; at least I changed my mind at the last minute and went back to graduate school at the University because I heard he was teaching there. Ten months went by without my looking him up. Instead—with a mixture of shyness and cunning he would have understood perfectly—I tried to make friends with his friends in the hope we would be thrown together. But before that happened he died.

I begin with these matters because they seem to me important: his appeal, particularly as a critic, comes in good part from the ability—rare in modern criticism—to make one *care*. This gift flowed naturally from his personality, whether in the flesh or on the page, and since his death it has kept alive the stories and memories that have been his monument. However, its net effect has been to obscure the more general interest and achievement of his work, and also to limit appreciation to the more endearing aspects of his personality.

The significance of Rosenfeld's work must be reckoned by the simple, classic standards that he himself used as touchstones for judging other writers: first, his "feeling

for life and his knowledge of it"; second, his commitment
to his times, in the sense that his friend William Barrett
formulated this commitment, as one of incorporating contemporary mind and feeling at their deepest levels. These
are not standards one applies to most modern literary
critics, and for this reason, Rosenfeld did not figure very
prominently in our famous "age of criticism." He looked
at literature too directly, insisted too much on its immediate relevance, to command much attention at a time
when the discipline of letters was everywhere concerned
with the detection of subtlety and order. While the more
famous critics were busy with the canons of explication
that could release in a jet of abstractions those meanings
that our age loves constantly to rediscover and re-encap-
sulate, Rosenfeld was content to read freely and write
about what he saw in a way that was congenial to him.
His preoccupations, in turn, were derogated as "literary
journalism." Well, that is what Rosenfeld wrote—mainly
book reviews for unscholarly readers. His simple, abiding
concern was for "the plain fact, the plain reality of
human life" as it was captured or missed or compromised
by a writer. His method, if he can be said to have had
one, was mainly Sainte-Beuve's principle that criticism is
"justness of characterization." Instead of a methodology
he relied on an exceptional literary and moral intelligence, and mainly by "taking a good look," as he liked to
say, he usually made his way to the center of the book
under discussion and then to the center of its writer's
oeuvre, often within 1,000 words. If he had any purely
literary goal, it was to restore the "confidence in our ability, within our right, to take a simply human measure of
literature," but he had no program and did not try to
become a "force." He merely wrote, and for fifteen years
helped to keep alive the fundamental reasons for bothering about literature at all.

Moreover, his criticism contains from first to last a
specific awareness of what was happening to the human
image and to the values of heart and mind that preserve
it, during what he called "an age of enormity."

In the 1940s, with its sense of "crisis," Rosenfeld was

thus a deeply representative figure; during the 1950s he
seemed to many of his friends quixotic and dated, an
"underground man" in an open and practical and not
unpleasant society. Today, as the complacent bets of
those years are going off the board and we find ourselves
at an even more fearful extreme; as we experience once
again, coolly or in panic, the modern dilemma of contactlessness, the inability to grasp the life around us, the
numbness and uncertainty toward the terror and vulgarity
it embodies—Rosenfeld's consciousness of contemporary
mind and feeling is once again pertinent. Like Camus and
the later Orwell, he knew what it meant to live in a completely politicalized age and what the few desperate truths
were that one had left to affirm. Like theirs, his courage
was his knowledge of our life; and his premature death, like
that of Camus and Orwell, meant that another precious
light had gone out, leaving us that much more in the dark.

As such, Isaac Rosenfeld was a more complex figure
than the legendary "Isaac" or even the biographical man
suggests. As he once wrote to a friend, "for the writer, as
for the artist, there is no real life without the symbolic
one," and what he stood for, what gave him his frontage
on experience and his values, is to be found most purely
and powerfully in what he took to be his role as a writer.
Another of Rosenfeld's own principles of criticism was
that "the imagination is the man." He meant by this, as
he says in his essay "The Two Gides," that "the whole
man is the interaction of a man and writer, and
each of these elements of the self is the result of the
other." The term he gave to this "whole man" was "character," which he believed to be as much a product of
imagination in any deep life as it was in fiction or drama.
This formulation is particularly relevant to the complex,
tragic fabric of his own character, for he lived, as well as
wrote, by his imagination, and one, therefore, can best
talk about the man in terms of the themes of his work.

In a tribute to Rosenfeld, published shortly after his
death,* Saul Bellow recalls a scene from their high school

* "Isaac Rosenfeld," *Partisan Review,* Fall, 1956.

days in Chicago—young Isaac, still in short pants, rising
before the debating club to read his essay on Schopen-
hauer. Much the same image of his adolescence is found
in his first novel, *Passage from Home*, the story of a boy-
philosopher, "sensitive as a burn," whose moral intuitions
are the more remarkably sophisticated as his actual experience of life is limited, even relatively retarded. A child of
the tidy and solemn and self-enclosed life of a *petit-
bourgeois* family on Chicago's Jewish West Side, Bernard
describes himself at the age of fifteen as a "fervent but
rigid little boy, nervous, fastidious, plagued by a sense of
order and propriety." But his imagination is that of a
rebel, and not very far from the drab streets of home is
the Near North Side where his aunt Minna lives in
splendid Bohemian isolation from the family.

> This small room which had little sunlight by day and
> air at night—my stepmother would have pronounced
> it unfit to live in—contained the world. . . . The
> pictures on the wall, their wild, broken colors and
> unrecognizable forms, took on meaning and welcomed
> me. Here dwelt that spirit which we barred from our
> lives. . . .

Bernard calls this spirit "freedom," and in time he runs
away from home to live with Minna and her lover, a clever
Gentile drifter named Willy, whom Bernard himself has
brought to Minna. However, he soon discovers that his
aunt's freedom contains little more than bitterness, and in
her tense and sloppy relations with life, he eventually
detects more misery and waste than there is in the de-
pressive, cautionary restraint of his father's and step-
mother's life together. (Rosenfeld was later to say that
the Near North Side wasn't really Bohemian but merely
a neighborhood of home-loving people without homes.)

In the end Bernard returns home, prepared to accept it
for its awkward, stern moralism that he has found to be
imprinted on his own spirit and for its close family ties,
with their occasional aura of love. However, his father,
the presiding spirit of "home," offers him neither righteousness nor love, and his homecoming is as much a failure

as his escape to Minna's "exile" was. His "actual longing," as he realizes in retrospect, "looked neither to home nor exile, but to a life foreign to both in which some beauty and freedom prevailed." He has had at least one glimpse of the quality of this life when he goes to the house of a Chassidic Rebbe with his grandfather and sees the face of the cranky, ineffectual old man grow radiant with joy and dignity in sharing the wisdom of Reb Feldman and the ecstatic dancing of his followers. Later, Bernard realizes that it is for these transcendent moments of full understanding and full connection that one must live. In a remarkable passage toward the end of the novel, he sees the alternative spelled out as he sits in a conservatory in which huge, tropical plants are kept. He senses that these plants have a "much stronger and more ponderous grasp of life" than he does, and that beside them, his own existence seems "ailing and cold . . . a form of death." At the same time whatever little life he has in himself is also merely part of their blind, unconscious cycle of natural growth and decay, subject to the same process of "meaningless non-being, counting for nothing." As Bernard goes on to realize:

> There was no way out unless one bore forever the vision of the jungle, of life's vast, meaningless profusion, and fought against it; fought against it by never sparing a moment of the true life and the true human beauty. . . . Such moments I had known, perhaps at home, perhaps in childhood. . . . But no matter . . . love was a meaning into which I would always have to inquire.

The autobiographical ground of *Passage from Home* is particularly apparent at these points of emphasis where character and theme intersect. It is also apparent in the emotional core of the novel, the hunger that lies behind Bernard's various strategies and gives the book its sense of ache and emptiness and aspiration for love. The figure of Bernard's mother, who had died when he was a small boy, seldom enters the novel explicitly and is but dimly conscious to Bernard himself; but the meaning of his behavior, particularly as it involves his mother's sister,

Minna, and the emotional tone of his sense of the world and of himself are both defined in good part by the loss that her early death represents. This loss was also Rosenfeld's, and though its influence on his own personality and values is as plain and as obscure as such things are in life, the characterization of Bernard under its aspect affords additional reason to read the novel as containing much of Rosenfeld's early "character."

In any case, Rosenfeld, like his young hero, believed that his values must derive from nature as well as transcend it. Like Bernard's encounter with the plants, this was a matter of experience rather than theory; as Rosenfeld later wrote in "Religion and Naturalism: A Personal Statement": "The natural derivation of value . . . must be experienced directly, the dependence of everything on nature must be felt concretely within one's own life, before naturalism can be anything more than an attitude, and a superficial one at that." Similarly, Bernard's early grasp of his "homelessness" in the world, his glimpses of that "empty space which . . . stretched between person and person, between ignorance and knowledge, between one hand and the other," his vision of the "divided and alien aspect of life" were for Rosenfeld some of the primary facts of his identity as a Jew as well as a writer, and from them came his abiding preoccupation with the problems of human ties and self-integration. Bernard also shares his creator's efforts to feel more directly and deeply, to define his life and its meaning mainly by his emotional attachments. Or again, the boy's notion of a freedom beyond self-indulgence, one that must be fought for against inner fluidity and inhibition, is found in Rosenfeld's prolonged struggle toward the same end. What he wrote of "The Young Richard Wright" was true of himself:

> Essential to his growth as a writer, let alone his survival as a man who sought liberty, was his need for accomplishing an individual act of liberation. . . . He would have nothing less than that which the truly free man, unencumbered by his own compensations, can obtain.

Finally, there are the terms of Bernard's "passage from home," which stand as a paradigm of Rosenfeld's own journey—that is, from the restraints of the parochial Jewish culture and the "essential sadness" of its life, to the "freedom of the world without God against which we shut our doors," and the effort to find in this world a measure of natural and spiritual satisfaction. But what gives this passage its special character is precisely the fact that it never ended. Just as Bernard's "passage" involves a return to the moral nurture of "home" and an acknowledgment that he resembles more than anything else the father he has fled, so Rosenfeld's character and writing involves a to-fro relationship between what he called "Jewish intellectualism" and a type of Reichian-method Bohemianism, the one with its cultivation of knowledge and moral reflection, the other with its passionate openness to experience. His goal, like Bernard's, was "full humanity," the most complete development of a nature that was as broad and contradictory as it was deep. Thus, he writes at one point in his journal: "To know, to know, to know . . . knowledge and love combined into the one ecstasy, the highest good of mind and body."

In 1941 Rosenfeld came to New York. He was twenty-three, recently married, and starting on a Ph.D. in philosophy at New York University. Within a year he left school to become a regular contributor to the *New Republic* and then joined its staff as an editor. By the end of 1943 he had established himself as a literary journalist of the first rank and a fiction writer of unusual promise. Almost overnight, this young unknown from Chicago emerged as the rising star on the New York literary scene and one of the key representatives of the post-Marxist, post-Depression temperament.

Looking back at Rosenfeld's early work, a good deal of which is included in this volume, it is not surprising that he should have taken precedence so rapidly. What is surprising—indeed astonishing—is the quality of almost every performance, the calm, confident strength of the writing, the intellectual grasp of his ideas, the richness and concentration that he brought to the traditional methods of serious literary journalism. One striking review follows another, whether the subject is the fiction of Nancy Hale or Anais Nin, the world of Sholom Aleichem or Jean Malaquais, the philosophy of John Dewey or of Kenneth Burke. When one realizes that the writer was still in his middle twenties—which, given the necessarily slow development of most critics, is still practically adolescence—the breadth and ripeness of his judgment is the more remarkable. If genius is the power to make the reader consistently shake his head in wonder, then this is what the young Rosenfeld had.

Which is not to say that he was an entirely inexplicable or even isolated phenomenon. He had been trained in philosophical analysis by such men as Eliseo Vivas and Rudolf Carnap, and when he came to write practical criticism, he was able to fortify it by a precise use of general ideas, without which book reviewing soon becomes a relaxed form of prejudice or advertising. He had also been at the University of Chicago during the late thirties, when radicalism ran strong and, as he was to write in retrospect in "Life in Chicago," "politics was form and substance, accident and modification, the metaphor of all things." Like many of the young writers who came out of the Depression, he had learned, as he says, "through political activity, to admire the vigor which a social orientation will impart to thought," and from the start his criticism was given vitality and point by his consciousness of what a given book was saying—implicitly and unconsciously as well as explicitly—about the times, about us. Thus he took positions, committed himself; his mind was most political in the sense that he distrusted "wisdom without thesis—the inexpensive kind." But if the young Rosenfeld's experience as a Trotskyite had made him aware of the traction and thrust of precise radical ideas, it had also made him aware of the ironies of fully accepting them. As he put it in his early story, "The Party":

> To us has been willed also a fortune; as yet it has
> no value except in our own circle. . . . But what a for-
> tune—the whole world! . . . Some day the world may
> actually fall into our hands! Then where would we run?

The thought and the tone are typical. Rosenfeld both
capitalized on and distrusted his skill in dialectic—first
in philosophy, then in psychology. He was too much concerned with judgment to rely on logic; instead he looked
to his intuitions and experience and sense of humor for
his point of view, and to his imagination for his tone.

At the same time, his own working interest in the
problems of writing fiction also checked his tendency
toward overintellectualization, though not always. He believed that "literature teaches us profound respect for
phenomena, it holds us among the many details of the
surface and keeps us from plunging at once after causes."
Thus he tended to work out a precise description of the
writer's image of life, trying to make it reveal as much
as it could, before he moved on to the more general questions that this image provoked. His criticism was practical
in the sense of operating within an awareness of the
limitations of what he called the writer's "grasp." Questions of structure and style were thus subsumed under
the question of what the writer was making of human
experience, how much of life was he able to hold up
and judge.

Rosenfeld had his own claims to make on fiction, involving his own attempts, particularly in the short story,
to deepen its treatment of character. But strangely enough,
his criticism was noticeably freer of preconception and
influence than was his own fiction, and his sensibility
operated in a more open and catholic, and often more
vivid, way. He had no critical system, as I've said; he was
less interested in the methodology of literary judgment
than he was in its commitment to open and relevant observation. "The strength of a theory of art," he once wrote,
"lies not in its structural underpinning, but in the directness with which it allows values to come into their own
. . . the virtue of the *Poetics* is that it rests on aesthetic
experience without intermediary, observing and analyzing

directly." This is the key to Rosenfeld's own achievement as a critic: the transmission of the immediate experience of literature onto the page. In this he was aided by a classic critical style—simple, limpid, but with enormous power of concentration. Into it flowed a rich interplay of his own traits: his directness and subtlety, his detachment and warmth, his taste for dialectic and for concreteness. Almost any passage brings this out; the following is from one of his first reviews, "Sholom Aleichem: The Humor of Exile":

> Sholom Aleichem has often been compared with Dickens. The comparison is superficially plausible, as far as resemblances in verbal humor and characterization are concerned. But there is a fundamental divergence between the two, which typifies the Jewish author's removal from the entire tradition which, in greater or less degree, has united all social novelists. Society, for Sholom Aleichem, was less the object than the source of his sentiment, and thus love, more than indignation, gave motive to his art. What he felt toward his people, toward their poverty and hopelessness, was always directed outward, as if proceeding from their, rather than his own, heart. He himself was perhaps capable of a greater individual expression than the one he achieved. But folk artists lose nothing by their sacrifices.

However natural was the cast of Rosenfeld's critical imagination, it was also fairly typical of the literary temperament that he found in New York: the firm, terse, intellectually ambitious prose, the fluent, sophisticated breadth of reference, the concreteness of idea—political at the core—the taste for epigram. It was a style, as Seymour Krim has recently pointed out, that young Jewish writers in particular aspired to control, and during the 1940s a good number of them succeeded. Besides Rosenfeld there were Bellow, Delmore Schwartz, Alfred Kazin, Irving Howe, Leslie Fiedler, Robert Warshow, to name only some of the more prominent ones. Their backgrounds in lower- or middle-class Jewish life gave them certain similarities in attitude and ambition that have come to be discussed a good deal in recent years; but per-

haps more crucial to their work was the legacy of political
and social awareness that they had brought out of the
thirties, and their common search for direction in the
dark and lonely years of the early forties. In another of his
first reviews, of Walter Morris's *American in Search of
a Way*, Rosenfeld sets forth in "Journal of a Generation,"
the situation of his generation in these terms:

> The frustrations he [Morris] encountered were the same
> that have turned almost his entire generation into
> underground men—men who are not so much beyond
> belief as below it, incapable of the desperate exertion
> of rising which an affirmation of our time demands.
> This is the generation which remembers the last war
> dimly, and the Depression clearly; which was sustained
> by the WPA only to see the rise and flourishing of
> fascism, the death of Spain and the disgrace of the
> democracies; which lost, in Stalin, the last hope of
> imminent socialism and in the present war the hope of
> its own survival. That such men, moral underground-
> lings, cannot affirm values which they never possessed
> is hardly a matter for wonder, and even less for blame.
> The affirmation of life in our time is an act only a
> transcendental man can perform . . . But ages and
> generations do not come that way.

Where to go now? What to live for? These became the
leading questions as the "economic crisis" of the thirties
faded into the "moral crisis" of the forties, and "the alienation of the masses" was changed by the war psychology
and the war economy into the "alienation of the individual." This is the period of *Partisan Review*'s series on
"The New Failure of Nerve," of Bellow's *Dangling Man*,
of Rosenfeld's story, "The Hand That Fed Me." The last
is a moving evocation of the new underground man. It is
done in a series of unanswered letters from a young Jewish intellectual—whom the end of the Writer's Project
and the coming of the war have made "irrelevant"—to a
working-class girl from a Russian family who had flirted
with him a few years before at a WPA office and then
suddenly dropped him, as he believes, for a dull but successful white-collar man. The political parable is fused

with a social one—the Jewish boy who goes on carrying
a torch for a Gentile girl, hurling at her indifference his
protests and solicitations, now proud and then humble,
now demanding that attention be paid to his injuries, then
offering himself all over again. The third theme of the
story is the unfolding of Feigenbaum's present loneliness
and frustration as one of the "bare, pared, essential" men,
desperately in need of some sense of personal meaning
and hope, who says near the end on a note of purest existentialist doctrine: "For that is happiness: the conviction
that something is necessary." With all the irony and sadness of the post-Depression blues, Feigenbaum concludes,
freeing himself from the girl for the last time:

> Be gentle to the unfulfilled, be good to it. We are
> accustomed to sing the joys of the happy, the fulfilled
> men. Let us also learn to sing the joys of the desolate,
> the empty men. Theirs is the necessity without fulfill-
> ment, but it is possible that even to them—who knows
> —some joy may come.

In the tone of the story, Jewish sensibility fuses with
the new existentialist one: for example, the little question
"who knows" tucked into Feigenbaum's bitter analysis of
his aloneness and freedom. In the early 1940s, the situation of the contemporary Jew adrift in a Gentile society
could be felt as a parallel to the aloneness of the artist and
the radical in a mass society. "As a member of an internationally insecure group," Rosenfeld wrote of the Jew in
1944 ("The Situation of the Jewish Writer"), "he has
grown personally acquainted with some of the fundamental
themes of insecurity that run through modern literature.
He is a specialist in alienation (the one international
banking system the Jews actually control)." But Feigenbaum's position on the extreme also provides a "comfort"
that, as a Jew, he knows in his veins. His wacky little
"who knows" is a murmur from the past, a remnant of
a long tradition of hope in misery, of the shrug between
adversities, that characterized a people who accepted
suffering rather than anything short of complete deliverance. Similarly, Feigenbaum's final statement to the girl

("But God, if you only knew, if you only knew how willing I am—always—to take the risk of my happiness!") is another ground-note of a religious culture which, as Rosenfeld wrote of Sholom Aleichem's comedy of endurance, had never learned in its unremitting hunger for Eretz Israel "to rationalize adaptation to the world." To the extent that he holds out, delivers himself up to the force of his desires, insists on receiving nothing less from life than full gratification and transcendence, Feigenbaum is a true son of East European Jewry, among his other roles. And he resembles his creator in nothing so much as in his faithfulness to the saving image of his expectations and in what he was willing to endure for it.

Like his unsuccessful alter ego, Feigenbaum, Rosenfeld was obsessed for many years by the familiar Jewish theme of salvation—or what Harold Rosenberg, in a brilliant reading of Jewish character, has called "the Jewish vertigo." Naturalist that he was, Rosenfeld saw the way out of the underground not through Jewish faith in another, redemptive place, but through the satisfaction of his natural desires. But he was a mystic for all that—and a Jewish one. He tried to bridge the gap between alienation and connection, depression and joy, secularism and transcendence, through the flesh rather than through religious experience, and he found his mentor in Wilhelm Reich. However, Rosenfeld's Reichianism, under the inevitable conditioning of his character, often reads as much like Hasidism. "To love all love," he writes at one point in his journal, "even the beloved partner's love for another. For then we see the world spelled out in letters of flame."

Most of his meditations on salvation through the flesh went into his fiction; in the meantime he wrote his reviews from the point of view of a man trying to remain level with his generation's experience, and so he cast about for signs of life, awareness, moral initiative in the cultural doldrums that had followed, in William Phillips' words, "the utter breakdown of values and distinctions and a failure of the will to independent radical expression." Rosenfeld believed that philosophical naturalism offered the best ground for the reconstruction of values but that it would first have to go beyond the finicky and narrow rationalism in which it was bogged down. In the contributions of Hook, Nagel, and Dewey (his own early mentor) to the "Failure of Nerve" symposium, he saw the failure of naturalism to confront the motives for the turn toward the obscurantism and consolations of religion by dealing with the yearning for belief "as an illegitimate form of inference." In "Philosophical Naturalism: The Failure of Verve," he states: ". . . Naturalism must itself be liberated, broadened, and extended over the regions of experience in which the dominant anxieties of our time have grown. . . ." Further, it must attend to, not simply deplore, the irrational in man as a dominant factor in human personality. Finally, he noted that orthodox naturalism in its adherence to the methods of science had missed "the richness, the variety, pleasure, tragedy, the sheer possibility of experience," and that in its commitment to the analysis rather than the assertion of values, there lay its own failure of nerve, or, as he put it, "failure of verve."

Along with its methodology, then, naturalism required what he called "the full moral temperament" to provide the motive and imagination for its doctrines. In the fiction he was given to review he saw much the same problems: a preoccupation with literary method or style, if not merely with the writer's own ego; a lack of felt experience. What was needed was again the inwardness and comprehensiveness of temperament that would allow the writer to grasp and respond to the daily losses that all defensible values were suffering, and a renewed vitality that came from the struggle for affirmation. The artist's primary task, as he wrote in "Jean Malaquais' War Diary" (1944), was "to bring together the human and the animal in man, to make an imaginative synthesis of what society has dismembered." In the work of Nancy Hale and Irwin Shaw or John O'Hara, on the one hand, or of Henry Miller or Kenneth Patchen, on the other, he saw little of this synthesis, or little chance of it. In the first case the human animal was reduced to his behavior, in the second to his fantasies and sensations. In general, the problem of the fiction writer of this period could be summed up as follows:

> You have a story to tell and you sit down to write it, and you might as well be wood for all the place there is in modern fiction for the fact that you are human. You are either hard-boiled or hysterical; you are either a grim little behaviorist, as objective as a sack of nails, or a natural gusher with a wild mouth or snakes in your hair. . . . Choose either pose and say nothing. Or choose surrealism and go to sleep.

In fictional terms, the problem was the reconstruction of character, the weakness of which in modern literature has continued to be a commonplace of criticism. However, behind Rosenfeld's treatment of the problem lay his philosophical point of view, which prevented his formulations from becoming merely a subtle restatement of the middle-brow reviewers' search for "real people" in fiction. "Character"—whether in the conventional literary sense or as the writer's self-portrayal—was for Rosenfeld not only the essential element of fiction but also the most telling index of the writer's intelligence and passion, his capacity for understanding and judging the world. Whatever the writer may or may not have achieved in terms of preserving or extending the so-called "art of fiction," his main responsibility was not to that but to the attitude with which he approached experience, and this attitude was most clearly embodied in his characters. Thus the trouble with Irwin Shaw ("A Left-Wing Middle-Brow") was that his characters were constructed from a false sophistication, a tissue of Freudian and liberal platitudes in the service of the "guts-and-dry Martini" attitude toward life, and from an affirmation that begins by accepting "nearly everything as it is." In a British novelist like Charles Williams the characters were weak because they were made up completely of writing. "Gross distinction [such as that between life and death] did not concern him," Rosenfeld writes in "Sensibility as

Fiction: Charles Williams." "His was too fine a sensibility
to be impressed by anything obvious. . . ."

In the characters of both Shaw and Williams, and of
the prominent schools of fiction to which they belonged
in America and England, respectively, Rosenfeld saw a
fundamental failure to grasp the human being's deep
commitment to struggle. "Were conflict entertained for
its intrinsic psychological interest," he wrote, "character
would emerge in vividness of emotion, in the ambivalence
of desire, and the unity of moral meaning." With this
attitude toward experience, character would emerge
again as both the dramatic and moral center of fiction,
and "experimentation" would become the writer's attempt to find his "exact position in the world, the symbol
that expresses it precisely, and the knowledge and the
comment you must bring to bear upon it."

Rosenfeld's own position remained that of alienation,
which he saw as unsatisfactory but inevitable in modern
society. In trying to create character from this position
he was most influenced by the example of Kafka, whose
alienated men were cast whole despite Kafka's full recognition of the forces of fragmentation that operated on the
contemporary individual both from without and within.
What drew Rosenfeld to Kafka was the comprehensiveness of his art and the singleness of his purpose: his
struggle to arrive at a "purely human freedom," wrested
from all the obstacles of the external world and of the
self. By his genius for combining and unifying disparate
traits of experience, Kafka had created characters of such
thick and complex texture that a figure such as K. could
stand for theological, moral, psychological, social, and
even political man; but even so, Kafka's description of
human nature was seen to be complete only when one
grasped that its "final cause" was the assertion of man's
irreducible freedom.

Such an affirmation appealed deeply to Rosenfeld. So,
too, did Kafka's method in its marriage of storytelling
and a philosophical order of thought. And there must
also have been an equally deep attachment to this lonely

but transcendent art produced by another neurasthenic Jew who had been able to sublimate his own and his people's needs and terrors in an absolute statement of the human crisis. The ghetto sensibility, which Rosenfeld himself loved, with all its hallucinations and hope and ironies both intact and transformed in Kafka's art, reached out in parables to comprehend and redeem the broken, fearful moral order of Europe. During the later forties, Kafka became a particularly relevant figure in this respect.

In 1944 Rosenfeld, in "The Situation of the Jewish Writer," had written that the recent sufferings of the Jews would lead their writers "to make certain inevitable moral discoveries. These discoveries, enough to indict the world, may also be crucial to its salvation." In the ensuing five years, as the first reports of the Nazi death camps mounted and later the memoirs and studies began to be published, Rosenfeld himself was making the discoveries he had predicted. In 1948 he published a remarkable review, "Terror Beyond Evil," of Jacob Pat's *Ashes and Fire* in which he argued that our "numbness" when confronted by reports of the screams of the dying Jews made us "no different from the murderers who went ahead and did their business and paid no attention to the screams." His point was that to acknowledge the facts in full, both of the screaming and the numbness, was to realize that the fundamental reality of Western culture was now one of absolute terror. All the rest was the blindness of wishful thinking, the comforts of complacence, especially the liberal assumption that the slaughter lay "within the realm of the explainable, the workable, the preventable," that is, of the old morality of good and evil. Another book he reviewed, on the Soviet labor camps, provided but another text for the moral.

In an essay of the following year, titled "The Meaning of Terror," Rosenfeld developed his proposition that terror had become the main reality by examining the current state of the culture. One recognizes today in his moments of truth that a civilization which killed six million Jews yesterday, or used the atom bomb on the civilian population of a defeated enemy, may very well allow sixty

million to die tomorrow—and further that no morally
vital culture survives the abrogation of its canons of good
and evil. To Rosenfeld this truth was already perfectly
clear in 1949:

> War is the model enterprise and the model form of
> communality. These are abstract propositions, but even
> so they are obvious; when we fill them in with experi-
> ence, they are overwhelming. Unfortunately, there is
> nothing else into which we can fit our experience—
> traditions are broken and culture is unavailable. . . .
> Our culture is an empty form, standing for a continuity
> of experience which is now discontinued, for the
> reality and inviolability of human values that are every-
> where violated and denied. . . . Today the cultured
> man is isolated . . . the cultural form that conveyed
> humanity and assured the transaction from one man
> to the next has been destroyed.

To bear witness to the terror was essential, if our sense
of humanity was to remain concrete and a culture be
initiated that conformed again to men's experience. With
this knowledge of terror beyond evil, one was forced to
give up the old and equally compromised and useless
notions of good and to realize that the only basis of renewal lay in a "joy beyond good." The ground of this
joy was love: the development of "a new capacity, proof
against terror, to experience our natural life to the full."

If the frame of Rosenfeld's analysis had been provided
by the moral categories of Nietzsche, the content was
strongly influenced by the writing, and therapy, of
Reich. Rosenfeld's Reichianism ran a course of nearly a
decade, and one can only touch on it here. In brief, he
found in Reich's theory of the orgasm the possibility of
carrying his search for freedom into the three sectors of
his character: his natural drives and the struggle against
his inhibitions; his intellect and its commitment to first
principles of thought and conduct deriving from and in
harmony with nature; his spirit and its thirst for the full
being and transcendence of ecstasy. At the same time,
Reich's theory that a self-regulated man and community
would develop from complete sexual freedom and satis-

faction seemed to Rosenfeld the most powerful means of transforming culture so as to remove its terror and its potential for further terror. The very extremism of Reich's system—as over against the Freudian—must have commended it in this time of extremity, just as the extremism of Trotsky often exerted a purer and more irresistible appeal to the radical temperament—as opposed to Stalinist revisionism—during the economic crisis of the thirties.

During the latter part of the forties, Rosenfeld worked on a novel that incorporated his ideas of terror and joy in a Kafkaesque method and perspective. "The Enemy" (of which only three parts have been published)* begins in a setting of prolonged and indefinite war; its hero, a pleasant intellectual named Brigadier, has been given the task of determining the nature of the enemy. When conventional methods—observation and interrogation, then torture and murder—are found to be unavailing, Brigadier disguises himself and takes on the new name of Pathfinder to travel into the country of the enemy and acquire definitive information. But the nature of the enemy remains obscure despite his best efforts; the intelligence he collects is mainly about himself, derived in good part from his experiences with asceticism and sex along the way. In time, the landscapes of repression—stockade and monastery—begin to give way to those of liberation—peaceful towns, green woods, and running water—and the character of Brigadier-Pathfinder begins to change. "The Enemy" was completed in 1951. The three sections I have seen are deeply conceived and beautifully written, but the novel was rejected by Rosenfeld's publisher, and then by others.

Whatever the publisher's reasons for rejecting it, by 1951 it was no longer a very "topical" book. The Kafka vogue had run its course; Reichianism was taking on an increasingly crackpot aura; and, more importantly, the sense of the age had turned. *Commentary*, which in 1946

* "The Brigadier," *Partisan Review* (March-April, 1947), "In the Monastery," *Kenyon Review* (Summer, 1951), and "In the Holy City," *New World Writing* 20 (1962).

ran a symposium on the crisis and alienation of the individual, was by 1949 asking its writers if the anti-Semitic tradition in English and American literature blocked their "full participation and integration in the tradition." The next year *Partisan Review* was asking its contributors if they felt culture could exist without a positive religion (a rather far cry from the tenor of the "Failure of Nerve" series of 1943). In 1952 came its famous symposium "Our Country and Our Culture," whose keynote was the reaffirmation and rediscovery of America. What all of this, and more, bespoke was a new political and social orientation on the part of the old radical intellectuals, which, in 1946, Rosenfeld noted as the shift from Marx to Freud, from "change the world" to "adjust yourself to it." He saw it as an orientation that "blesses the bourgeois in all of us" by shifting the perspective from a radical and historical understanding of contemporary society to one of accommodation and apologetics and by trading in the lonely sense of differences for the "ecstasy of belonging."

This was not the way out of the "terror," and Rosenfeld resisted it. He continued to believe that if indeed the end of alienation had arrived, it lay simply in the fact that society had fulfilled the intellectuals' worst fears and expectations, thereby ending their sense of being outside of it. He did not worry about the problems of integrating and participating as a Jewish writer ("So they won't name any streets after me"). He held out against the refuge of religion and took the risks of the margin of freedom he guarded against the encroachment of politics. Eventually he went away to teach at a university, but he did not confuse its quiet atmosphere, its orderly intellectual interests, its highly developed manners, with the different tenor of American life and culture outside the academy. The new interest in social codes and manners that had gone hand in hand with the embourgeoisement of the old radicalism seemed to him largely beside the point, whether of fiction or of contemporary society. Responding to Lionel Trilling's argument that manners were indispensable to the novelist

for the "hum and buzz of implication" they gave to
character, Rosenfeld described this argument as a "variant
of the old claim for the necessity of a traditional society"
which was becoming popular again in the academy.
"Within its shelter," he wrote, "the hum and buzz of
implication can still be made out. Off-campus an age of
enormity is in full riot and the roaring in the ears is
bloody murder."

In bearing witness to his vision, Rosenfeld did not
let it harden into a holistic pessimism. He was less interested in the decline of the West than in simply "coming alive" again and writing about books and men and
life's better possibilities; he did not wish to bring in the
Jew's "indictment" but to tap out his message of "salvation." Furthermore, he knew that any moral dialectic
must look to the ground between its extremes if it is to
supply immediately relevant values. In "Mind, Body,
Spirit: The Road to the Castle," a review of Hesse's
Magister Ludi and Moravia's *Woman of Rome,* he used
the core of the two novels to prescribe a type of fiction
that embodied this credo: "Health, naturalism, the joy
of love, the preservation of secular culture, these small
and still very shy little devotions to enlightenment shall
have to provide the dominant movement of fiction if
drama is to mean a real adventure, not a crack-up, of
spirit."

This statement foreshadows much of the important
criticism of his later years. To be sure, the values he
lists were apparent in the point of view with which he
had set up as a critic, but they became increasingly
dominant in the late 1940s. He gives up the old stance
of the underground man ("Who needs *two* such worlds?"
he asks in "Sartre's Underground." Politics is already
"the underground of our time"). He also loses some of
the alter image—the brilliant young writer taking possession of a varied cultural heritage, clearing the way for
his own work, and otherwise frequently expressing his
views on a wide range of subjects. One sees in the later
criticism—of Hemingway, Faulkner, Orwell, Henry

Green, Gandhi, Cahan, Simone Weil, Stendhal, Sartre, and others—a deepening of both the natural and moral perspective, a more patient and exhaustive effort to analyze literature, politics, and religion in terms of their life-giving or life-denying possibilities. Rosenfeld continued to rely a good deal on the analysis of character—both of the personages and of the writer himself—as it reveals the writer's grasp of life, but this too is carried on at a deeper level and with a more explicit attempt to explore the relationship between the instinctual drives and strength of feeling and of values.

However, except for a spate of reviews in the *New Republic* during 1952, he did less and less writing. His literary interests seem to have given way to more pressing concerns in his life as they did in what work he managed to finish. Like many writers who begin in a blaze of achievement and recognition in their twenties, Rosenfeld ran into writing problems later on. The rejection of "The Enemy" was a serious as well as bewildering setback and he was a long time recovering. He had not used his early success to armor himself against the possibilities of failure, and had remained a poor caretaker of his career. He had left the *New Republic* after a year, relying on his writing for the serious, low-paying journals and, later, on part-time teaching at N.Y.U. to support himself. Despite his reputation, his relations with the literary world remained as marginal as they were with any other. His two children came early in his marriage and he settled down, after a fashion, in the Village; in 1952 he went to Minnesota to teach and after two years moved on to Chicago, which he was on the verge of leaving at the time of his death. But no matter where he was or what job he had, he kept himself in the clear, taking the risks of instability and independence, of uncertainty, sterility, and failure. Like Feigenbaum he carried his place in the world within himself and followed the steep emotional curve of his nature. "I have no refuge apart from the satisfaction of my desires," he said of his life in 1950, and added, "—I am not speaking of a happy life, only of a deep one."

One literary critic who had a brief but intense friendship with Rosenfeld thought of him as "the last Bohemian." Another has described him to me as a "Chassid." At the end Rosenfeld spoke of himself as a *luftmensch*. Such definitions are incomplete but they all point to the same attitude toward life and society that kept him free of the lures and snares of accommodation, kept him, that is, at his full value.

His main interest came to be in figures such as Gandhi and Tolstoy who had succeeded in transcending their limits by a sustained action of will, imagination, and feeling that carried them beyond the given habits of their character into a new domain of personal freedom and power. In the achievement of "self-realization beyond the ego" he found the sources of Gandhi's triumph over politics, along with his capacity for love and joy that had survived what seemed to be a crippling inner life. Judging by the opening section of a book on Tolstoy that he began writing in the early 1950s, Rosenfeld was embarking on a similar investigation of Tolstoy's style. He felt that the sources of the great Russian novelist's power over life and art derived from the continual encounters of a strong sexual nature and a no less strong religious one, which drove Tolstoy to fuse nature with morality in his work and, by-passing the struggles of the ego, to give himself up to his grasp of the great themes of existence. Similarly, he saw ("Reflections on Orwell: Decency and Death") that Orwell's approaching death had had the effect of forcing the writer of *1984* to surrender his "life-long image, the character and style and habits of reason and restraint," and by the force of his own passion and imagination to succeed in "expressing the totalitarian agony out of his own."

To acknowledge one's instinctual life, to educate the feelings, to be thoroughly onto oneself, to struggle against the pettiness and defensiveness and prevarications of the ego for the larger claims and possibilities of existence; to understand the enormity of the modern world's encroachments upon the natural and individual life and oppose them by the force of one's desires and intelligence and hope—so Rosenfeld continued to live and to write. He found a positive example in Stendhal; a negative one in Hemingway; a mixed one in Faulkner, Sartre, Simone Weil. In his own fiction he was trying to break away from the large, symbolic design of Kafka and write about his own experience in the world in more immediately concrete ways. However, this work, too, went slowly and fitfully. These were the years of "the fat gods," in Saul Bellow's phrase. It was not an age that Rosenfeld felt at home in, and he fought against it, as Bellow wrote in his *Partisan Review* memoir, trying to maintain his faith in "health, naturalism, the joy of love, the preservation of secular culture." And, according to Bellow, he paid the price in "boredom and deadness, despair, even madness." All of this he kept out of his work and remained, for the most part, silent.

Bellow believes that he won in the end, and there is some indication of that in his writing. Toward the close of his life he wrote a story about a king, a rather non-descript and homely Jew, to whom both love and wisdom came easily. In his Solomon, Rosenfeld was able to create a character who embodied Feigenbaum's anguished assertion of ten years before—that "some men are capable of rising out of their own lives. . . . Their only secret is a tremendous willingness—they do not struggle with themselves!" It seems that the creator of both characters was approaching this much peace after the long passage that had lain between them. Similarly his last few reviews and articles have a simpler touch, a more direct sense of the man who wished to write "so truthfully that only I, as I actually am, will appear on the page." But where he was going in his work is another question, one that perhaps only his journals will disclose.* For now what we have is the record of the passage itself, of a luminous and affirmative mind through our dark and cynical times. As he wrote at the end of "Life in Chicago," the piece he was working on when he died, he looked for

---

* I have seen only the entries for 1948. The whole of his journals comprises, I suspect, an extraordinary document of the man and his times.

the everlasting in the ephemeral things: not in iron, stone, brick, concrete, steel, and chrome, but in paper, ink, pigment, sound, voice, gesture, and graceful leaping, for it is of such things that the ultimate realities, of the mind and the heart, are made.

And he was right. For this *"luftmensch . . .* with a thirst for water" produced the most enduring kind of criticism. His "ephemeral" book reviews and articles offer, it seems to me, the most sustained example of the human uses of literature in recent American letters. What "Isaac" did for his friends, these pieces will continue to do for his readers: their humanity touches the spirit, restores us to our better selves, and makes us happy.

✑ AN AGE OF ENORMITY

✒ Journal of a Generation

Perhaps what I think is peculiar to myself is common to most all of us.—*Walter Morris at the age of twenty*

AMERICAN IN SEARCH OF A WAY is the journal kept by Walter Morris from his twelfth until his thirty-fifth year, terminated only by his induction into the Army. It is a full record of a life, of an intellectual, emotional, and moral history. Touch this book, and, as with Whitman, you touch a man.

He was born in 1907 in Johnstown, New York, and spent most of his life in nearby Gloversville. The early pages of his journal show him as a mischievous boy and although a diarist, normal in all respects and not particularly introverted. A few years mark the improvement of his spelling and his intellectual awakening. He has talent for music, drawing, and writing. In 1928 he enters the University of Michigan at Ann Arbor, and two years later his Search proper begins.

Tonio Kröger to the contrary, Morris's early development showed an increased participation in the life about him rather than a growth of detachment. From the start his sensibility made him the representative, not the exceptional, man. He had his share of loneliness; but his isolation was more a matter of circumstance than an alienation fostered by a mournfully indulgent ego. That this casts him into the type of the American artist, one cannot say. But there is a sturdiness to his temper which persists through his later years, giving equal sway to the artist and the man.

At Michigan he began to write poetry and fiction, and his teachers encouraged him. At the same time he showed

an aptitude for philosophy and was drawn to Plato and
Santayana. He speculated on Pure Being and a life of
ascetic devotion while recognizing the demands of matter
and the claims that his own appetites put upon him.
Eventually, he resigned himself to the duality of flesh
and spirit. But the resignation, much like the original
preoccupation with the Ideal, was a reflection of his dis-
couragement. Unable to attain his goal outside himself,
he had erected the unattainable within. So with his
philosophical realism, where frustration also had a guiding hand. Poverty, which would never leave him, had
already made itself felt. Rejection slips were beginning
to pile up. Ideal conflicts have their counterpart in the
mundane, and into the reconciliations which a man seeks
among events as among ideas, the same sad note creeps
in. Fortunately, sections of his journal won him an Avery
Hopwood Award in 1933 and 1934. But thereafter he
was on his own, and he left the Graduate School without taking his M.A. The frustrations he was to suffer
were to be all the more bitter for involving simple needs.
Men want wives, families, and decent jobs, but Morris
felt himself unequipped to make a satisfactory adjustment, and he did not know what he would do with himself in this world. "Apparently, one may as well howl
for the moon." For a while he worked on the HOLC in
Detroit, which bored him. Finally, in 1935, he went
back to Gloversville, where he was to stay seven years
until his induction.

It was in Gloversville that his agony began—Gloversville, a small town where, "by conservative estimate, Mrs.
Grundy peeks from every third window." He was close to
thirty, unsuccessful in love, penniless, and dependent on
his father. He suffered from severe sinus headaches, in-
somnia, and depression. "Many in my generation," he
writes, "have become State psychiatric charges, with no
disgrace." But as he watched the spreading waste of his
life he began to see in it the ruin that was falling everywhere upon the world. The war in Spain had begun, and
with it the betrayal of the democracies. Gradually his
political orientation took shape. At first he found it a

mild process after the dilemmas of the spirit. But in the
end he joined the Communists with a strange zeal that
was half conviction and half guilt. He left the Ivory
Tower (which he had never inhabited—guilt makes
curious confessions) and stabled his White Charger.
"Goodbye, Mr. Yogi," he wrote, addressing his old self,
and he vowed to read no more "leisure-class literature."

He joined with the Communists for the reason most
men join: he was a man of good will, sincere in his concern for the world. But after a year he left in disgust.
He left for the reason that most men leave: he had remained sincere, a man of good will. The role of the
GPU in Spain, the Moscow trials, and the absence of
democracy in the Party were too much for him. He was
disillusioned with the entire Marxist movement in America, Trotskyist as well as Stalinist. The Marxists, he suggests, are the expatriates who never left home. Their
ideology and motives are predicated on Russia's foreign
policy, nowhere suited to the needs and interests of the
American working class. The only Marxist group with a
native tradition that he could find was the Socialist Labor
Party, the smallest and least effectual of them all. For
himself, he retained only a belief in liberal socialism,
democratic, free of violence, and opposed to the Jesuitical
doctrine of the means justifying the end.

But in the Party he at least learned a trade. He had
become an accomplished mimeographer; and now set up
the Mimeo Shop in Gloversville to make himself independent of his father. He began to write again, and he
had a love affair with a Jewish girl named Bimba. But
the returns of the Mimeo Shop were scant; the stories
made the round of *Harper's,* the *Atlantic, Story Magazine*
to no avail, and the novel he had written was promptly
rejected. And Bimba, whom he had loved for two and a
half hopeless years, proved too much attached to her
home and her parents' anti-Goyism to marry him. He
had had affairs before. It was marriage that he wanted,
and a family, a fully adult adjustment, but this never
came. Frustration seemed his constant lot: economic,

literary, and sexual failure. And then the war broke out and he felt it would soon be over with him.

But a man grows for all that. In leaving the Party he returned to himself. Zest came back to him at the moment one might have expected his resources to be at their lowest point, and his journal picked up new vitality. He had learned, through political activity, to admire the vigor which a social orientation will impart to thought. Now he will become a composite individual finding good in all men who can build—engineers, architects, technologists—and asserting them all in himself and in his work. Spirit had not left him. The bite of failure was dulled, but only because he had learned to suffer it and had turned, maturely, with a disillusioned joy, to the affirmation of life:

> Something almost pounds at me these days to keep clear of the religions of despair, of the art and literature of what is variously called "fin de siècle," "coterie," "decadent," and of what I now call "alienating" philosophies. . . . I do not want to be alienated from reality, intellectually, by an epistemology; or alienated from life, emotionally, by a religion or an art or a philosophy. I will keep to the realism of the average man, sharing his "animal faith" so far as that is possible without sharing his uncritical assumptions.

He had found his Way. Then, as though in reward for his faithfulness, the very journal which marked his progress was accepted for publication. Shortly thereafter he was inducted into the Army.

His journal is not only remarkable for the experience it records—it is Everyman's story, the experience of an entire generation—but also for the display of the resources Morris brought to counter his experience. Morris did more than learn from his life—an empirical wisdom after all the easiest to come by. He withstood it, a braver accomplishment. The frustrations he encountered were the same that have turned almost his entire generation into underground men—men who are not so much beyond belief as below it, incapable of the desperate exertion of rising which an affirmation of our time de-

mands. This is the generation which remembers the last
war dimly, and the Depression clearly; which was sustained by the WPA only to see the rise and flourishing
of fascism, the death of Spain and the disgrace of the
democracies; which lost, in Stalin, the last hope of im-
minent socialism and in the present war the hope of its
own survival. That such men, moral undergroundlings,
cannot affirm values which they never possessed is hardly
a matter for wonder, and even less for blame. The affirmation of life in our time is an act only a transcendental
man can perform, one who would be mad for his joy, "a
psychiatric charge, with no disgrace," were he incapable
of transcending his experience. But ages and generations
do not come that way. Man, for the most part, is either
below his experience or level with it and *"kann nicht
anders."* That Walter Morris, whose frustrations were of
the deepest, could survive honest and unbroken and still
capable of joy, makes his triumph all the greater, giving
it a fidelity to life which surpasses the very experience
entered here.

New Republic, January 11, 1943

✑ Class Fiction: Frustration
at the Barricades

As LIKELY A PAIR of opposites in the season's reading as *The Little People* and *The Prodigal Women* it may, at first face, be difficult to find. Down the line it goes. Author: man—woman; subject: "insignificant" people—"important" people; style: slangy, stumbling, free—heavy, correct, tight. And yet reconciliation is soon at hand. For slave and master are both bound, and the small dreams and the great ones awake to the same ruin. It is the one synthesis our society knows: opposite social classes are reconciled in an equal frustration.

The Little People is [Albert] Halper's best book in that it carries itself without prodding, a little vaguer and wiser than heretofore. It is about the workers in Sutton's, an exclusive Chicago department store, the hatter, the elevator boy, the shipping clerk, the salesmen, and the salesgirls. They are all powerless; they have no hand in their lives. Job, Boss, and Routine control their souls. They may squeak or rage, but Sutton's walls are thick and their own complaints die in their ears. Ambition gnaws at them, or simple hope, or the need of survival. One wants a hat store of his own; another, a girl of his own; a third, a husband, a little dignity, a chance to live like a *Mensch*. They go on dreaming: some day a break may come, luck may change, they may have at least enough power to maintain a personal identity, enough riches to support an ego, an opportunity to hit back. But luck will not change because, for them, each level has its own frustration, and if a man rises he will face a new doom.

Nancy Hale's *The Prodigal Women* is about life on the other side of the tracks, the people who are in the swim and in the know, who take up social space. Its heroines, Maizie, Betsy, and Leda, are rich in love, experience, and power, respectively. Maizie, the D. H. Lawrence woman, must absorb her man through submission, feed on his virility, and dominate in surrender. Her husband is a painter, cruel to her, selfish, rebelling as a man, and justified. Maizie is doomed. She passes from years of illness and hypochondria to eventual insanity, the devouring woman who, losing her object, devours herself. Betsy, Maizie's lavish younger sister, runs her course in the twenties and the Prohibition thirties, believing the New York Myth, rising in the world of ladies' magazines and Powers models, sleeping around town free and adventuresome, but her heart untouched. Then she falls in love. Betsy is doomed. Her lover, later her husband, is a paranoiac who tortures her, digs into her promiscuous past, degrades her, and beats her. She is dirt under his feet, but Betsy loves it.

This, for her as for her sister, is love and submission; she is robbed of her power and licked for good, but because she can give herself, and because experience, for once, can touch her, sink in, and have personal meaning, nothing else matters, neither her lover's religious mania, his brutality, nor his lack of human worth. For all this Betsy has a masochist's gratitude; a whipping at least bears a sting. Leda devoted her life to the acquisition of power, social status, and poise. She was cold, she played a nasty, calculating game. In the end, at the top of the pile, she catches a chill. What has it got her? The answer, of course, is nothing. She is alone, without love, bereft of her own talent for poetry, the third in a trilogy of self-willed doom.

And so, both books level off at the frustration point. For when our prodigals, done spending, realize that they have spent not themselves but a foreign substance, when they find that their wasted values were not really their own but impositions on the spirit, this discovery leaves them frustrated instead of free. Then it may be assumed that the antithesis of classes is not a durable one, and that cleavage does not necessarily represent an opposition in society. For if the little people worship the big, then social values are continuous. And if both, in their essential capacity, can meet only frustration, then each on their own side of the barricade will fall too exhausted and self-injured to struggle with the other.

But this, too, is a deceptive appearance. Class war goes on even without warriors. No matter how weary the prodigals, how disillusioned, their values still hearten them. A whiff of perfume at the nostrils and the beaten spirit revives. And if the little people still believe in luck then, even if they no longer believe in themselves, they still accept the rest of the social mythology, and they are out to get even when luck changes. It is a war of values for both.

But the values may change, and the antithesis may emerge elsewhere, decisive and basic. In an article on Ferrero in *Partisan Review,* Ignazio Silone makes a profound statement. "A society," he says, "is renewed when its humblest element acquires a value." That is, when it acquires a value of its own. Then the continuity is broken and men know where they stand. The reigning values of a society are rejected, and the values which that society rejects are reaffirmed. These are the values of the spirit, the only values of renewal which, in times of corruption, only the humble possess. It is for this reason that the proletariat, the *cafoni,* the elevator boys, the honest poets and intellectuals, in a word the little people, constitute a potential revolutionary class. They are men already alienated from society; but some day they may be alien only in virtue of their devotion to the morality which their society despises. And then, sick of wallowing and wanting nothing of what the enemy calls success, they will seek to rise only by first humbling themselves, and the little people will become the prodigals, men of lavish spirit who burn defiantly.

❧ Nancy Hale: Fiction as Method

A NOVELIST'S SHORT STORIES often stand in a revealing relation to his major work. The scale is reduced, the writer practices an economy wherein he is forced to proceed without cover, exposing himself at every turn. Thus his method, which in a larger work is often obscured by space and time, here plays a distinctive role—in Nancy Hale's stories, the dominant role. Her stories are all method. Reading *Between the Dark and the Daylight*, you will understand precisely where and why her best-selling novel, *The Prodigal Women*, failed.

Her method is largely an academic, unoriginal adaptation and attenuation of the professional short-story form too much in vogue these days. She conveys her effects by measuring them in advance, calculating the stress each point can safely bear. Thus: an introduction must be brief, concrete—a few objects, a house, a tree, an observation, are enough. Then on with the story—a few strokes set the limitation of the heroine's personality within which the developing conflict or narrative will obediently keep its bounds. The climax is secured through a summary of psychological strains, a suggestive recapitulation, emerging in a moment of capture, resolution, or breakdown, then underscored with a line, a perception, a thought.

These are well-formed stories—any one of them could serve as a model for a short-story course. But none is satisfying, for none is freely expressed. The form of these stories is not so much a form that has been mastered as one that masters, controls, determines, like an a priori category, the perceptions and the emotions which may enter it. Miss Hale writes under the onerous obligation of meeting her own requirements.

The stories in *Between the Dark and the Daylight* deal with the anxieties of children, the lushness of adolescent life, and with women, young and old, unhappily married, insane, defying the conventions, rejecting society, making an effort to break through the lies and brutalities of their middle-class surroundings and emerge free and true. But while Nancy Hale's rich subject matter is one of intense conflict, her treatment is almost purely neutral; the modern tradition of restraint (which has made a virtue of repression) keeps her from committing a single passional act while she writes. A writer's access to character may be facilitated if he can suspend moral judgment; but not if he lacks it. Miss Hale's preoccupation with surface, with the mere texture of narrative, suggests this lack. In her stories the surface tension mounts, as in a glass, reaches its climax, breaks, spills over—but at no point is it more than water.

The title story is perhaps the best. Treating of a young girl (here her method finds its most appropriate expression), she captures the conflict between an adolescent's desire to return to childhood and her awakening to the sexual world. The young girl gets out of her sick bed where, in fancy, she had nostalgically recovered the buried but warm self-center of her childhood, to sip a soda with a girl friend. She is conscious of the drugstore cowboys' stares, and is pleased. Sipping her soda, she knows she can't turn back to childhood; sensing the young men about her, she no longer wants to. This story is written with the adequacy of perception which always takes on a dimension of truth. The conflict is seen, the moment is captured and held. But, simple as this perception is in its appeal to sensibility alone, it requires a strong, a passionate sensibility to sustain it. Nancy Hale's sensibility is formal.

This weakness kept *The Prodigal Women* from attaining the pitch of realization at which it would have become more than good writing, more than competence.

The conflict and the suffering were there, the perceptive flashes, but not the great sensibility itself which can fill a page of Conrad with revelation. Judgment, the artist's personal passion, was absent—the inward struggle toward affirmation which makes even Drieser's sketchier and clumsier stories monuments of an individual's growth. Only once, in *Between the Dark and Daylight*, does one encounter perception at this level (in a story of insanity, "Who Lived and Died Believing," which she treats on the whole with intimate though too literary a feeling): "Hell is not heat or cold, it is banishment to the ultimate ego." The rest of her work is lost in a clarity which throws no relief, a smoothness, an order so regular it would be destroyed by growth.

New Republic, July 12, 1943

ᴀ§*The Trouble with the Short Story*

SUPPOSE THERE WERE no short stories. We would have memoirs, sketches, extravaganzas, tales, long or short, humorous, serious, lyrical, or trashy. The impulse to write would still be present and, presumably, the impulse to edit and reject, to assemble the year's best work. Superficially, it would make little difference if short stories as such disappeared from the market: the other short forms would easily fill the gap. But if short stories disappeared from the mind; if the psychic entity, "idea for a story," were free to express itself in a variety of forms and to call upon new energies and new designs, the writing of our day would be rewarded by a grant of liberty, a release of imagination.

Look at the year's best work [*The Best American Short Stories of 1943*]. Though of a somewhat higher average level than last year's collection, the present stories continue the same trend. They deal, among other themes, with childhood sustaining a shock of revelation from the adult world (William Faulkner, "The Bear"; Wallace Stegner, "Chip Off the Old Block"); a miscellany of sexual conflict (John Cheever, "The Pleasures of Solitude"; Vardis Fisher, "A Partnership with Death"; Mary Lavin, "Love Is for Lovers"; Eudora Welty, "Asphodel"); the war as a topic of current events touching on the anxieties of the civilian front, actual fighting not included (Vicki Baum, "This Healthy Life"; Kay Boyle, "Frenchman's Ship"; Irwin Shaw, "Preach on the Dusty Roads").

This covers a very wide range of subject matter, timely

54

as a form of literary comment, but by no means critical or urgent as far as the actual experience of American life is concerned. But though the range of subject matter is wide, the treatment is in most cases almost identical. Loose as it is, the short-story form is highly conventional, and though these conventions have not yet won full academic recognition and support—some stories in the collection might still be considered "advanced"—this is sure to come, for our writers have already succumbed to an academic outlook of their own making. Only two stories out of the thirty deviate significantly from the currently accepted form—a sketch, consisting of childhood reminiscences, "Samuel Blane," by Murray Dyer, and a prose poem, "Threnody for Stelios," by Peter Gray. A third, "An Argument in 1934," by Delmore Schwartz, thrown in as a concession to the avant-garde, had all its paragraphs numbered when it first appeared in *Kenyon Review*. Martha Foley lopped off the numbers, altering the story's appearance but not its basic orthodoxy. The rest of the stories in the volume were already written long before they were conceived—an a priori category engulfed them.

These stories were gathered from fourteen magazines, from the *Saturday Evening Post* to the *Antioch Review*, from *Mademoiselle* and *Harper's Bazaar* to the *Yale Review*—a fairly representative sampling, though the slicks and near-slicks are in the majority. Despite her disregard of *Partisan Review*, where at least three excellent stories (too long!) appeared during the year, I have no great quarrel with Miss Foley's editing. The most she could have done was to produce a better collection. It is not her fault if she fails to inspire better stories. Then whose fault is it if story after story runs along in the same vein, the same words, the same pattern?

I believe the short story itself is at fault. Some stories are told, others are made. The first have a natural pattern, illustrated by Sherwood Anderson's best work. The second are based on a study of technique, and it is with these, where technique is learned but never discovered, that my dissatisfaction lies. Evidently, the way to write such a story is first to get an idea for one. A chance recollection or a chance encounter, sometimes a name or a title, or the suggestion of a scene, will do. The present collection offers very little evidence that these ideas symbolize crises in perception, moral anxieties, themes or fantasies deep in an artist's life: they lack the obsession of the personal. Such ideas are afloat in a tradition, and make only an ineffectual entry into the awareness of literature, for they already bear the stale literary semblance of a bookish birth.

Another fault, the greatest one, is that the contrivance of character in a well-tailored story is identified with the contrivance of narration. Short-story characters are receptacles for the flow of narrative and they never overflow, nor do they receive their fill. In Robert Gibbon's "Time's End," for example, a story about a plantation owner's failure to move two old Negro women, deeply attached to the soil, from their house in the swamps to a more productive section of the plantation, neither John, the protagonist, nor Mub or Glow, the heroines, have a speck more of reality than is demanded by the minimal conditions of action. Only with Curtis, the incidental villain *ex machina,* a truck driver called in to move the two women, do the outlines of character appear even dimly, and only because he says "nigger" and tramps heavily on the wooden floor.

This is the common failing. Short-story writers divide character delineation between two techniques: description (often no more than the hook of a nose, the line of a mouth, size, shape, hulk) and action (a peculiarity in smoking cigarettes, a way of blinking or walking), and between the two methods reality is constantly running out. The structure of character, its strains and conflicts, are ignored and its emotional pattern which, of all traits, should serve as the fundamental means of psychological identification, is violated in the very act which substitutes the heavy innuendoes of behaviorism for the simple feelings of the inner life. Character becomes no more than a point of density in a story. Where individuals are needed to sustain dramatic tension, up they spring from their bed of words, meeting all requirements but their own. It would be better not to raise a story to dramatic pitch but let it lie lax in the easy tone of sketch or memoir, if the very tension of conflict which creates character is also the means which destroys it. For conflict, in the contemporary short story, is a platitude and a technical device, something which happens when two people get together, in no way involving the will's deep commitment to struggle, a mere trick for getting a story started. But were conflict entertained for its intrinsic psychological interest, character could emerge in vividness of emotions, in the ambivalence of desire and the unity of moral meaning.

It surprises me that stories with so wide a range of subject matter should suffer from faults reducible to a common denominator. For which reason I suspect the form. "The actual technique of story-telling has seen no startling innovations during the year," says Miss Foley in her foreword to the volume. Evidence, I believe, that the form has settled down to a middle-aged conservatism of thwarting the imagination.

New Republic, October 4, 1943

❧ *Philosophical Naturalism:*
The Failure of Verve

I HAVE BEEN WONDERING, while reading *Partisan Review*'s series on "The New Failure of Nerve" (January-February through May-June, 1943), whether there actually is such a thing. In one sense, of course, there obviously is—there is panic on the Left and a feeling of hopelessness which comes from the defeat that liberalism has suffered in the years preceding and attending the war. Yet the movements, philosophies, and tendencies which Professors Hook, Dewey, and Nagel attack are by no means nerveless ones. They are the familiar movements of philosophical, religious, and political reaction, the cults of mysticism and obscurity, the flirtatious mythologies of quasi-fascism, the doctrines of the Catholic Church. These are audacious. A study of the contemporary failure of nerve, it seems to me, would have to examine the motive for man's allegiance to the obscure as well as the doctrine of obscurity itself. The war, I imagine, makes such an assessment of motives difficult. It presents us with a set of motivating factors—all of them bearing on political defeat—which are at once self-evident, no matter how unclear they may be.

The discussion of the New Failure of Nerve is thus a critique of an old phenomenon rather than the discovery of a new one. But there have been many defeats (there is a defeat to correspond with each issue at stake in the war). One can find, for example, motivation for retreat in the purely moral losses the race has suffered. A study of this kind, "Conversation with Nazis," by Roger

58

Caillois (*Commonweal*, June 25) presents some of the data which Professor Hook ignored in accepting the obvious motives for surrender at their face value. Mr. Caillois points out one victory the Nazis have already achieved: over our assumption of the universality of moral order and good will, of the spiritual community of compassion, kindness, dignity, and honor. They have overthrown the ethos of the West not so much by violating it (to violate is still to accept, just as to hate is to resemble) as by showing that the forbidden conception of a moral world completely in reverse is feasible. Even the strongest nerve responds to evidence—evidence of this sort is appalling.

We are inclined to take for granted that demoralization will always be of benefit to the enemy. Why this should be the case, and why the Right, and movements such as Thomism, mysticism within and without the Church, and the whole obscure doxology of reaction should gain from our defeats we are at a loss to explain. No one expected the causes which have contributed to the failure of nerve to create a swing over to liberalism, naturalism, and reliance on scientific method. But surely these movements should have something to gain from universal crises, as revolutionary movements, we remember, at one time did gain. The reason, I'm afraid, is that liberalism in thought, as in politics, is equipped to capitalize only on minor catastrophes, itself falling a victim to major ones. Men develop an interest in methods, in problems of means, evidence, and validation so long as they enjoy a minimal security for their basic beliefs. When that security is gone, and with it the beliefs, they lose interest in methods of implementation, rushing to find new beliefs. The naturalist and liberal traditions have been losing out in recent years because considerations of means and methodology have lost imaginative appeal.

This is not to suggest that naturalism is responsible for the failure of nerve. But surrounded as it is by areas of

waste emotion in which the will is forced to exchange
truth for security; existing in a period when cultural
breakdown (not to be confounded with historical ana-
logues) has reached a new level in human loss, naturalism must itself be liberated, broadened, and extended over
the regions of experience in which the dominant anxieties of our time have grown if it is to counteract the
failure of nerve in the most important sphere of its actual
occurrence—precisely the sphere of nerve, of will. But
observe the exposition of naturalism which Professors
Hook and Nagel develop.

Central to their exposition, as it is central to the philosophy itself, is the problem of methodology. Scientific
method is presented as the only reliable one (which in
fact it is) of validating claims to knowledge, of confirm-
ing propositions, and of evaluating evidence and determining means for the implementation of values. Loss of
faith in scientific method is thereupon established as a
symptom of the failure of nerve. This is true as far as it
goes—men in intellectual panic have abandoned the
methods of science and empirical naturalism. But they
have exhibited other traits, other symptoms: they have
felt anxiety not only for the truth of certain propositions
but for the world itself in that nonpropositional, vague,
metaphysical anguish which is nonsense technically, yet
morally often the watershed of sanity. Or they have, at
the point of death, begun to yearn for immortality, God,
and "eternal things," discovering a religious emotion
which, even though it be the mask of fear, still bears the
features of genuine experience. These yearnings may be
transgressions of the scientific or empirical temper of
mind, they may, surely, be obscure, but as experiences—
not as doctrines—they are on a level with all immediate
experience and no more obscurantist, nor allied to reaction, than any involuntary apprehension of the spirit.
These data neither invalidate nor surpass the claims of
scientific method. But for that very fact I can see no
reason in ignoring their status in experience, or in attempting to eradicate or correct such tendencies by a

recital of the methods of scientific inquiry. Except as whipping boys, they have received no recognition. The central problem of the failure of nerve is seen as the knowledge-relation—as though yearning were to be dismissed as an illegitimate form of inference.

What is at fault here, in an avowedly nonmetaphysical philosophy, are certain metaphysical hangovers. The empirical tradition, which has devoted itself to the critique of rationalism, has nevertheless taken over from rationalism one of its uncritical premises: the supremacy of reason. This results in an oversimplified construction of the human personality. It is assumed, in the greatest degree by Professor Nagel, that the formal exposition of the program of reason will be a sufficient condition for halting the flight from reason. He therefore finds it unnecessary to devote his attention to the irrational, not only as a constituent of the failure of nerve but as a dominant factor in personality. He is satisfied to show that the intrusion of irrationality into thought results in error, forgetting that men live primarily by their mistakes. Thus what exists in the human personality as emotion and need—the need for moral security, for belief —is acknowledged in his philosophy only as a deviation from an arbitrary standard of rational behavior, while its intellectual expression is dismissed as nonsense.

There is a narrowness of doctrine in the official position of empiricism which the more difficult emotions betray into perplexity. Normally taking little account of esthetic, imaginative data, of the sources of poetry, art, and playfulness, as well as of suffering, the official position fails both in its assessment of the causes of the failure of nerve and in its appeal to sensibility. It offers only methods and canons at a time when the Church offers salvation, when fascism, mysticism, metaphysical sociology, or even simple cloud-gazing, dangerously unrivaled, offer emotional values. There is an admirable stoicism in its adherence, in default of wider accommodations, to the methods of science—but it is the stoicism of simple diet. Somewhere it has missed the richness, the variety, pleasure, tragedy, the sheer possibility of experience. It has overlooked man's legitimate spiritual orphanage in attacking the false asylum of the Church. And it has had its own failure of nerve—or better still, a failure of verve.

↩ Second-Generation
Perspectives

A PROVINCIAL (who is every man until he has loved the world) one day cried, "Nothing human is foreign to me," and learned to love spaghetti. This is a parable. Go wherever men eat and you may have spaghetti. Or chow mein, or kosher corned beef, or whatever you like. Only by the width of our stomachs have we missed taking the foreigner to our hearts.

The same people (dagoes, sheenies, hunkies, greasers —our language is enriched from giving them bad names) who in coming to our green and pleasant shores have as often found their humiliation as their home, are nevertheless admired and acknowledged by us for their quaintness and their color. But this is a sociological, not a human, acknowledgment. I, for one, grow angry when I hear human beings call one another "quaint" or "colorful." These words mark the tourist's mentality, which a man need not travel to acquire.

Nevertheless, what is the tongue tempted to call Jerre Mangione's *Mount Allegro* but colorful? Color has been deliberately selected and added—so much so that Mangione himself seems partisan to the traditions of popular sociology—the better to set off the old story of the immigrant's heartbroken, comical fortunes.

Through his narrator, a young boy, Gerlando Amoroso, Mangione depicts a Sicilian family and its innumerable relatives living in Rochester, New York, in the squalid industrial district nicknamed Mount Allegro. Gerlando's early experiences, his juvenile gang life, and his encounters with Northern Italians make him aware of the

63

social stigma reserved for his people. The first thing Sicil-
ians encounter upon coming to this country is their poor
reputation, prepared in advance by other, and particularly
Northern, Italians, in co-operation with the never reluctant *Americani.* And so young Gerlando learns that the
world expects him to go about armed with a knife, ready
to do violence on the least provocation. His father, the
world's best pastry cook, Peppino Amoroso, forbids him
and his younger brother to carry so much as a jackknife;
with the result that the youngsters must suffer from im-
puted sins at least to the extent of being prevented from
joining the Boy Scouts, who, it is known, are knife bearers.

Reading on, one meets Uncle Luigi, with his passion
for rich widows, who never come his way, and his love of
experimental theology. No sooner had Luigi landed in
America than he was fascinated by the variety of religious
denominations. At once this errant Catholic became a
Baptist for the sufficient reason that the Italian Baptist
minister who converted him was the first cleric he had ever
met who looked happy. But Luigi could not restrain his
religious *Wanderlust,* and he entered other folds, deriving his greatest delight from visiting as many different
houses of worship as he could find, from the Church of
the Holy Rollers to an orthodox synagogue. Then there
is Uncle Nino, jeweler, loafer, and ne'er-do-well, who
never missed an opportunity to deliver orations in the
purest Italian studded with quotations from the great
Dante. And so one becomes acquainted with the members of this prolific, noisy, hospitable, and gregarious family, their dinners and banquets, the squalling children
and the flowing wine.

Mangione's material is so much alive that the only way
he can keep it from running together is by imposing the
external rank and order of topics; accordingly he follows
the adventures of his family and friends in terms of their
responses to typical conflict situations—their struggles
with the American language, their attempts to meet misfortune through recourse to superstition and the cult of
the evil eye, their difficulties in adjusting their strict sexual morality and system of arranged marriages to the

freedom of the American environment. But Mangione's concessions to form end with his chapter divisions. He makes few generalizations. The pattern of social response and adaptation which is the underlying theme of these memoirs is to be pieced together out of vivid items, in themselves more memorable than the theses they illustrate. For example: the father, insanely jealous of tradition, who bites the ear of his daughter's American boy friend.

Nevertheless, the overtones which Mangione catches are a little disconcerting. His characters, while overdrawn, are insufficiently realized. They appear wistful, eccentric, pathetic, or comical, but are known less through themselves than through the author's frequently remote medium. It is this which points indirectly in the true direction of his story. For while Mangione is illustrating the process of social adaptation, he himself is writing as a member of the second generation, more affected by that process than any of the individuals he portrays. He has already become an outsider, in whose eyes the old folks have lost their finality. For if one eye is Sicilian, the other is American, and he cannot help but look beyond his people, sensing the comparisons he is too loyal to draw. The objectivity he once may have sought has now become unavoidable. Instinctively he has made his narrator a young boy, for it is only in that guise that he is still at home, a participant, in Mount Allegro.

But whatever the distance that separates him from his origins and prevents a more inward rendering of the Allegrans, Mangione remains essentially a man of two cultures. Thus, when he pays a visit to Sicily, not only does he recognize the inexorable accommodation that has made him an American, but he gains final insight, through his own alienation, into the nature of his people. Over all of Mount Allegro has lain the nostalgia of the immigrants for the old country, growing greener and more tender with the years of separation and hardship in the United States. But Mangione finds Sicily a bleak, starving country, its wretchedness exceeding the worst American slum, its poverty resulting from official neglect, and its spiritual impoverishment the consequence of deliberate Fascist techniques of social control. Poverty now becomes for him a source of illumination—it is the signature of Sicilian culture, for the warmth and exuberance of Mangione's countrymen have always known destitution at their heart, and their extraordinary gregariousness and joy of life is a solidarity against death. But in Sicily their festivals are desperate, for the shadow of Mussolini's jaw falls upon them—that broken jaw of their lost kingdoms. Within two months of his departure Mangione is back in the United States. His generation has accepted America and only waits for her, in turn, to take to her envious heart the warmth that foreigners have brought in their own strange persons.

New Republic, March 22, 1943

❧ The Situation of the
Jewish Writer*

ALL DISCUSSIONS pertaining to the Jews must begin with some very gloomy observations. The Jews are, everywhere, a minority group, and it is a particular misfortune these days to be a minority group in the United States. A conscious member of such a group is necessarily over-conscious: he is distracted by race and religion, distressed by differences which in a healthy society would be considered healthful. The very simple state of being a Jew—and it should occupy no more of a man's attention than any ordinary fact of his history—has created traumas, fears of violence, defenses against aggression. These are about the worst conditions under which an artist could seek to carry on his work. An artist should first of all have the security of a dignified neutrality. He should be able to consider himself a *mensch mit alle menschen gleich*—that is, an equal, a man among men, a representative even if extraordinary individual. But a Jewish writer unconsciously feels that he may at any time be called to account not for his art, nor even for his life, but for his Jewishness. Only a brave man can be a brave artist, let alone a good one, in a hostile world. It is therefore clear to me that whatever contribution Jewish writers may make to American literature will depend on matters beyond their control as writers.

But the position of Jewish writers—artists and intellec-

* Written in response to a series of questions on the role and problems of Jewish writers in America which had been asked by the editors of the *Contemporary Jewish Record*.

tuals in general—is not entirely an unfortunate one. For the most part the young Jewish writers of today are the children of immigrants, and as such—not completely integrated in society and yet not wholly foreign to it—they enjoy a critical advantage over the life that surrounds them. They are bound to observe much that is hidden to the more accustomed native eye.

The insight available to most Jewish writers is a natural result of their position in American life and culture. Jews are marginal men. As marginal men, living in cities and coming from the middle classes, they are open to more influences than perhaps any other group. I vaguely recall a Yiddish proverb to the effect that bad luck always knows where to find a Jew; and as a barometer of political calamity the Jews in this country are second only to the Negroes. But even gentler influences, short of fatality, know where to find Jews—in the middle, in the overlapping area where events converge. And the middle position has its cultural correlate, that of being centrally exposed to all movements in art and in thought. This position of cultural exposure gives the Jewish writer the advantage of access. (There is much more to be said about this point—more than I have the space or the knowledge to disclose. But, generally speaking, the position of Jewish writers illustrates one of the strangest phenomena of modern life. Since modern life is so complex that no man can possess it in its entirety, the outsider often finds himself the perfect insider.)

Close as they are to the main developments in America, some Jewish writers may retain more than a little of European culture. Either through their position in the Jewish community, their childhood, or the influence of their immigrant parents, they may possess a sense of reference to an earlier community. I don't know how widespread this old world feeling is among Jewish writers. But if it is at all common, I should say it is a valuable thing. Jews in America have relatively little contact with country life, with small town folk and farmers. But through cultural retention, through a subliminal orientation to more primitive surroundings, they may still find in themselves access to rural life, understanding of its character and traditions.

But it is one thing to consider the Jewish writer's social equipment, and quite another to regard his actual position in society. As a member of an internationally insecure group he has grown personally acquainted with some of the fundamental themes of insecurity that run through modern literature. He is a specialist in alienation (the one international banking system the Jews actually control). Alienation puts him in touch with his own past traditions, the history of the Diaspora; with the present predicament of almost all intellectuals and, for all one knows, with the future conditions of civilized humanity. Today nearly all sensibility—thought, creation, perception—is in exile, alienated from the society in which it barely managed to stay alive.

But alienation from society, like the paradox of the outsider, may function as a condition of entrance into society. Surely it is not a condition for the Jew's re-entrance into the world that has rejected him. But persecution may lead him, as it has in the past, to a further effort to envisage the good society. No man suffers injustice without learning, vaguely but surely, what justice is. The desire for justice, once it passes beyond revenge, becomes the deepest motive for social change. Out of their recent sufferings one may expect Jewish writers to make certain inevitable moral discoveries. These discoveries, enough to indict the world, may also be crucial to its salvation.

I do not want to make too much of alienation. It is the only possible condition, the theme we have to work with, but it is undesirable, for it falls short of the full human range. Besides, in every society, in every group, there are what Saul Bellow has called "colonies of the spirit." Artists create their colonies. Some day these may become empires.

Contemporary Jewish Record, February, 1944

❧ Sholom Aleichem

I. The Humor of Exile

THROUGHOUT Mr. Samuel's book [*The World of Sholom Aleichem*] there is a tone of patient, literal, laborious, and repetitive explication which, though certainly poorer than Sholom Aleichem deserves, is nevertheless justified. Mr. Samuel, true to the title of his work, is writing primarily about a world; and though "worlds" are large and public entities, universally knowable or known, here, however, is one which in the space of hardly fifty years has all that vanished. It is the world of *Golos* (Diaspora) further dispersed, existing at present only in reminiscence, and only in vestiges of religious or communal tradition. At one time it was the center of Jewish learning and culture. The East European settlements, in Poland and in the Pale surrounding Kiev, of which Sholom Aleichem wrote, were great communities, flourishing as well as misfortune, repressions, and pogroms would allow. But it was in the nature of this world to die. Even without pogroms, without Chmelnitzky and Petlura, who failed, and Hitler who succeeded in destroying it, it would have died, a victim, even of an innocent history in whose changes it neither had, nor wanted, a part. Mr. Samuel has, therefore, done well in making his exposition careful and clear and detailed. He should certainly have shown, as I imagine he possesses, a more philosophical understanding of his subject; and, since he was dealing with one of the greatest folk artists, he might have devoted more attention to the individual stature of the man and the techniques of his craft. But by way of capturing and translating into the English language traits and qualities of a culture which was lost in social translation, Mr. Samuel has succeeded admirably.

There have been many Jewish worlds. The one known through the novels of Sholem Asch (*Three Cities*) or I. J. Singer (*The Brothers Ashkenazi*) represents the breakdown of traditional folkways under the influence of industrialism, and the emergence of a Jewish proletariat and a modern middle class. This aspect of history the Jews of Asch and Singer share with the rest of the world, and their story has successfully been translated because their life was itself in process of translation. But the life of Kasrilevke (Pauperville), Sholom Aleichem's arch-typical village, was too far removed from the origins of social change, too limited in its access to history, and too faithful to its own traditions to endure without breakdown the eventual adjustments that were forced upon it. Kasrilevke was guarded but exhausted by an old religion which had never learned to rationalize adaptation to the world.

In Kasrilevke, religion, like mud and chicken feathers, clung to one's very boots. Let alone the Sabbath, holidays, ceremonies, and learning—even haggling involved Scripture. Sholom Aleichem's Jews, it is correct to say, were a religious group. Of necessity their religion was more than a dogmatism, unrelated, or in winking contradiction to the life they led. Their religion affected their most familiar and intimate emotions—the perpetual insecurity, fear, and nostalgia of the homeless—fortified them with parables, and provided a metaphysics of sentiment as well as an immediate guide to the conduct of life. Besides, it was fundamentally a secular religion, for it provided the only available basis for culture. But while this religion embraced the world, it was also profoundly alienated from it, and acknowledged Kasrilevke only as society, never as a homeland. All thought and expression, even the most trivial modes of intercourse among the Jews were permeated with yearning for Eretz Israel, for home. Even the Yiddish language, as Mr. Samuel shows in a brilliant chapter, was never allowed to develop affinity for the natural world; it was poor in object names, recognizing only the few miserable species of flower and bird whose existence alone the exiled, for fear of forgetting Jerusalem, permitted themselves to acknowledge.

Sholom Aleichem's humor drew upon the phenomena of alienation. He himself was a man of "Western" culture, born of a landed middle class family (rare among Russian Jews), to whom the progressive and revolutionary traditions of the nineteenth cenutry were perhaps even more available than the traditions of Kasrilevke. But though he belonged outside the world in the depiction of which his greatness lay, his own alienation fostered his sympathy for the less sophisticated exile in which his characters lived. (Here, his sympathy, one of recognition rather than of surrender, followed an instinct of wise artistry. He did not identify himself with the life of his people; rather, he recognized the identity in pattern between their lives and his own—a distinction which proletarian novelists have never understood.) His humor was preoccupied with poverty—poverty, the visible symbol of man's alienation from the world. He constructed a comedy of endurance, balancing the fantastic excess of misfortune (always short of life's complete destruction, yet always threatening to attain its end) against the precious but useless resources of the human spirit which can make equally fantastic accommodations, can even overwhelm the world with its enthusiasm, and yet remains no less impotent than the despair it sedulously avoids. In this respect, Sholom Aleichem was in the great tradition of Chassidism, to which he provided the secular counterpart. Enthusiasm and ecstasy are the ideal limits of his humor, just as they were the final values of the Chassid's worship. His was the humor which loves the world from which it seeks to be delivered.

Deliverance is a familiar theme in Jewish thought, and remains, however disguised or modified, a basic concept in its social philosophy. We would naturally expect the social, as distinct from the religious, meaning of the term to imply a rather clear set of values, a sense of injustice and indignation, and a program of rectification. But the peasant tradition in literature, especially in Sholom Aleichem's time, reinforced as it was by the influence of Russan populism, introduced several complications, religious in origin, which had a natural result in offsetting social thought from the centrality of the thesis of class struggle. Sholom Aleichem, like Silone today who also celebrates poverty, would seem to suggest a fundamental ambiguity in man's desire for salvation. This ambiguity results from the double function of alienation, to both of whose meanings Sholom Aleichem subscribed. On the one hand, suffering and privation leave men alienated from the world, free to act, in default of possession, toward the reconstruction of the social order and the redistribution of worldly goods. On the other hand, their alienation from objects produces an alienation from values, deprives them of enthusiasm for action, and leads them back to their poverty as the only trustworthy and familiar, if not the only possible, locus of values. Men's original indignation is sapped by a loss of faith, and leaves a residue of pity and self-love which no program of rectification can draw off. So Sholom Aleichem elaborates the symbol of poverty, which he identifies with the Jews' particular plight, their alienation even from the class struggle, the alienation, when all else is restored, of remaining homeless on the earth. While awaiting deliverance, he is skeptical of all other alternatives. He will not venture farther than the values immanent in his love for his people.

For Sholom Aleichem, I should judge, there was no valid distinction to be drawn between reformism and revolution in politics. Extremes could never catch the only important issue between them, nor gradations, subtleties, or concessions of thought. Only one doctrine could strike the point of possible cleavage between the world of Kasrilevke and the world at large, and that was the doctrine, Zionist in whatever form, that not until the Jews once again had a home could they hope to attain, without foregone futility, the values and responsibilities of modern life. Consequently he could find no standard for evaluating the variety of revolutionary theories which were beginning to appear even in Kasrilevke. He could extend his sympathy to all of them, but his hope to none. The breakdown of Jewish life could only be accelerated by participation in the class struggle (a participation which he nevertheless approved). But for the Jews even the most basic revolution in society could only be reformist in scope. Their revolution would first have to be historical: the history of Diaspora would first have to be brought to a close. Until then they had not even chains to lose, nor, since chains imply fixation, even the hope of acquiring a few.

Sholom Aleichem has often been compared with Dickens. The comparison is superficially plausible, as far as resemblances in verbal humor and characterization are concerned. But there is a fundamental divergence between the two, which typifies the Jewish author's removal from the entire tradition which, in greater or less degree, has united all social novelists. Society, for Sholom Aleichem, was less the object than the source of his sentiment, and thus love, more than indignation, gave motive to his art. What he felt toward his people, toward their poverty and hopelessness, was always directed outward, as if proceeding from their, rather than his own, heart. He himself was perhaps capable of a greater individual expression than the one he achieved. But folk artists lose nothing by their sacrifices. He would not instruct, rouse, organize his people toward any perspective available only to himself; he would not go beyond the limitations they themselves could not transcend. But it was not so much selflessness as an extreme self-development through love which reinforced his original fidelity to the sources of his growth. He could see the hopelessness of his people's traditions from the liberation of his own knowledge; but he also knew, through the identity of personal experience, the hopelessness of their lives. And it was his love, not only his uncertainty, which made him cling with them to a faith he had abandoned, and to celebrate, with as great a joy and tenderness as possible, the impoverished world within which they built, and later lost their lives.

Partisan Review, May-June, 1943

II. The Blessings of Poverty

IT IS NOT THE Butwins' fault that their translation [*The Old Country*] of twenty-seven of the better known and loved of Sholom Aleichem's three hundred stories falls so far short of the original Yiddish. The quality of Sholom Aleichem's Yiddish, for reasons that I shall try to indicate, is well-nigh incommunicable. Besides, whatever the defects of this translation, its mere existence calls for gratitude: this is the first time, as far as I know, that even such a small part of Sholom Aleichem's great work has been made available to the English-speaking world.

What, after all, is translation? It is the fault of our literary pragmatism that we so seldom ask this question. For ordinary purposes it is enough to say that translation is the finding of word combinations in one language to stand for word combinations in another. But this will not do as a definition. First of all, it begs the question in supposing that we already now what language is; the fact is that an important property of language is disclosed only in translation. What this property is, is made clear by the second shortcoming of the usual notion of translation, the assumption that the language of literature is wholly devoted to communication. Again the fact is otherwise, for writing, even in the strictest sense of naturalism, necessarily contains, if it is art at all, an irreducible element of expression. Expression is what the translator must trust to more than the luck or skill of his sense of poetry to recreate in his own language. The conveying of the expression of one language in the words of another ultimately depends on the congruence of separate cultures, philosophies, and ways of life. The translator, in an age when the internationalization of culture is an absolute imperative, is the philosopher *par excellence*. The entities with which he deals are paramount in metaphysics, recalling its simplest, but most difficult, its first, but most neglected, task: our need to know one another.

It is in this expanded sense of "translation" that the

translation of Sholom Aleichem is such a hard, hopeless, even tragic enterprise. There have been some successful translations from the Yiddish—Sholem Asch and I. J. Singer are excellent examples; but whereas the works of these authors, whether they are concerned with the origins of Christianity or the working-class revolution, involve familiar themes of Western history, Sholom Aleichem's work is almost deliberately at cross purposes with English and with the history the language subsumes. His idioms are entirely of another world (illuminated, but not "translated" for us in Maurice Samuel's brilliant *World of Sholom Aleichem*); they are of a Yiddish whose survival in the form that Sholom Aleichem made use of was no less remarkable than the survival of the people who spoke it, and one of their greatest accomplishments.

Language itself, the mere prose of daily life, is already the greatest poetry. The extraordinary poetic of Sholom Aleichem's Yiddish is its consciousness of what is peculiarly Jewish in existence. The language has a facility for singling out the most disparate and incongruous objects and catching precisely that quality wherein they reflect the destiny of the Jews. A turn of phrase, an additional syllable, and what would have been, as in any other language, a report of experience, becomes in Yiddish a comment on Jewish experience, say a reference to Diaspora, a veiled reminder to the Lord of the promise of deliverance and perhaps an expression of despair at its coming. The liberal sprinkling of Hebrew performs in an inverse way the same function that the presence of "foreign" words performs in the secularization and internationalization of the language: Hebrew, as the language, historically, of the true home and the faithful tradition, lends poignancy to the half-tones of exile, and an incongruity that mirrors in its humor the whole incongruity of Jewish dispersal. When Tevyeh the Dairyman, for example, refers to his wretched horse by the Hebrew word *sus*, he takes advantage of a usage available only in Yiddish to transpose the objects of the familiar world into a context equally familiar to the speaker but unrelated to his immediate concerns, so that the latter are trans-

ccnded, viewed historically, and implicity judged. The
same horse that drags Tevyeh's wagon along carries us
back thousands of years. Yiddish is a kind of consciousness
in verbal form, call it historical paranoia or call it truly
mystical, that interprets the whole creation in terms of a
people's deepest experience and intuition.

Sholom Aleichem's language is full of the intimate
quality of the life he loved and described so well. For this
life, as for his specifically surcharged words, there is no
equivalent in any other life or language. But to the extent
that transmission is possible under such inauspicious
circumstances, the essence of his work communicates itself
concretely in portrayals of the Jewish character which is
so faithfully rendered that it must, in some poetic part,
have been created for his people by the author.

Take Tevyeh the Dairyman. His closest Western cousin
is perhaps Sancho Panza. There is the same earthiness in
both of them, the same familiarity with misfortune, the
same wisdom expressing itself in proverbs and misquota-
tions. But Tevyeh is a Sancho without Don Quixote, unless Tevyeh's Knight is God Himself. Tevyeh is moved
by God's will as Sancho by his mad master's; it is to God
that Tevyeh complains, to God that Tevyeh looks for
help, and it is God who is the author of Tevyeh's misfortunes. But there is parity between Sancho and Don
Quixote in so far as they are the two faces of the same
coin, and the space between earthbound reason and
ridiculous faith that divides them is also the one that joins
them. Don Quixote's faith is superior in its madness precisely because it does not fear the ridicule it was doomed
to provoke. But how does God come to be mentioned in
the same breath with ridicule, or how can there be
parity between God and Tevyeh unless the dairyman has
something of the divine in him? It is precisely this conclusion, that Tevyeh has something of the divine, which
is demanded by the effort to understand the dairyman
and his brothers. God may well fear his ridicule, or at least
his wit as it expresses itself in prayer and complaint; and,
though it is nowhere suggested, for Tevyeh is a pious Jew
who would never utter such blasphemy, the possibility

remains open, when one considers the life that God has ordained for Tevyeh and his people, that there is a streak of madness in Him. Moreover, Tevyeh, like Sancho, when he rides his spirited reason, becomes his own Don Quixote; he is full of a ridiculous majesty which brings him closer than ever to his Master.

Tevyeh approaches the divine first of all in his irony which—no other word or degree for it—is absolute. (The English translation misses most of it.) It is present in every sentence he speaks, in every phrase and word, its extreme development being the measure of his moral courage. So highly developed is it, and so far pushed past all frontiers of ordinary caution, retraction, or qualification in God's favor, that it becomes something mystical, and it is no wonder that Tevyeh's worship, conducted always in the ironical mode, attains the immediacy of the direct vision and communion. It is irony that links Tevyeh with God, that brings together the patient and the author of suffering.

The chief cause and acutest form of suffering in the Jewish Pale was poverty. But the poverty of the Jews, like the Yiddish language, was itself a symbol and a kind of symbolism; in its final extension it was a sign, in the true religious sense, of God's ordination of the world. Deprivation of material means was the symbolic counterpart of the Jews' historical deprivation; they owned little of the world, not even so much as a home in it, and the continual struggle for food was like the unbroken prayer for deliverance. The Jews owned little of the world, but their hunger was the true dimension of all their longing, and their disappointment, which need not even have been felt inwardly, so close to the quick were its external provocations, was the clue to their great expectation—for were they not the Chosen People? Yet Tevyeh says we were chosen to suffer—it is for this that the world envies us. The irony here does not destroy the bond between man and God. The strain draws it tighter and lends pride to the perceptions of the poor—for now they know with Whom they are struggling. It is in poverty that man turns to God and in poverty that he turns away from Him, mistrusting Providence, or knowing it all too well. And yet his poverty is his strength and his blessing, it is the source of the irony that enables him to endure his faith in God, and of that great, tenacious will to life which, even if only an ironic victory is possible, at the cost of misery and misfortune, nevertheless chooses irony for the sake of triumph. It is in this faith, which is also faith in themselves, that the Jews have triumphed, and that they have revealed themselves to be still a warlike tribe. Sholom Aleichem's poor dairymen and tailors, shopkeepers, teachers, hapless speculators, *luftmenschen,* and *shlimazolim* are our foremost warriors. They have fought the longest and costliest war in history—the war, simply, with history itself.

It is this poverty as richness, as the rarest symbolic blessing, which ultimately proves to be untranslatable and which underlies the particular failures of the English phrase to do justice to the original. When Tevyeh says *"ligen in der erd un backen bagel"* to express destitution ("To lie in the ground and bake doughnuts")—not that bagels, strictly speaking, are doughnuts, or that *"ligen in der erd"* means lie *in* the ground or lie *on* the ground— it has a sense compounded of both, as when we speak lightly of a living death; very wisely the translators did not attempt to render this phrase in English—when Tevyeh speaks in this manner he shows a veteran contempt for poverty and proclaims his mastery over it. Likewise, when a character in the story "Hannukah Money" is called a *"farshleppte krenk"* (a "chronic ailment," wildly mistranslated here in a sentence that uses the word "zany," as if the Jews of Kasrilevke had already reached Broadway) and thereby set down with the power and finality of an imperious gesture, we must assume something of Jewish history to know how suffering can impart mastery of the world. . . . Such are the clues, lost in a lost culture, to the blessings of poverty. Its ultimate beatitude in Chassidism is truly ineffable.

Insights such as these gave Sholom Aleichem, the humorist and folk poet, also a philosopher's stature, so well did he know the confluence of personality and God.

He defined a peculiar intellectual and spiritual province of the Jews, revealing the hidden vitality of their religion and the historical viability of their culture. It is a province which is lost to the majority of us today, who know nothing of such blessings, even as that which was once our world, with Kasrilevke its Jerusalem, was lost to the world that engulfed and destroyed it.

New Republic, July 22, 1946

‌The Anger of
James T. Farrell

To GET AT THE THEME of James T. Farrell's Danny O'Neill books you might well go back to one of the concluding passages of the second volume of *Studs Lonigan*. Danny played only a minor role in the Lonigan trilogy and his life and character were no more than sketched in. But he was Farrell, and perhaps even the truest portrait of the artist Farrell would ever draw. Danny, at the age of twenty, having lived in squalor and brutality and survived, has at last established his identity, wrenched out of the bitter heart of the world that he knew. It was a world of lies,

> . . . a world of misery, neuroticism, frustration, impecuniousness, hypocrisy, disease, clap, syphilis, poverty, injustice. . . . He wanted to be a writer. . . . He wanted to purge himself completely of the world he knew, the world of Fifty-eighth Street . . . the hates it had welled up in him. . . .
>
> He walked home, carrying a briefcase full of books. Studs Lonigan, Red Kelly, and Barney Keefe passed on the other side of the street. They called him goof and told him to leave it alone. He didn't answer. Some day he would drive this neighborhood and all its memories out of his consciousness with a book. . . .

Thus the Danny books were born out of anger, and it is only fitting that the fourth, and apparently final volume dealing with Danny's life in Chicago, should be entitled *My Days of Anger*. But while anger is Farrell's sustaining emotion, giving impetus to his writing, it does not provide the whole intended measure of his theme. To begin with, there is very little anger in *My Days of Anger*. Furthermore, while there is a doggedness and bitterness in everything Farrell writes, these qualities are merely the elements of anger and not its dedication. The dedication, the innate goal of a man's anger, is never clearly expressed, for the dedication is personal, and Farrell cannot express himself. He can only indicate, through a violent aspiration, the values he wishes to attain, in the hope that the surge of his feeling will carry him there. The artist must stay on close and gloomy terms with what is in the world in order to get a sense of what life can be. His intentions may be poetic, but his method will deny itself all access to poetry; he will go on criticizing, never invoking, and what he attains as his own possession is "torn out of the guts of reality." Farrell will show, over and over again, what the reality is against which he plays off the heart's angry knowledge of the better life. But as he envelops it from one point of view after another, from character to character and incident to incident, reality envelops him until his anger is gone—and with it goes the knowledge. He would purge his memory, but scenes keep spawning in the foreground of his consciousness and he cannot forget. He would let his anger carry away the burdens of his experience, but it only makes his burdens heavier by calling them back to life. In the end he neither forgets nor hates. His purgation leaves him more deeply involved than ever, but the emotion it sets free is no longer sheer hatred. It is a kind of grim, grinding sympathy, an allegiance he owes his document for having dwelt on it so long.

In *My Days of Anger*, Danny O'Neill reaches young manhood. His first accomplishment is breaking away from Catholicism and becoming an atheist. It is at the University of Chicago where he liberates himself, and where also he comes into contact with the intellectual life which has so long been denied to him. He had been pampered and spoiled by Uncle Al, Aunt Margaret, and Grandmother, giving his father, Jim, deep concern that he would turn into a dude, a damned O'Flaherty. But now that his father is dead, Danny, taking a hand in the support of the

surviving O'Neills, has been working for several years—
first at the express company where his father had been
employed, and then as a filling-station attendant. Con-
scientious and serious, he has earned a scholarship at
the University. He has given himself over entirely to his
ambition, formally, to become a lawyer, actually, to become a writer. But while he has found in himself a central urge, a unifying obsession, he remains all too human
and he is still subject to distraction. Thus, Danny's ever-
present desire for prestige and status leads him, first, to
make an unsuccessful bid for a fraternity; later, after
dropping his job at the filling station in order to write, he
fritters away his time and winds up as a campus reporter
for *The Chicago Inquirer*—a Hearst paper interested in
obtaining scandalous stories and photographs of coeds'
legs. He still goes off on a bat now and then; he has his
share of whoring and knocking around.

All this, while it goes into the presentation of the true
character of Danny, undoes the purpose of Farrell. For
Farrell, as well as Danny, is distracted. The theme of
awakening, the growing, singing consciousness of identity,
the courage a man gathers for survival are all undermined.
Farrell is obliged to push Danny back, time after time, to
the edge of his consciousness, and the anger which Fifty-
eighth Street had drawn and sustained is dissipated.
Danny shakes his fist at the sky—but there he no longer
sees the face of Studs Lonigan. It is difficult to feel anger
when you are writing about yourself.

At least one might feel generous toward the ego, offer
it at an advantage of intensity, involved, at an extreme
point, with feeling and thought. But while Farrell writes
about himself, he is a severely repressed and, for all his
outspokenness, a very circumspect writer. He will admit
no thought, no feeling until it has been carefully inspected
for relevance, its social antecedents on Fifty-eighth Street
certified. It is as though Farrell shared the ethnocentrism
of the old neighborhood—the stranger has a hard time
getting by. And whenever a theme foreign to the surface
of his environment—an abstract issue, an emotion with
philosophical overtones—is admitted, it receives only

superficial attention. Thus, Catholicism is pinned down by only one trait, superstition; and Danny's breaking with the Church, his denial of God, though Farrell introduces an unconvincing nightmare of guilt, are on a level with declaring that the earth is flat.

So seriously does Farrell take the tradition in which he writes that he forgets it is, after all, only a tradition. It is a tradition of social documentation, and while it suits his temperament, the method which he derives from it unfortunately elevates temperamental limitations into criteria of procedure. In any case he would have difficulty in getting at the heart of the matter, in marshaling enough poetry to foreshorten, and varying his tone to convey the temporal and intellectual processes of growth. But he does not even strike for the heart: chapter after chapter of the Danny O'Neill series is given over to the documentation of the thesis that basic attitudes are formed through social contact—a fact available to a writer's immediate intuition. He is forever filling in the background and writing introductions to the few sustained dramatic episodes that mark the climax of his narrative. His characters are so much in character, so heavily plastered with the steady pat-pat-pat of the trowel that they emerge at once absolutely accurate and utterly unreal. In *My Days of Anger*, where the point of view is for the first time limited to Danny and the method of diligent accretion finally abandoned, Farrell, having relied for so long upon it, cannot avail himself of the greater freedom and concentration he now has at hand.

But Farrell's obvious technical shortcomings themselves constitute a form, a form suited with a wry perfection and exactitude to the expression of the sluggish inner potential of the meanings with which he deals. These meanings, always embodied in a social situation which moves to an increment of suffering, do not themselves move to an increment of clarity. If at one pole of his system of social psychology the individual strives toward, but never attains, a concrete conception of the good life, so at the other pole, where he is concerned with the mass of men, movement toward the good society is also frustrated. Clearly, the end is socialism, but it never becomes a clear end. Danny has not yet come to understand socialism—but must an ideal forever be limited by a receptive capacity? The characters in *Fontamara* have, of course, experienced the class struggle more deeply than Danny O'Neill. But Silone has the greater projective capacity; it is clear what he is striving to say, and he need not strive so bitterly to say it. Striving remains identified with its proper object, the ideal itself, which, while urgent and impulsive in Silone, in Farrell, when he comes to it, will probably result in another documentary effort, the clear face of it crabbed over with notes.

But it is the document which predominates in Farrell, the experience labored over and recorded, the toneless transcript of the world as it is. A strayed Catholic, he believes in his document as a Baptist in his Bible. He feels his effort has been ultimate, so long as it has been honest; and that his document is exhaustive, if no single part of it is false. He will remain sworn to his document; he will never give up the transcription of experience, the bitterness of memory which can never relieve itself. *My Days of Anger* ends in 1927; as Danny comes into the present, he will gain in time, and another two years may find him seven years advanced. For Danny is always encroaching on the present, the times in which Farrell, as grown man and writer, finds himself. This is his real, if undeclared purpose—so to enter the present within which Farrell writes, as to force upon his contemporaries an awareness of the reality they are too weak to remember. Already Danny has come to the threshold of the Depression, and the years which lie ahead of him, the most crucial in the experience of the present generation of young men, will show him carrying forward the memory of fear and the reality leading into war which the tin-horn optimists of our time have already forgotten. How will they account for all the rest, if what little this document says is true?

New Republic, November 8, 1943

ᴄ₰ *Ramón Sender's*
Chronicle of Dawn

José GARCÉS was an officer in the Spanish Loyalist army
who escaped to France before the final collapse of the Re-
publicans and was interned in a concentration camp.
While Madrid and Valencia held out, his hope held out;
he continued to study engineering, and would say, "they
are resisting in the Center, and one day we shall be sent
for." When it was all over with the Loyalists he threw
his engineering manual into the sea. There was nothing
left to live for; it had been a war to the finish and the
vanquished must pay. Garcés resisted all his friends' attempts to obtain his release. He threatened to use his
liberty only for the purpose of surrendering himself to the
fascists. Death was the only worthy door by which he
might leave the camp. And he left by the door worthy of
him, but not before he had written down his recollections
of his life.

It is by this device (which is not really a device at all,
but a measure of honest necessity) that Ramón Sender
sets down the adventures and mishaps of a young boy,
presumably himself, his first love, his conflicts with his
father, his fledgling egotism. Like all childhood narratives which gain their point by drawing away from the
present, *Chronicle of Dawn* achieves an idyllic effect.
The recorded episodes by themselves—whippings admin-
istered by a righteous father, scrapes with the neighbors
and with his girl Valentina's father, gang fights bordering
on delinquency, getting lost in an underground gallery
lined with tombs and torture chambers—are almost as
much reason for calling this an unhappy, as a happy,

childhood. But it is the tone in which remembered experience is set down and the purpose these scenes serve which give *Chronicle of Dawn* its quality of delight. It is the prisoner Garcés' last possession and Sender's own refreshment. At the heart of his story is the theme of early love. And it is this—even more than the beauty and objectivity he achieves—which gives this book its extraordinary poignancy, as if death's own memoir were simply a love story.

After reading *Dark Wedding* and a recent short story, "The Eagle," which appeared in *Partisan Review,* I was particularly struck by the renewed ease with which Sender handles symbolism in the present book. His symbolism appeared to be getting out of hand, even at times symbolizing nothing so much as itself in an iconography run riot, religious in its overtones but wary of the reality to which it owed some final commitment. *Chronicle of Dawn* is to my mind a very welcome reconstruction of the symbol. Sender here uses narrative itself as a symbol— which, after all, is its natural function in the generic sense, as distinct from the particular genres in which men write.

For narrative itself is the supreme symbol in *Chronicle of Dawn.* Else why should a man like Garcés, crushed, hopeless, at his life's end, cling to the narration of his life? It is, as he says, a means of making himself "a man of substance." Garcés has a right to this remnant of faith, just as he has a right to his otherwise complete hopelessness and to his condemnation of the victors (and the neutrals) of the Spanish war, of whom he says:

. . . the generation now in power everywhere is a corrupt generation, a generation of liars. Few of will live until the succeeding generation, our generation, takes command of things. . . . But even if we live, it is not certain that the rising generation is not contaminated. It seems that to reach the level of power, you have to lose everything first.

Garcés' reconstruction of his childhood is therefore not an escape from political responsibility, nor even a simple flight from hopelessness. It is, rather, a justification of the hopeless. The vanquished must be willing to pay with their lives. It is hence their duty to admit defeat; to find solace in half measures, in catch-penny, penny-caught optimism, is in fact the greatest betrayal of the ideal. Only through the reconstruction of the times and experiences in which the ideal had meaning—the childhood of hope—can one examine, with the most unsparing honesty, the significance of the ideal, and know, without delusion, precisely what was lost when "all was lost." A research in lost life is the artist's counterpart for semantics, which goes looking for lost words in reconstructing the ideal. Sender would find himself; and if the source is intact only in memory, so much the better for memory.

Chronicle of Dawn is in many ways the coming full circle for Sender. In his first novel, *Pro Patria*, the hero, Viance, is left, "his life entering infinity," precisely where Pepe Garcés must now begin. Viance had survived years of poverty in his native country and the slaughter of the disastrous Moroccan campaign. He returned to Spain to find his very village washed away, buried under fifty feet of water. This was the last blow for him, but not for the rest of his generation, who outlived their first undoing at the hands of the state by recognizing the enemy and joining the revolution. But what remained for them after the triumph of the fascists? In *Dark Wedding* Sender examined the possibilities of a pure idealism which must consider all revolutions well lost, for the realization of the ideal necessarily entails its destruction. But I believe he has now undertaken a rewriting of idealism, transferring it back, just as his symbolism has shifted, to the development of the ego, where it may, perhaps, be justified again. Many writers today in search of a belief broader and more reliable than politics regard this as their only alternative: to go forward by going back into themselves. And even if this is not the only means for making themselves "men of substance," still they will have found a means. And if this be to die, then "to die is different from what anyone supposed, and luckier."

New Republic, April 24, 1944

✒ Jean Malaquais'
War Diary

I SHOULD LIKE TO SAY what I must about Jean Malaquais' war diary with the humility owing to a man who
has been through hell. I do not know who, faced with
his hardships, would have reacted differently, nor do I
suppose there are many writers alive today who could
remain artists when, in addition to the common misery
of war, they had to bear the further burden of exhausting
concrete-construction work in the company of unmitigated
boors. But for all that, a man is on his own. He may
not be able to control what experience shall make of him,
but for the attitude with which he approaches experience,
the complete man who exists before shock tears him apart,
he is completely responsible.

Jean Malaquais went to war the way almost everybody goes to war—none too eagerly. The suffering he
bore, the discomfort, annoyance, fatigue, and boredom
that he felt, are universal, known to all soldiers. Nevertheless, the diary that he kept during his term of service
with the French army, from the outbreak to the collapse,
is, for the most part, a curiously inappropriate and inadequate, an almost too individual, commentary on war. It is
as if the author of *Men from Nowhere*, taking the
surreptitiously public view of private life to which writers
are prone, had said, "let's see what Jean Malaquais has
to say about this affair." And thus, throughout at least
the first half of his diary, there is a constant fluctuation
between writer and man. Hell breaks loose; Malaquais
puts it down in his diary—and adds, I am right here on
the spot, recording this. The writer's self-conscious

89

promotion of the man, his reiteration that the man is in full attendance, makes you feel that the man is, somehow, a little remote from it all.

War Diary, however, is more than a record of the incidental agonies of war. It is also a self-portrait and a political document. Malaquais's political opinions are, of course, independent of the particular traits of his character. But what is true of his character is true also of his beliefs: in each the man and his failings are contained.

"The majority of the unfavorable judgments which I form about people," writes Malaquais, "have to do almost exclusively with their intelligence, rarely with their heart." This statement gives the key or feeling-tone in which the diary is written. But I take it for more than that. I also regard it as one of those outcroppings of character, hard and definite, that reveal something of the substance of a man. Other passages, such as, ". . . the men with whom I am forced to live. God how I despise them! And how, through them, I despise myself!" acquire deeper meaning, even losing some of their fastidious exasperation, in view of the unsparing things he says about himself. In spite of which he still indulges himself, as one need only read *Men from Nowhere* or the theory of art he sets forth in the diary, to discover.

It is obvious that he is a writer of predominantly intellectual temperament (regardless of his intellectual development, which is not exceptionally high or abstract). But more important than the kind of temperament Malaquais may happen to have is the fact that this temperament is limited by a peculiarly intellectual failing—mind's failure to understand the heart. The irrationalist tradition to the contrary, this mind is capable of doing. Witness Dostoevsky in Siberia, the pages of *The House of the Dead*. But Malaquais is dealing with phenomena that need, perhaps, less to be understood than fused. It is the artist's task to fuse, to bring together the human and the animal in man, to make an imaginative synthesis of what society has dismembered. Of course, among soldiers, "dead men on leave," there are bound to be brutes and morons. But the observation of human degradation is

itself a kind of blindness in the writer if it does no more
than emphasize his sense of aloofness. Malaquais's aloofness (which differs from the detachment a writer must
school himself to achieve) betrays a basic lack of energy,
a fatigued impulse deflected from art to a finicky preoccupation with the wounds of the ego.

But for all the vacant areas that the war has blasted in
his soul, Malaquais is still equal to depicting the climax
of all hopelessness, the fall of France. In passages that
are at last free of self-indulgence, he records the futile,
disorderly resistance and the disorderly retreat, gathering
momentum, dragging a whole world after it. I hope it is
not heartless to say that it is not until he reaches the
abyss, the greater image of the death which has been
growing in him, that Malaquais feels at home; not until
then does he become the representative figure he could
not be through sensibility alone, the man whose suffering is related to his time.

His political opinions—and this may be said for his
sincerity—are of a pattern with his personal cut. He had
enough sense of history to know what was required by
the times. The war, he knew, would not end by
Christmas: destruction was in the air; spring would bring
it on. He saw the world "slowly rolling toward the abyss,"
and had no hope in the outcome. But he dissociated himself from this world "completely, absolutely, without
reservation."

This withdrawal may have been politically motivated,
but the withdrawal supersedes the politics. He does not,
like a Marxist, go to the Third Camp—there is no more
Third Camp. The real enemy is fascism, but the enemy is
everywhere, and Hitler is but the perfect exponent, the
epitome of the bourgeois world. I do not know anything
about Malaquais's political past—but he need not have
had any at all. It is because so many of the radicals in
Malaquais's position—"oriented" but lost—are Marxists
who have abandoned their faith, that the faithful attribute disorder to the defection from Marxism, while
the skeptics attribute it to the original mistake of holding
the Marxist position. All of which is error as far as

Malaquais is concerned, for it is not so much a position as an idealism, belief itself, the capacity for life, that he has lost.

No, politics is life, after all, and whatever a man write about—his opinions, his comrades, his boredom, his fear —he risks the same defeat: the defeat of not knowing what there is to defend. That is the real loss: that out of this war there should come so great a forgetting among the very men—the artists—who, in the face of death, could always distinguish themselves by their own, peculiar bravery: the knowledge of what life is.

New Republic, February 28, 1944

⟞ Louis MacNeice
and the War

REREADING MacNeice's *Autumn Journal,* I was struck by the way in which a period of writing, that is to say a style, approximates a period of time. The same history is common to both, and each may be read in terms of the other. In the case of MacNeice, as with Auden, Spender, and Day Lewis, taken as a group before their present divergences appeared, history is as indispensable to the poetry as the paper it is written on; more than subject matter, it is the very form, the language and the words, the rhythm and the attitude—all, one might say, but the poet himself. Take a distance short enough, and most modern poets are fellow travelers: through depression, the rise of fascism and the threat of war until the first great terminal, Spain. Nearly all the poems of this period are journal entries, covering the way; even the most personal lyrics in their setting and context are close to the headlines and look forward to

> Not the twilight of the gods but a precise dawn
> Of sallow and gray bricks and newsboys crying war.

And yet how like an irrecoverable past this recent period, this style, has already become! The simile, "dead as 1938," occurs at the end of *Autumn Journal;* the poet, writing it, must have known that it would apply to the whole journal, the like of which he would never be able to write again. For the events of the autumn of Munich, and their counterparts in feeling, were crying war, to whose actuality the poet, like Achilles in his unreal pursuit of the turtle, could come only so close without

93

ever passing beyond it. The war was the sudden leap, the absolute break which no prophetic mood could ever really encompass. Everyone knew what was coming, but for that very reason no one was prepared; in which respect men are always victimized by history, even when they have mastered its principle, for how shall we go on being ourselves when our prophecies come true?

MacNeice's informal style could only have become formalized (it had already begun to turn in the long stretches of the *Journal*), and his relaxed antipoetic line on which, side by side, hung classical devices and the idioms of modern speech could only have stiffened and by an anachronistic poetics bound the poet of the flux of things. So too with his attitude of mind: the resignation, the protest, the urbanity, and the complaint; the ability to steal a lyric moment from the sense of doom and the determination, always a little awkward and repetitive, to strike a new note, the constant resolution to come to a resolution. With the end of the prewar years in sight, this vein was exhausted; this mine closed down while men streamed back to the actual coal pits.

In the poems of *Springboard* we find MacNeice paying greater attention than heretofore to the problem of commitment and risk in belief. The certainty of the simple position, the emotional security of being able to assert the general value and virtue of commitment in default of a specific one, is no longer available at a time when circumstance, more powerful than the individual's power to choose, has pushed him to where he is without having had to consult the will. Simplicity—mere moral energy or belief in belief—has become all too simple. And while the title of the book may suggest the transition accomplished and the point of take-off toward further things already attained, the title poem qualifies MacNeice's position more exactly, preserving its inherent conflict. The heart of the problem is the individual's risk in war. He stands on the springboard, knowing that the leap to sacrifice and belief is called for, yet he is there only because he has been pushed—he does not believe.

It is impossible to make a decision, a free choice, on such narrow, perilous ground, let alone its not being worth it. "And yet we know he knows what he must do." He will make the dive

> One man wiping out his own original sin
> And like ten million others, dying for the people.

Technically, this poem is the high point of the volume, if we overlook a dangling modifier, a solecism which usage has certified as a device. MacNeice tells us in the dedication that "the velvet image . . . the lilting measure" no longer convey his meaning, and that "I am compelled to use/Such words as disabuse/My mind of casual pleasure." In "The Springboard" his conversion to war-time writing has been made at a profit. The line is drawn taut, but its resilience does not let one feel the strain. Though writing in closer quarters, he still has the same ease, and for that matter—true of many war economies—the present constriction may well be preferable to the roominess of his earlier work. It was always the casual accuracy, the offhand precision of images that was original and important in his writing; the rhythmical patterns, for all their freedom, were more a matter of contrivance, and therefore less integral to the conveying of his effects than they appeared to be.

The title poem also succeeds in gathering together under a specific philosophical image those aspects of the problem of responsibility that are dispersed through the other poems. MacNeice is quite ungenerous in his less philosophical statements of the case against his irresolute contemporaries. In "Bottleneck" the objective source of moral indecisiveness is completely forgotten—unless one is to believe that he had not yet arrived at the under-standing shown seventeen pages later in "The Spring-board." The passivity and impotent neutrality of the man who "would never make a soldier or a servant" are made entirely subjective things and blamed, completely without sympathy, on "the permanent bottleneck of his highmindedness." In this poem, as in other sketches of moral types, "The Satirist" and "The Libertine," the conscience of his satire is clouded in self-congratulation, which suggests that he may be scotching a few of his own snakes.

Personalism, the discovery of the value of personality as an absolute entity, is, however, a frequent concomitant of philosophical reconstruction; MacNeice's preoccupation with personality types is therefore an essential activity, necessary to the new account he is trying to give of himself. It serves him as a basis of negative definition (the satires depict what he is not) and as a testing ground to try the run and scope of his ideas. In "The Kingdom," a long poem that ends the volume, MacNeice makes his first sustained effort to state directly and embody in personality the principle of his resolution. The Kingdom is of

The incorruptible souls who work without a commission,
The pairs of hands that are peers of hearts, the eyes that
    marry with eyes,
The candid scholar, the unselfish priest, the uncomplaining
    mothers of many . . .
These, as being themselves, are apart from not each other
But from such as being false are merely other. . . .

The Kingdom

. . . has no king except each subject, therefore
Apart from slaves and tyrants and from every
Community of mere convenience. . . .

                    And they are many. For go,
Go wherever you choose, among tidy villas or terrible
Docks, dumps and pitheads, or through the spangled moors . . .
Everywhere you will discover the men of the Kingdom
Loyal by intuition, born to attack, and innocent.

There follow six portraits of men and women who belong to the Kingdom, whether they know it or not: a squire who is a man of nature without a squire's presumption; a devoted mother; a drunken soldier; a girl "with a pitcher of ice-cold wild emotions . . . filled . . . at a lost well . . . of the remembered Kingdom"; a scientist and an honest preacher.

These are the people who know in their bones the answer
To the statesman's quiz and the false reformer's crude
Alternatives and ultimatums.

There is a fault, an important ambiguity in "The Kingdom" which, to my mind, prevents it from realizing the very excellent intentions of the poet. The fault is not in the lines as such, some of which are among MacNeice's best, but in the mystique that emerges from them, a kind of humanistic creed lacking in poetic differentiation. While I cannot help feeling that MacNeice's position is in its main respects the only possible one that can be held by a rational poet and a good liberal, determined to write with a minimum of distortion, I am disturbed to recognize in it the obvious trademark of the modern myth of The Common Man, which has lent itself to so many abuses, to say nothing of its intrinsic shortcomings, that its presence in serious poetry is almost an initial disqualification. There is both dignity and banality in this mystique, a true instinct, a half-true rationalization, and a complete falsehood: it is true in being homocentric, in its regard for man; half-true in its making of the merely human a positive value in all contexts, where it serves also as a rationalization for the absence of other values; and false in being democratic by coercion, forcing an identification of the common with the best. That it is all things to all men may be seen in its political implications which run all the way from a mild reformism of good will through totalitarianism to extreme anarchism. For The Common Man is the great empty vessel of our time which remains empty although all manner of doctrines and assumptions, words and slogans and genuine human hopes flow into it. It is disappointing that so fine a poet as MacNeice should not have left a purer, more definite and personal residue in the common concept. As it is, "The Kingdom" seems but to underwrite the formless rational mysticism which is fast becoming, for liberal writers, the style that approximates the present age.

And yet MacNeice, especially in his more critical poems, including those which already belong to the past, does come close to fulfilling an ideal condition of modern

times: the ideal of a rational poetry. As I have been trying to show, his writing is not without distortion, but it
is a distortion incidental to the conception of poetry and
not of its essence. He has remained faithful to the
principle with which he began: to conform sensibility
with wit and intelligence and fully express his individual
nature so that no part thrives at the expense of another
part. Pursuing his principle, he has deviated neither in
the direction of a religious nor a political disavowal of the
supremacy of the modern intellectual tradition, liberal,
skeptical, and humane. He is one of the few examples
we have of a poet who has managed to live more or less
without repudiation.

It is no easy thing to be a rational poet. In a sense, the
very notion is oxymoronic, and even if we carefully
explain what it means, and set forth the conditions under
which a rational poet is still possible today, rationalism
itself conspires against us. Rationalism is an economical
form of thought, consuming little heat, and can keep
going quite well by itself, with no actual need for poetry.
Observe, for example, that MacNeice can coolly posit
the value of human personality on its own terms without
having to say with Blake that everything that lives is holy.
A rationalist, moreover, is committed to a faith in means
and intelligence, a belief in the possible success of human
ventures that gives him a curiously optimistic coloring,
abhorrent to poetry, which admits only hope. Paradoxi-
cally enough, the more difficult it becomes to hold up
the rational mirror to the face of history, the more
optimistic the rational poet grows. "The Kingdom" offers
sufficient evidence that this is true of MacNeice; there,
the minimal belief in the incorruptibility of individual
human nature looms as a maximal commitment, if only
because historical pressures, having cracked all other
articles of faith, have made this one imperative. In another
poem, "Explorations," the optimism is even more pro-
nounced, for it is read into a naturalistic account of the
descent of man. Speaking of the lesser animals MacNeice
observes that their apparently happy instinctual adaptation to environment need not be envied by man since

> their imputed purpose
> Is a foregone design—
>
> And ours is not. For we are unique, a conscious
> Hoping and therefore despairing creature, the final
> Anomaly of the world, we can learn no method
> From whales or birds or worms;
> Our end is our own to be won by our own endeavor
> And held on our own terms.

It seems to me that "the final anomaly of the world" is too strong an expression to be used of man if he can win and hold his own end. But the statement "man is the final anomaly of the world" is necessary to the poem as poem, for it is the only one which is poetically true in a group of biological truths. It is one of the defects of a strictly reasonable account of things, too great perhaps for any poet to correct, that the truths of poetry do not always mingle with the truths of mere natural experience. All poetry can do is declare the final anomaly of the world and trust that reason will restrain itself. A rational poet is still a possibility, but a rational optimist is a dead duck.

New Republic, October 22, 1945

⋘ The Young Richard Wright

BLACK BOY is Richard Wright's own story of his childhood in the South until his seventeenth year. Reviewers
are fairly well agreed that it is his best book and that it
is besides a valuable contribution to the literature of
American race problems. There is no doubt in my mind
that it is these things; but I would say that it has an
additional value, rare among books that have race as their
theme or deal in general with the individual's suffering
because of his status in an oppressed minority group.
Black Boy is also the story of a man's rise to artistic
consciousness—or at least the beginning of the story—
and as such, while it in no way furnishes a solution to
the Negro problem, it does contain within itself the
principle of such a solution: the end which the oppressed
hope to achieve in liberation. Wright presents, in limited
but unmistakable form, evidence of his knowledge of
freedom, an earnest of his conception of human dignity
made all the more valuable by the bleak background
against which it stands out.

His early memories are of violence, poverty, and
hunger; he recalls fights, beatings, his father's desertion of
his mother, his mother's unsuccessful attempts to provide
for the family—days and months and years spent with a
constant gnawing in his belly. His first contacts outside
the home were with black children similarly underprivileged; and his depressed environment, long before he had
learned to read and write, had already imparted the
typical poor child's precocious knowledge of vice. Over
all his formative experience lay the hazard, which he was

soon to learn with the black man's full risk, of transgression against the whites. Wright learned his place in Southern society with particular bitterness, for his humiliation as a Negro was bound up with his efforts to find and hold a job. It was on the job, even when he was barely into his teens, that he learned to smirk and grin and say "Mister" and "yes sir," and be a good nigger who knows what's good for him. It was a hard lesson for him to learn—and all the better proof of his instinctive sense of freedom (though perhaps his early rebellion against his father's authority may have been a presocial influence that determined this pattern) is the fact that he never did learn it. For all the external concessions that he was forced to make, his will to freedom and dignity never died. As with all Negroes and all men who are born to suffer social injustice, part of his humanity found itself only in acquaintance with violence, and in hatred of the oppressor.

His schooling meanwhile was sporadic, interrupted by frequent moving from town to town as his mother sought to improve the family's lot. He was taken to live with his grandmother when his mother suffered a stroke, at an early age, which incapacitated her for the rest of her days. Life at his grandmother's was in many ways the climax of his misery—for while their economic position was somewhat improved, it was here that he encountered, full force, the oppressed man's self-oppression in the form of religious fanaticism. Grandmother and her household were Seventh-Day Adventists to the letter. Richard was forbidden to work on Saturdays—the most important day of all for one who must support himself while attending school—and was subjected to a zealous, unrelenting campaign for the salvation of his soul. He resisted with all his might; his early experience had already made him a "realist," and so it was a matter of simple realism for him to observe that as far as his own life, and that of most Negroes, was concerned, the existence of God made absolutely no difference. He converted Pascal's wager to the support of atheism: if there is a God, he will be amused by my efforts to deny him; if there is no God, then I am right. So far as he knew, he was only drawing the most reasonable conclusion from his experience in resisting religion; but perhaps there was also an irrational drive, inseparable from his desire to become a writer, that made him stand aloof from the immediate spiritual community of his people. He says in an early chapter—it is almost a premise of his own creative activity—that the emotional life of the Negro is widely misunderstood. Where most whites see the black man as a gay, carefree, passionate creature, he is in reality a man of impoverished spirit whose apparent *joie de vivre* is no more than a desperate fiction for survival. The white prejudice at this point would seem to favor the Negro—we think, almost automatically, of spirituals, jazz, swing, folklore, religious ecstasy, absence of sexual inhibition. But Wright claims a deeper insight which holds all external expression invalid, so long as the inner spirit is not free. Essential to his growth as a writer, let alone his survival as a man who sought liberty, was his need for accomplishing an individual act of liberation, and he could not follow his people in accommodating himself to a life of known or concealed enslavement. He had to find a more abstract and general conception of freedom, a more generic emotion, applicable to all mankind, even if in so doing he would seem to abandon the cultural resources most immediately available to Negroes. His mistrust of religion, his "realism"—the lesson he had learned from poverty, hunger, and humiliation—was the expression of a basic mistrust of all compensatory emotion. He would have nothing less than that which the truly free man, unencumbered by his own compensations, can obtain. As he remarks apropos of his religious crisis (which is applicable to his entire consciousness) he felt that his honesty made him religious enough—more so than the zealots who turned the evil of their enslavement against themselves.

A poor youth, Negro, living in the South, rebelling against authority, and wanting to become a writer faces a twofold peril: of ostracism from his own group and death at the hands of the whites. He became increasingly aware of the danger in which he lived, and while his energy drove him beyond compromise with the South and toward preparation for his subsequent literary life (a brief catalogue of the writers who opened a new world to him is one of the most touching, however typical, notes of authenticity in his story) he also made himself ready to flee to the North. The book ends at this point, after describing some of the events in which his pride and sense of his own worth brought him into dangerous conflict with the white world. He is prepared to go North, eventually to become a writer, but above all—and here he can succeed even if he fails in some measure as a writer—to find for himself, and therefore for his people, a true statement of human liberty, transcending color and class even as it transcends the individual man himself.

Jewish Frontier, June, 1945

ঌ Southern Fiction and
Social Reality

SOUTHERN WRITERS have produced the nearest thing in America to a genuine, contemporary folk art. Other regions have their spokesmen, but only the South has stood still long enough for the best writers to catch up with it. The ingredients of a folk art are there, still undisturbed by the progressive industrialization of the country. The South has legend, history, and tradition, a relatively primitive folk culture among the Negroes and poor whites, a bourgeois culture in the cities and the trappings of a decrepit but still pretentious agrarian aristocracy; all of which elements put the Southern writer in a position somewhat similar to that of the Russian novelists of the nineteenth century. It is no accident that the South has produced the leading regional writers.

Eudora Welty and Carson McCullers are surely among the finest of their generation of Southern writers. But it is curious to see how each in her own way makes what one might call an attempt to escape from the South. I don't mean arbitrarily to assign to Miss Welty and Miss Mc-Cullers the intention of achieving folk art, only to call the absence of a true folk quality in their writing an "escape." Each has her own distinctive aims as a writer, which it would be foolish to surrender to folk demands. I do, however, mean to point out that Miss Welty and Miss McCullers cannot utilize all the resources of their native regions; the reasons for this may have some bearing on American regionalism and folk literature in general.

My report on Eudora Welty's novel [*Delta Wedding*]

must begin with a confession of embarrassment, namely, that I was not able to get through more than a hundred pages. I found the going too dull; and since the most moderate demand one can make of writing is that it be interesting, I feel justified in having let Miss Welty's book go without further struggle. What I have to say applies, therefore, only to the first hundred pages, with the understanding that I may have missed some meaningful dramatic developments important to the evaluation of her novel as a whole. Moreover, there are kinds and degrees of dullness, some of which only very good writers can attain. Eudora Welty's writing is always imaginative and perceptive and miles above the generally prevailing level, even if, on a particular occasion, it does not happen to make an interesting novel.

In *The Wide Net*, Miss Welty's last collection of stories, she had reached an extreme point, beyond which, apparently, she found it impossible to go. There she had, as it were, forced an exchange of centers with the world, had evicted objectivity and moved into its place with an elaborate esthetic furniture. Though interesting and readable in a way that I have not found *Delta Wedding* to be, her last stories seemed withdrawn into a sort of fixed, interior esthetic contemplation, devoid of the life and color and preoccupation with Southern character that had marked her earlier work. *Delta Wedding* is in some ways a return to the earlier mood. It is a novel of Southern family life, full of characters with distinct personalities and idiosyncrasies: the children, the aunts, uncles, Negro servants, etc., of the Fairchild family, all of whom are drawn together in the preparations for the wedding of Dabney Fairchild. The action is placed objectively and is reported in a variety of ways—through direct narration, conversation, and the points of view of the leading characters. *Delta Wedding* has, in short, the full structure of a novel, and its lack of interest is not due to faulty construction.

I think the dullness of Miss Welty's novel may be traced to the fact that though she draws upon social resources of custom and speech, it is not really a society that she is dealing with, but the sensations of one. The events occur discretely, as they would to someone who, though situated within this society, did not have any ongoing, extended relationship with it. Transitions are not keenly felt, and therefore the experience of connection, which is the essence of a society, does not enter the novel in the form of a clear, continuous, dramatic line. This also affects the emotions of the characters; the Fairchilds are presented each within his own separate sensibility, and are held together only in external relation by the overflow of the author's sensibility. The density of atmosphere and the many family details do not serve to establish a true family connection. It is as if Miss Welty had unlearned the lesson of Tolstoy, that the history of a society is the history of the innermost emotional interactions of its members.

Carson McCullers' novella, *The Member of the Wedding,* stands in more or less the same oblique relation to the South. It is the story of Frankie, or F. Jasmine Addams, in her thirteenth year, cut off from her girlhood friends and from the life around her. Frankie is a member of nothing and belongs to nothing; she is insanely bored. When her brother returns on furlough from Alaska to marry a local girl, Frankie gets the idea that he will invite her to accompany them on the honeymoon. This notion fills the great gap in her life, and the novella shows how she enlarges on her fancies, building them up out of nothing, until the inevitable disappointment. The interest here is more readily maintained than in Eudora Welty's novel; the dramatic line is stronger and more clearly drawn, the anticipation mounts in spite of some padding with which Miss McCullers has filled out her slender story, and there is an over-all irony and detachment that reinforces the emotional quality of the writing. But in relation to the South and to the folk material that is so liberally used, *The Member of the Wedding* is also oblique and self-centered. It presents not so much Southern life, as a parable on the life of the writer in the South, the alienation and withdrawal the sensitive Southerner must feel.

It is this aspect which these two books, otherwise dissimilar, have in common, and I think it is of some significance. In both novels, as in much of Southern writing, there is an unavowed double standard which divides the material used from the personal uses to which the author puts it. The subject matter, the color, the speech, the characters are all taken at firsthand, from a deep social involvement; but the meanings that the author wishes to express are not so closely related to the Southern environment and share little more than its surface values. At the level of personal expression, the author withdraws, turns inward to the sensibility, as Eudora Welty does, or to the theme of alienation, as with Carson McCullers. Though both have taken a wedding as their theme of symbolic unification, it does not unite them with a folk or traditional society, as such a symbol might be expected to do, but serves rather to indicate their degree of withdrawal —which, in terms of the values involved, is solipsistic in relation to the South. It is an inevitable withdrawal, for the serious American writer cannot but be alienated from American society, close though he may be to it, and much though he may wish to belong. And it is this, I think, which is responsible for the fact that though we have regionalism in abundance, it will never attain its goal of folk art. This contradiction is all the more clearly seen in the South, where the folk material is richest and the folk appeal strongest. But the social contradictions of the South are also the greatest you will find in this country; and they are such that the whole society may be called the antithesis of art. I do not see how a serious Southern artist can really and truly feel at home in his home.

New Republic, April 29, 1946

✍ Psychoanalysis as Literature: The Case of Anais Nin

THE VIRTUE OF Miss Nin's writing, in a time of "human winter," is that by its exclusive preoccupation with the intimate problems of feminine psychology, it is concerned with an aspect of human values as such. Her style, moreover, in its use of fairly broad emotive language and in the expression it gives to feeling and sentiment, possesses a certain *Innerlichkeit*, an air of immediate reality, for lack of which so much of modern American writing is dying such a hideous, choking death. But Miss Nin approaches the human by way of psychoanalysis, which, as I shall try to show, leaves a great deal to be desired for literature.

Anais Nin treats of whole life histories, even though her stories are restricted in time and in scope to the present mood and atmosphere of her characters. Implicit in the narrative condensation is the psychological, if not specifically psychoanalytical, premise that personality undergoes a continuous development, with childhood experience its most important factor. Her fictional interest is not so much in the character as in the neurotic predicament of her heroines; her writing is therefore more illustrative than creative—illustrative of the wars and wounds of life history, and the dangers, particularly sexual in nature, that loom before women when their development is thwarted.

There are three stories in *This Hunger*: "Hejda," "Stella," and "Lillian and Djuna." Hedja is an Arabian girl, Stella, a Polish actress who becomes a Hollywood star, and Lillian and Djuna are mature American women —and yet the four women and the three stories in which they occur are all fundamentally the same. One basic pattern emerges from them: the woman, hampered in the expression of her sexuality by her fear of the male—which fear is the anxiety that he will not allow her to achieve her proper expression, or that he will fail to fulfill his own role—a fear, that is to say, of his strength and his weakness—turns aggressive and tries to wrest his dominance from him. It is out of this struggle that her hunger arises—the need for fulfillment through her own nature, which she has made herself incapable of attaining.

Miss Nin almost completely neglects the dramatization of this conflict, so eager is she to state it in terms of immediate feelings, or so certain, apparently, that the mere statement implies dramatic realization. The task she assigns to literature seems to be no more than to present and amplify the insights of psychoanalysis, lay them around the core of woman's self-knowledge, and fill in with details of character and feeling the blank spaces of abstract psychological understanding. It is her preoccupation with such details, disproportionate to the amount of real importance that she assigns to the accidents of human existence, that retains for her attitude its title to literature—submersion in the flux of feeling, even if the writer drowns, does give her a kind of posthumous status in reality, which, at a time when most writers are dead anyway, is almost as good as being alive.

But one must insist that fiction live. The reason that Anais Nin's fiction dies in the writing is not only that she fails to transmit her literary feeling directly and dramatically, but—a curious thing—that she is a thoroughgoing mechanist, for all the apparent intuitiveness of the subject matter with which she deals. The aesthetic protest against the aggressions of intellectualism, and the counterclaims of poetic impulsiveness against the detached, scientific observation of life, sometimes develop a positivism all their own, in the practice of which the writer resembles nothing more than the thing he means to avoid. No fact of naturalism was ever so much a fact, a concrete abstraction or a pointer-reading, as the facts of the soul with which Anais Nin puts together her stories.

Woman's being crushed by her effort to cope with man is made to appear a kind of natural doom, ordained with all the authority of natural law. But this doom is derived not from a universal truth, but from a particular selection of events. Woman is shown only in the succession of shock and recoil that certainly fills, but just as certainly does not exhaust, her life. Wound and resentment, hurt and retreat—these are the only modes of interaction with men and with life that Anais Nin allows her women. Which, while it suffices to show the destructiveness of woman, does not let Miss Nin attain the further objective that she has set for herself—to depict woman's struggle to understand her own nature. The struggle for understanding is conducted completely without benefit of mind. Consciousness, in this new mechanics of feeling, is an epiphenomenon all over again.

The objection I am making is not to the portrayal of women as inevitably conducted by their anxiety into a helplessness against which it is useless for them to struggle, but to the unconscious systematization of human subject matter that underlies this portrayal, and to the belief, apparently held by Miss Nin, that such systematization does not distort the reality which is revealed in immediate feeling. Miss Nin's procedure involves the reductive fallacy, rare in literature, which is most commonly found in metaphysics. She begins with the end product of psychoanalysis, the selective breaking up of personality into its component drives, and then reads the resultant back into her subject as if it constituted the whole motive force of human nature. This rests on a confusion of depth psychology with character psychology, in which the latter is taken to be reducible, without residuum, to the former. That such is not the case is evident from the four heroines of *This Hunger,* all of whom, while intimately projected from within outwards, emerge, without personality, as mere personifications of neurotic anxiety. The gap between personification and personality is literature, which no amount of psychoanalysis, or sensitive writing, or combinations of the two, can fill.

❧ The Amusements of
Kenneth Patchen

"New writing" makes for conservative criticism. Whenever a departure from the usual takes place, there is always an effort on the part of critics to restore the continuity of literature; the canon of criticism must be extended and saved. And so, no matter how sympathetic a critic may be, and even if his intention is merely to explain the new work before him on its own terms and reserve judgment, he is at once involved in the creation of an abstract standard of value and form to which, in time, the new work itself, and its imitations and successors, will be expected to conform. To explain is to conserve. Now despite the pejorative connotations of the word "conservative," I do not deplore this procedure, but consider it perfectly natural and wish that something of the kind had already been done for works of the neoromantic, quasi-surrealist, egotistical genre of which Kenneth Patchen's prose is typical.

Thus far, all the criticism that Patchen's prose writing has received, whether favorable or not, has been, to my knowledge, of the impressionistic rather than the analytical variety. (Largely the same, I believe, may be said about Henry Miller, in spite of all the attention he has aroused.) If one were to take Henry Miller's unreliable word for it, *The Journal of Albion Moonlight* stands alone "in all English literature. . . . The most naked figure of a man in all literature." Probably nothing so enthusiastic can be said, even by the most confirmed admirer, of *The Memoirs of a Shy Pornographer,* but like its predecessor it is bound to engage more of the emotion than the discrimination of its readers. Needless to say, Miller's enthusiasm for Patchen is of the "kick-in-the-pants-for-art" category. He fastens on that which is anti-cultural, anti-traditional, anti-intellectual, which subverts form and allows the writer to emerge as the permanent center and concern of all writing—"to hell with characters, look at me, I'm the big thing," etc.

The trouble with this is that it is absolutely no good for advancing advanced writing. The writer discovers himself, pen in hand, and asks, "Whatever can I be doing with this object?" Which, like all cultivated expressions of naïveté, is a complete falsification. Such writing is in a culture, in a tradition, marked by a preoccupation with a definite class of subjects and objects, written in a typical style, with typical attitudes and gestures, and is really no freer from social assumptions and values than the work of any other school. It is one of the worst habits of avant-garde writers to pretend a disdain for literature, and of the critics who are concerned with them (I am thinking of George Orwell's and Herbert Read's essays on Henry Miller) to substitute exposition and political admiration for concrete analytical evaluation of literature as such.

A representative chunk of Patchen will contain references to immortality, God and death of the gods (à la Nietzsche), capitalism, anarchism and pacifism, sex, murder and blood-guilt, and any number of generally unacknowledged leanings toward and derivations from psychoanalysis. All things conspire to facilitate the outward projection of the ego. Guilt is vague and huge, meant rather to fill space than time, that is, to constitute a hypostatized object rather than lead to the analysis of personality. Accordingly, Patchen's terrors are always on tap. Though he appears to draw upon the subconscious as the source of his images and obsessions, he actually uses it as a storehouse for artificial props, constructed, I dare say, quite consciously. His purpose is to provide a setting for himself, a backdrop which will be mistaken for the action. He sets out to play all the roles that he knows to lie beforehand in the unconscious, and thus when he presents himself as murderer, god-slayer, guilt-seeker, or penitent, the effect, on me at any rate, is one of self-deception rather than self-knowledge. Experience will never support so ambitious a claim to vast acquaintance with the nether world; for no traveler returns from it, at least not unscathed.

These remarks will appear to be more apropos of *The Journal of Albion Moonlight* than of *The Memoirs of a Shy Pornographer,* for the latter is a more "conscious" narrative. But the same setting and devices of self-projection are to be found in *The Memoirs,* placing it in the same tradition. The shy pornographer is one Albert Budd, born in Bivalve, New Jersey, a naïf who does not understand the nature of his own book, or why it should be such a great success, especially among the women who mob him and rape him at the cocktail parties. He is in love with Priscilla, a crippled girl who lives in the country, and he is convinced that he can make her walk again. She agrees to marry him if he succeeds, but dies before their wedding day and before you have a chance to decide whether the green deer, the agent of her recovery conjured up by Budd's faith, and the other magical appurtenances in which the book abounds, have actually succeeded in putting her on her feet. Budd, overcome, uses the injection that a friend of his, the inventor, Donald Wan, had given him before his death. He turns into an angel and goes to heaven, where he meets Priscilla and the child they were going to have, and they all live happily forever after.

It is often said that toughness, an excessive violence, is an inverted form of sentimentality. *The Shy Pornographer* seems to support this proposition, for here the violence of *Albion Moonlight* is gone and in its place we find a mushiness which is the more direct expression of the same thing. Another source of its sentimentality may be found in its personality type (to personify a book), which is distinctly Oedipal. The crippled Priscilla is the tabooed mother, her love a heaven of unattainable bliss. The nightmarish obstacles that come between Budd and Priscilla, preventing their union, represent the son's fear of punishment and his guilt—the book is full of castration symbols—all of which is further borne out by Budd's occupation, for as a shy, unsuspecting pornographer he is in the typical Oedipus position of entertaining forbidden desires toward the object of his love. Therefore such love as he is able to express is sexless and overidealized, presented in religious guise or simply left to stand in the sentimentality of its deflected impulse.

But there is a good deal of excellent comedy in Patchen's took and it certainly succeeds as an amusement. Some of the fun is of a fairly common sort—punning, the acting out of gags, sexual exaggerations—but the best passages owe their humor to a surrealist technique; and surrealism, if it has done nothing else, has put new resources at the disposal of comedy. It so happens that we are all more faithful to reason than the current vogue of irrationalism will let us admit; surrealism owes its appeal to the hold that reason still has on us, for whatever serious symbolic meaning surreal transformations and incongruities are supposed to have, the effect of a sudden frustration of a logical pattern is to make us laugh.

The fact that the tradition in which Patchen writes depends to such a large extent on surrealist maneuvers deprives it of a good deal of the power and wisdom it claims for itself. It has staked all on a sleight-of-hand, a trick of symbolism that actually throws out the deeper human context that it is supposed to provide for literature. Patchen's politics, for example, a kind of anarcho-pacifism, uncompromisingly opposed to capitalism and war, is the nearest thing to an escape from politics that can be contrived in political language. Of this whole school of writing it may be said that it will succeed most among people who do not believe in it. Skeptics will be tolerantly amused by its show of fireworks, but the prophets of this new revelation will be left with nothing but their huge egotism gone sadly to waste.

New Republic, December 3, 1945

❦ Henry Miller in America

IF IT IS STUPID of a reviewer to refer to the dust jacket of a book in the course of his review, it is all the worse for him to launch his observations with an initial splash of such bad taste. But Henry Miller (and I personally think it is one of the best things about him) is on a perpetual holiday from taste, always inviting us to join him. Besides, the dust jacket of *The Air-Conditioned Nightmare* is singularly appropriate, and says something about Miller in a way not said before.

It is a photograph. In the background stands a sky-scraper, of white stone. Superimposed on the base of the skyscraper and occupying the foreground is a shanty—sharecropper's hovel or miner's hut, a decrepit thing. This is the portrait of America that first confronts us in Miller's transcontinental travelogue.

What has this photograph, reminiscent of a type of wordless social comment of the thirties, to do with Miller? With the Miller of overstatement and overwriting as principles-in-themselves, and the overflowing surrealist cocktail? Who f . . . ed himself clear of the world and called on us to stare in a desperately exalted trance of contemplation at the cracks between our toes?

The photographs of the thirties were meant to fill the empty spaces that mere words were supposed to have left in our consciousness. You saw their faces, and these

115

became the bitter underscoring of the text. And then the text itself disappeared, sinking without trace into the hollow cheeks and eyes, the holes of the clapboard cabins. This was more or less the time that Miller pulled out for France. He has returned to pick up a state of consciousness and a habit of mind more or less where he left them.

Miller's America, his air-conditioned nightmare, is also a series of images, without text. He has already said all that he has to say; has caught the images, a few of them memorable, and has no more to catch. His own peculiar kind of comment, the comically overdone, and perhaps seriously under-felt, indignation, is already a dated and vacated thing; and the images that stood out in it have been taken over by the photographic slicks, either tamed and spruced up, or outdone in savagery in the weekly spreads of *Life*. America of the glaring contrasts, of riches and poverty and tons of food wasted, has become a household notion. The American nightmare has taken the place of the American dream, and it is as sentimental as its predecessor, as popular and as widely believed in. We all know our shame and our disgrace by now; they have blended with the breakfast coffee. Miller is in the position once ascribed, if I remember, by Mencken to George Bernard Shaw—parading, stripped to the waist, with a placard that reads: Man is a Mammal and has an Umbilicus!

There is, nevertheless, an element of novelty in Miller's nightmare—novelty, that is, as far as the average American bad dream is concerned. He makes his protest from the standpoint of the artist and Bohemian, whose sufferings are ignored in the popular version of our *cauchemar*. It is a serious indictment (better expressed in his *New Republic* letters and *Plight of the Creative Artist in the U.S.A.*) and there is much truth in it. But it is the truth of the self-sufficient man, a little smug in his righteousness, who doesn't have to take account of more than *he* already knows. He is at once spokesman and poseur ("I prefer corduroys"); he is honest while he fakes and a faker in his honesty, and has not been able to resist playing the lion to all the woolly cubs, and creating a cult with each angry swish of his tail. Perhaps the greatest homage one can pay him is not to take him too seriously.

The limitations of Bohemianism are all too obvious. (Miller himself may be aware of some of them—*vide The Colossus of Maroussi.* Or was that the supreme Bohemian effort, the gesture at faith?) He has nothing to say of American society and politics that his pose and his gesture have not already summarized. Anything not fully covered by his pose is included in his prayer for the immediate destruction of civilization—a device whereby silence can be made to say everything.

But despite the persistence of his Bohemian grimace, Miller shows signs of softening up. He has heart-to-heart talks with convicts, painters, children, desert rats, automobile mechanics, etc. (spoiling some of these passages, as he frequently spoils the best of his pieces, by running off a surrealist coda, or indulging himself in the delight of the obvious moral he has drawn). His conversations, and his witty or whimisical moods, when he forgets about his toothsome snarl and lets himself go, are better than what one expects of travel-talk, and there are some occasional pages of the simple, lively prose that he does so very well. Miller, you sometimes begin to feel, is really the homey sort.

It may be the onset of age, or in some way the effect of America, but Miller back-at-home is not the same old Henry. The image he created for himself, among the despairing ecstasies of *Tropic of Cancer,* of a man, flashlight in hand, peering down a vagina, is hard to connect with the motorist peering through a windshield. It may be because America is everything he says it is, the very same sterile horror (how else account for the Miller cults?) that his indictment bears no weight. He falls so readily into the American stride, the tricky, self-advertising gait, that he becomes merely a conscious citizen, disgusted by his society, but by no means dissociated from it. Miller, the decultured man, can thrive only on the ruins of ancient cultures. Without traditional or classic setting, his pose is no more than another American eccentricity.

❧ Two Modes of Fiction

PIPE NIGHT is so much a book of the times that it is at
least fifty years out of date. [John] O'Hara tries to catch
the mood and character of everything—as Wolcott Gibbs
says in his preface to the book—that is "bounded on the
east by Fifty-second Street and on the west by Hollywood
Boulevard." And so he takes short runs on buses and
trains, picking up servicemen and civilians, men and
women who frequent gin mills and night clubs and fall
in love and get married and divorced and lead stodgy
and respectable or colorful and disreputable lives, in the
course of which, whether it be trying to sell a set of golf
clubs or sleeping with the latest lame-brained movie
actress, they give themselves away to the observant eye
and the sensitive ear. But there is nothing new, unique,
or particularly revealing in O'Hara's insight, for all the
importance he attaches to what he sees, hears, and under-
stands; nothing that does not go back at least to the
reporter's sketch pad of the twenties, if not straight to
O. Henry.

These thirty-one short stories are derived from a journalistic tradition of popular culture—the "human-interest
angle" that helped build up the circulation of the metro-
politan dailies. "Human interest" is ostensibly devoted to
combating the anonymity and insignificance of life in the
present-day world. It holds that there lives nowhere an
average citizen with life so dull that some moment of it is
not worth knowing. The whole technique is to reveal this
moment—with as great an economy of time and detail as
drama or plot will allow. As a result of which the insig-

nificant citizen is left no richer, no better named, than he was before; on the contrary he has been drained of the minor importance that life has let run his way. Not he, but the city, the composite anonymity, is the real hero; and the short-short story, which sets out to censure the world's heartlessness, ends by flattering and affirming it.

It seems to me that O'Hara is doing precisely this sort of thing. Society is given; his object is to see how the man in the street or the bar, who need no longer be a "real" character, makes out in a typical social encounter. The method followed is the same: there is a dramatic moment in which something happens—the eye can catch it like a camera—and in this moment all significant details of character are revealed. And of course the moment, thus captured, constitutes a story; all the necessary attitudes, the tensions that go on in society and enter into particular situations, are already known; they are furnished by the times.

From which it follows that such writing is essentially conservative. It hoards the legacy of its own and preceding generations, making only such adjustments as popular culture itself may demand. It does nothing on its own, never analyzes, never ventures an evaluation of the times. The social criticism that does enter into O'Hara's stories, as when, for example, he lets the irony of a solecism or a misquotation stand as an indictment of a philistine, is sheer class mentality—the sophisticate's sense of security within his own milieu—and Sinclair Lewis all over again.

Toughness and sentimentality go together in these stories, for a very good reason. While the style is presumably keyed to fast life, ruthlessness, and the hardboiled truth, and the writer's basic assumption would appear to be that men are nasty, selfish, and unsparing, the tradition demands pathos, the contrary touch of deepdown softness or indecision. But the tradition is ruined by what it demands, and is doomed to moderateness. And thus the outstanding impression you are likely to get from these stories, if it is not their monotonous resemblance to one another, is the moderateness of every point they try to make. Men are, after all, only moderately nasty, moderately selfish, etc.; stronger emotions, more meaningful situations, cannot be shown on a moment's notice or glimpsed in a moment's time. O'Hara, very careful to avoid extremes that might break up his narrative pattern, sticks to popular culture and its provincial sophistication, as modern and mediocre as the latest song and as little related to the real culture of our times.

It is as unfair as it is instructive to strike a contrast between O'Hara's book and the short stories in *Fireman Flower,* by William Sansom, an English writer. No contrast could be so great, or so unfavorable to the former, and it should be discounted somewhat by acknowledging an inherent difference in genre. But the point of genuine contact between these two widely different methods of storytelling lies precisely in the relationship of the writer to his culture. Sansom's stories are not particularly of the present, being located, for the most part, in unspecified time and space. But they constitute a fuller and more relevant commentary on our times than anything that has recently been done, or remains to be done, in the behavioristic tradition. Sansom is quite openly a Kafkaist, to the extent, not that it matters, of imitation. What is important with Sansom is that he has found through his study of Kafka a method of controlling his sensibility so as to present his private symbolism in the widest possible frame of reference that he knows how to construct.

It is in itself exciting to find a writer who can be excited by general problems. Unrestrained by the niceties of repression that pass for objectivity he can set down a moral proposition as it does in fact occur to the human mind, and by allowing himself intelligent expression— the place of "ideas" in fiction is a problem that a writer who does have a few can well afford to ignore—he manages to say a good deal directly, and to create a drama of implication much more moving, to my taste, than the tensions of literal strain and stress. A recurrent theme in *Fireman Flower,* for example, is that hope is the ultimate enemy of human purpose. Thus, in one story, four groups of prisoners are sentenced to wring a long wet sheet bone dry. The work is arduous; the prisoners' own sweat, dripping onto the sheet, nullifies their labor. Three of the groups fail; the fourth succeeds because its members have kept in mind the true purpose of their otherwise meaningless work, which is to restore their freedom. And when they have wrung the last drop of moisture out of their section of the sheet and apply to the jailers for their release, the authorities turn a hose, full force, onto the sheet, and declare, while locking them in, that purpose is everything and that in keeping alive the hope of their freedom they have already obtained it.

This may be another way of saying that you can't win. But the difference between saying it O'Hara's way and saying it Sansom's way is the difference between calling life a racket and a tragedy.

New Republic, May 14, 1945

◆§ Chopping a Teakettle:
E. B. White's
The Wild Flag

THE FLOWERS OF THE EARTH are the wild flag, the true banner of internationalism. There is a better phrase for it in Yiddish: *hacken a tcheinik,* which means to chop a teakettle, or in American idiom, to talk up a breeze—of nonsense. E. B. White, in these paragraphs testifying to the *New Yorker's* conscience, proves himself a master craftsman; not only does he chop away with an unfailing stroke, but he manages to keep a cloud of steam issuing from the spout as he works.

There is no such thing as urbanity without partisanship. Appearances to the contrary, the *New Yorker* has always upheld a set of values—the values, to be sure, which are sacred to its own bourgeois sophistication. Until recently, cuteness has been this magazine's only form of prayer; it has worshiped its own tone with the cute, the coy, the cunning remark. The scheme of its prayer has been not to call forth but to conceal the god. The *New Yorker* did not believe in committing itself bluntly, and it made cute fun of those who do. But with the advent of the war, conscience, which where the middle class is concerned is best defined as the fear of dispossession, demanded that it justify the ways of its god to man. Then behold, the Lord of Park Avenue and suburbia, the Supreme Profile, revealed His full face and declared Himself in favor of world government.

But He has need of His cloud, which is where Mr.

White's services come in; for if it is His own fear and trembling that the cloud hides, still it will appear that it hides His wrath. ("These editorials . . . were written sometimes in anger," says Mr. White.) "A Chinese farmer in a rice paddy would have to feel, between his toes, not only the immediate wetness of his own field but the vast wetness of the fertile world," saith the Tea-kettle, apropos of the obligation that world government would put on each man to take "the entire globe to his bosom." "The special feeling of an Englishman for a stream in Devonshire or a lane in Kent would have to run parallel to his pride in Athens and his insane love of Jersey City." Note well this last parable. A false god would have said Brooklyn; but only the true Teakettle, than Whom there is none more uptown, would have known when to say Jersey City.

The *New Yorker's* task is to convert its own apostates: they whom it sustained in archness and in coyness and in the *bon ton* of small talk, on whose middle brows it laid its blessing, exalting their emptiness—they shall now receive the Word. Thus it is that we have world government praised and national sovereignty denounced on every page, but nothing about actual politics. It is *bon ton* to mention fascism and racism and come out against them. But capitalism, imperialism, world markets, the profit system, exploitation, revolution, socialism—these words have a sweaty air; they suggest crowded downtown East Side meeting halls with their folding chairs and smoke in the dingy room, the stain in the armpits of the excited speaker. (And if these images are clichés—for which reason, among others, the *New Yorker* avoids the reality for which they stand—they are no triter than the more aseptic middle-class images that the *New Yorker* does employ: politics must keep abreast of science, our ideas must be as long-range as the latest bomber.) The limits of tone are the limits of class. There is a good reason why the *New Yorker* liberal must simper as he does. What his sense of urbanity allows him to say corresponds exactly with the limits of what his sense of politics—if he had any—would allow him to do. A fundamental revision of society, a practical consideration of the revolutionary measures necessary to the establishment of world government are in bad taste—and small wonder. The bourgeoisie will never give up its tone without a struggle.

But Mr. White asks very little. "If these topical paragraphs add an ounce to the long-continuing discussion of nationalism and throw even as much as a flashlight gleam on the wild flag which our children, and their children, must learn to know and love, I am content."

Block that metaphor!

Nation, December 28, 1946

~§ Silone's Spiritual Journey

ALTHOUGH SILONE'S PLAY [*And He Hid Himself*] is based on *Bread and Wine*, it is closer in spirit to the later novel, *The Seed Beneath the Snow*. The distance Silone has traveled, "coming from far and going far," is indicated by the transformation the character of Pietro Spina has undergone in *And He Hid Himself* and the accompanying change in the familiar theme of "the spirit of man . . . forced to save itself in hiding." In *Bread and Wine* Spina is primarily a revolutionist, sobered though he has been by the failures of the revolutionary movement in Europe. But in disguising himself as the priest Don Paolo Spada, to hide from the Fascist police, Spina takes on thematic as well as strategic vestments, and the strategy of his pose itself poses the problem that is to occupy the rest of his career: what is the justification of Marxism; why is one a Socialist; what are the ends that socialism serves? Spina now professes a deeper moral commitment than in his early days as a Marxist, and he tries to justify his Marxism in terms of what he believes to be the higher and broader morality of the Christian tradition. But his position is still expressed in the form of a natural morality, and its relation to Christianity, which he regards as an ethical heritage, though intimate, is one of consonance rather than derivation.

It is in *The Seed Beneath the Snow* that the priestly habit of Don Paolo Spada becomes a habit of Spina's soul. The Christian justification of Marxism has turned toward a fusion of the two traditions, and it is now as a Christian that Spina goes among the peasants of the

126

Abruzzi. His political acts are acts of brotherhood and humility. The strength of the Fascist regime and the unpropitious time have forced him into a retreat from direct politics; but it is a retreat that he regards as a forward step. Before a step can be taken, it must be prepared. To prepare the way by an examination of conscience, by a purgation of soul, by devoting oneself to acts of brotherhood in the example of Christ, is also a political task—for how shall there be just politics without a living justice among men? Christianity is now more than a heritage that natural morality may share with the Church Militant. It is also the essence of the message that Spina has to transmit to the Italian underground, and Christian righteousness is the source and the authority for the values that he upholds under the Fascist terror. Accordingly, Silone's imagination draws more freely on Christian symbols. In *The Seed Beneath the Snow* we encounter the hide-out in the manger, the donkey, the germination of the grain of wheat; Silone's peasant humor is blended with a Franciscan humility and love, and there occurs the ultimate Christian act of sacrifice in the form of Spina's surrender to the police, for the sake of the village idiot, who represents the mass of men.

This development in the direction of greater explicitness in the use of Christian symbolism, and in the transformation of metaphor into literal Christian meaning, is carried farther in *And He Hid Himself*. In the introductory note to the play Silone says that the modern drama presents "a new element in the guise of protagonist: the proletarian." (As Silone uses the term, drama denotes both the theater and man's consciousness in general—an ambiguity which is of some importance in the analysis of his play.) The proletarian is a new protagonist because modern Christian man recognizes in his "hardships and his destiny . . . the stuff of history, thought, or art." We recognize him as such because "between the ancients and us there has come Jesus Christ."

I should like to quote extensively from the introduction for its importance in establishing the dual context in which the play can be read:

> The characters of this drama are men of today, but they "come from far and are going far." They belong only incidentally to the chronicle of time. Their existence bears witness to the spiritual journey of the author and . . . a considerable number of men of his generation, in these last years. . . .
>
> The rediscovery of a Christian heritage in the revolution of our time remains the most important gain that has been made in these last years for the conscience of our generation. . . .
>
> It is a heritage weighed down with debts. A living, painful, almost absurd heritage. In the sacred history of man on earth it is still, alas, Good Friday. Men who "hunger and thirst after righteousness" are still derided, persecuted, put to death. The spirit of man is still forced to save itself in hiding.
>
> The revolution of our epoch, promoted by politicians and economists, thus takes on the form of a "sacred mystery," with the very fate of man on earth for its theme.
>
> The tasks of the economic and political order are by no means obscured or dissimulated thereby; they are indeed the first and main tasks. But the men called on to carry them out must know that they come from far and are going far.

I find a puzzling ambiguity in these statements. On the one hand, Christianity is said to be a heritage, and as such, presumably, its rediscovery represents a gain to the revolutionary movement *from without*. But it is because of Christ, on the other hand, that the proletarian occupies his dominant position in the drama and the consciousness of our time—which gives Christianity a central position *within* socialism. Thus socialism is independent of Christianity, to the extent, at least, that it can draw on it (and restore it and carry it on as part of its general aim at the re-establishment of human values); at the same time it is dependent on Christianity as an essential foundation for its values. The latter half of this ambiguity takes on even greater literal meaning in the play.

And He Hid Himself is a "Good Friday" play, in a setting made familiar by the novels. The main action is concerned with the episode of the informer Murica, as in *Bread and Wine*. Murica, a young student member of the underground, betrays his comrades to the Fascist police; tormented by his conscience, he seeks to redeem himself by confessing to Spina. It is not punishment that he fears so much as the possibility that he may escape punishment. The distinction between good and evil cannot consist merely in the distinction between that which society rewards and that which it punishes; for if a technique of betrayal were perfect, there would be no detection, hence no punishment, and therefore no distinction between good and evil. It is this which Murica cannot endure, and he confesses to Spina to be judged, and thereby restored to the human community. Spina spares him and accepts him back into the party.

One may note that up to this point neither Murica's nor Spina's acts require motivation in terms of literal Christianity. Spina's compassion, his identification of revolutionary activity with the highest moral engagement, and his discussion of the motives a man may have for becoming a Socialist, from frustration in the bourgeois order to a thirst after justice; the guilt Murica feels, his horror at the possibility that he may feel no guilt, and his desire to be restored to humanity can all be explained by natural morality, which can also provide a distinction between good and evil which is not wholly dependent on social approbation or disapproval. But in the further development of the episode, the natural aspect of the situation is transcended imaginatively; Silone draws on the Passion for the construction of a Christian parallel, and Murica becomes a Christ figure whose death, at the hands of the state police, is a recurrence on earth of His agony. Murica has taken sin on himself and has expiated his sin; by offering himself as a sacrifice in death he has redeemed mankind—at least to the extent of influencing the peasants to join the underground, who were at first very reluctant to do so.

I do not insist that the parallel is perfect, or that it must be taken literally. But that it is intended by Silone is evident from the many references he has the villagers make, during the final scenes, to the death of Christ, finally likening Murica to Him. It is significant that Murica's full redemption is obtained not in his confession to Spina, which is explicable in natural terms, but only by a Christlike death. I do not think it is going too far to say that Silone, after the fashion of myth, and without a historian's commitment, puts the Christian drama at the center of man's history, making the Passion epitomize the struggle of man on earth. It thus becomes the basic historical event, "the stuff of history," which every other episode in time, in so far as it is related to man's struggle and has moral significance, recapitulates as a "sacred mystery." Human aspiration toward justice acquires its meaning and its direction from this event, and it is thus that Jesus Christ raises the proletarian to his dominant position in our "drama."

And He Hid Himself is not a successful play, either in its own behalf or as a dramatization of *Bread and Wine*. Much of Silone's feeling for peasant humor and wisdom is present, but not to the degree of the novels. Pietro Spina remains the great creation of love and gentleness that he has always been, but the play does not allow him sufficient scope as a person. Spina's shifting from revolutionary to priest is necessarily presented without modulation, and a good deal of the irony of his position is lost. The scenes of the play are too episodic and static, and the exits and entrances constitute practically all the action that occurs on stage. By far the best scene is Murica's confession, which achieves an intensity nowhere else attained; but it does not come as a true climax, for the resultant action introduces extraneous material by way of the Christian parallel, which is not closely enough related in tone to the rest of the play.

Technical reasons may be the most important for explaining the failure of *And He Hid Himself*. But there is also something else involved, which has to do with the ambiguity that is apparent in Silone's conception of drama. Drama, as noted at the outset, pertains, for Silone, both to theater and to general consciousness. *And He Hid Himself* is both a play by itself and a presentation of critical episodes in the growth of a Christian Socialist conscience—the latter being not merely an implicit meaning of the play but an element structurally distinct from it. The success with which the novels join action and conscience is not achieved here.

The play, moreover, has the over-all quality of secular drama. So much of the resolution presupposes a direct response to the underlying Christian theme, and its emotional effect depends to such a large extent on the passion with which the spectator responds to the Passion, that the play as a whole becomes virtually a secular enactment of the Christian drama. Now it is hard to see how there can be a secular form in a time when drama—again used ambiguously, as above—is primarily naturalistic. The distinction we are accustomed to recognize between the sacred and the natural is an exhaustive one for our time, allowing for no middle ground, such as the secular. A secular theater presupposes the existence of a Christian society.

Thus the play, in its own terms, reflects the ambiguity of Silone's religious position. As he has stated in the introduction, Christianity is a heritage for the revolutionist to draw upon. But as Silone's development as an imaginative artist indicates, Christianity is not so much an ethical heritage for him as a living tradition, the symbolism and literal meaning of which are becoming the basic sources of his work. This, I am sure, must present a difficulty to all his old admirers. The world from which Silone comes as a radical, and whose conscience he now represents more clearly and more personally than any other living writer, insists, as a matter of its own tradition and its own inner necessity, upon a natural morality, and conceives its struggle as neither sacred nor

secular but entirely self-sustaining, a drama in which
man is the sufficient character. And yet Silone's examination of natural morality and the questions he has put
to the revolutionary conscience, asking it precisely how
far it has come and how far it is going, remain the most
searching that any man has posed in our time.

From Marx to Freud:
Adjusting to Belonging

THIS $10,000 PRIZE-WINNING NOVEL [*Wasteland*, by Jo Sinclair] is an epistle to the Jews who are poor in spirit. Our St. Paul, who becomes Saul again, is Jake Braunowitz, alias John Brown. Because he has a pain in his back, is ashamed of his family, and ashamed of being a Jew, and because his sister, Debby, insisted he should go, he consults a psychiatrist about his troubles. For eighteen years John has been hiding his Jewishness from his Gentile women, his Gentile colleagues at the newspaper where he is employed as a staff photographer, from himself and society at large. Nevertheless, he is unable to break away from his family and gefilte fish. Lacking identity, he can identify himself with nothing; at thirty-five he is still unintegrated and obsessed with a sense of waste, hence "wasteland." One reads his story as it comes out in weekly, and later in bi-weekly, interviews with the psychiatrist.

The poverty and degradation of the family are rather well sketched in—the stingy, dirty, irresponsible father; the beaten, semi-illiterate mother; sister Roz with her promiscuity, Italian boy friends, and night clubs; brother Sig with his cars and cigars; and above all, sister Debby. Debby, who has taken over the male role abandoned by her father and become a Lesbian, keeps company with colored girls, listens to classical music, writes stories about the poor and oppressed—cripples, social outcasts, Negroes, and Jews—for the *New Masses* and literary magazines, and knows what the score is. She has identified herself, inwardly and outwardly, with the people, and

133

it is the example of her courage and resolution together
with the psychiatrist's sympathetic understanding (clichés
intentional) that pull Jake-John back on the road to life.

The therapeutic procedure followed by the psychiatrist
is mainly that of prodding the subject with questions
and suggestions, and letting him talk it out. It works
wonders. No sooner has John got down on record the
story of his family's poverty and humiliation, and the
hatred he feels toward it, than his *tzores* drop off one
by one, the pain in his back disappears, and he calls
himself Jake once again. The new Jake is a kindly fellow
who photographs his parents and his brother Sig, takes
his nephews to prize fights and hockey games and gets
them jobs on the paper, introduces his sister Roz to his
Gentile friends when they visit the night club in which
she waits on tables, gives blood to the Red Cross, enlists
in the army and asks the Four Questions at the *Seder*.

If there is any literary moral to be drawn from this
drab but profitable little poem in celebration of the
beatitudes of psychiatric social work, it is, perhaps, that
naturalism is the best method of describing adversity,
but God protect it from good fortune. The political
moral and the moral concerning Jewishness are, however, of much greater consequence.

The noteworthy thing is that the secular priest who
works redemption is now a psychiatrist. Not so long ago,
in a novel of this sort, he would have been a Party
organizer, and Jake, if he were to lead his family at all,
would have led them to the barricades. The difference
is significant, for whether or not Miss Sinclair is herself
a fellow traveler, and it's no concern of mine, the piety
of her book is oriented toward the Jerusalem of a recent
Party line, now known as Browderism.

Wasteland comes to an end in an ecstasy of belonging. Jake's Jewish blood has been accepted, it has
mingled in the Red Cross station with the blood of
America—Negro blood, it is hoped, will soon be allowed
to join the stream—and Jake has become Everyman. (It
doesn't hurt, by the way, to perpetuate a few little

racisms on the side of blood; it makes the final mingling so much more poignant and exciting.) The only ghetto in America is your own. (In all the eighteen years of its concealment, Jake's Jewishness was never once suspected, and he had the good fortune, apparently, never to have heard an anti-Semitic remark.) As for the ghettos elsewhere, the war will wipe them out. Though some have *Seders* and others have not, at heart all people are people. But everywhere belong! And as for psychiatry (in the critical work of this period, a good deal was made of the unification of Freud and Marx, with adjustment becoming a very respectable word), psychiatry will change the world into a playground and a settlement house.

There is a superficial attractiveness about this position that has, I imagine, proved tempting to many Jews. It blesses the bourgeois in all of us, and is kind, in particular, to the Jew's self-hatred, with an indulgence that passes for understanding. The line removes the stigma from assimilation, presenting it, to a degree, as a duty and a positive good, and is moderate in its demands on residual Jewishness (John becomes Jake, but Brown does not again become Braunowitz.) To show that it recognizes human frailty and has our interests at heart, the dispensation lets redemptive activity down to an easier level—one runs fewer social risks in working for brotherhood than in working for communism. And above all, it dangles the eternal carrot of belonging before our noses with a "Bravo, old donkey, and an end to alienation!"

Fortunately, the human imagination cannot make too much of a good thing out of a bad thing. At least novels fail when they dish out this pap, and parties, too, have a way of succumbing to their own poison. For poverty is a friend of truth. What about the terrible poverty of Jake's family, which was so important in the diagnosis of his ailment—why has even mention of it disappeared from the cure? Are we really back to the origins of free enterprise, blaming poverty on shiftlessness and (new term) neurosis? No, not quite. Miss Sinclair has, or at least had, her answer for that one, too. WPA, we are told, was a respectable thing; it was in its own way a project for reclaiming wasteland. But now that you are back on your feet again, stay out of the red, plump for a people's government, learn to wear your Jewishness and your other differences correctly, as you would a suit of clothes, and you, too, can be a well-dressed man.

I am aware that as far as novels at the imaginative level of *Wasteland* are concerned, the shift from Marx to Freud is no more than a shift in clichés; resumption of the earlier allegiance would not necessarily raise the standard of literary quality. The same, however, cannot be said of the social orientation of which popular fiction is but a single manifestation. Here, it seems to me, a real sacrifice has been made. The transformation of "change the world" into "adjust yourself to it" has had the effect of abolishing concern with the kind of society that is worthy of our adjustment, and of removing the discussion of social problems from a historical context.

Treatment of Jewish problems in these terms absolves the world of responsibility for what the Jews have suffered as a people, and breaks up their integrity as a group by requiring them to adjust themselves as individuals. As in *Wasteland*, bourgeois society is taken for granted as possessing in itself all the norms of successful adjustment, all the conditions that the Jew, rid of the inner burdens of his Jewishness, shall be expected to meet. Nothing need be said of the historical context of anti-Semitism, of why the world permits and encourages it; for here we touch upon the guilt of bourgeois society, *its* alienation from humanity, and adjustment, as the program of the bourgeoisie, is designed to encourage forgetfulness.

Once again, the Jew is scapegoat, except that in this case, in return for the sacrifice of his interests, he is allowed to forgive the world by coming to terms with it. All of which tends to make liberalism synonymous with reaction, concentration on individual psychology and limiting the social problem to issues of racial brotherhood serving as a strategy for masking and maintaining social injustices at a deeper level. It is not inappropriate that a novel embodying this theme should have won the generous Harper Prize—for this theme happens to be the program of wealth in search of a conscience.

Commentary, March, 1946

✑ A Left-Wing Middle-Brow

IRWIN SHAW'S FICTION, as Faulkner says of Popeye's face, has "the depthless, vicious quality of stamped tin." But Mr. Shaw must not be dismissed with a single sentence. One must be patient, persistent, willing to point out the faults of his kind of writing for all to see, in the hope it may do some good. Just what is it that makes Mr. Shaw's fiction so bad and even, in a public sense, so dangerous?

There is his position to consider, though this is not the ultimate thing, for the fault ultimately is his own— his position as a representative of a generation of writers, and as a summary of a period in American cultural life. Mr. Shaw belongs to what has been called the "middle-brow movement," a movement embracing such figures as Norman Corwin, Bennett Cerf, the editors of the *New Yorker,* the Luce publications, and the local geniuses of Hollywood. There are many differences among these men; I doubt if they have an altogether conscious program, and yet they are all united in their kind and quality of talent, and in the public which they seek to exploit. They direct their work essentially to the middle class, taking care not to offend too deeply the prejudices of their audience. They believe in writing for the people, in writing clearly and distinctly, that all may grasp their social message.

More specifically, Mr. Shaw belongs to the left wing of this movement. This left wing calls itself liberal, is opposed to discrimination and racial intolerance (how adroitly the *New Yorker* made it *bon ton* to be against anti-Semitism—though it has not as yet been able to forego a peculiarly bourgeois pleasure in the charming malapropisms of colored maids); it is for the United Nations and for reaching an understanding with Russia, etc., etc. I find nothing objectionable in such ends. But the means which both the left wing and the movement as a whole have chosen are extremely vulgar, and exert an effect on literature not unlike that described by Gresham's Law: bad money cheapens and drives out the good.

What is so vulgar and harmful in this group, and in the member now under discussion? (Let it be understood—an essential point—that Irwin Shaw does not stand alone.) First there is its rationale: the belief that only the mass media, as presently constituted, can carry a message to the people. Thus, to criticize whatever they think deserving of criticism in American life, the middlebrows must begin by a defense of some of its worst aspects: Hollywood, after all, reaches millions of people, and so does the radio and the press, and there is no time to lose, no time for improvement now (come out of that ivory tower!), improvement must come when it can. So, to change anything, we must begin by accepting nearly everything as it is. Thus the condition for criticism is the suspension of criticism. This is one reason, among others, that these liberals have been called totalitarian: their habit of mind bears a great resemblance to the world outlook of Stalinism.

Irwin Shaw's style is what is very loosely and inexactly called hard-hitting. It is of a familiar American genus, sprung from Hemingway and his forebears, but lacking their clear rhythms, cleanness, and skill. The following hunk of sentence is typical of Shaw (I am making it up as I go along)— ". . . with the sun coming straight at you, and the girls on the beach in their wide, flopping straw hats, casting a lacework of shadows over their sloped, bronzed, sea-salted shoulders, remembered the taste of beer and the tuna-fish sandwich sharp to the tongue, now mocking it in the Italian mud, and the light in the hotel window and the clerk's easy, complaisant grin, and later, on the way home, the wind at your back and the night lying slick in a puddle of neon in the wet streets." The point in making this up, rather than selecting an actual quotation (e.g., p. 9, last paragraph; p. 128, antepenultimate paragraph; p. 179, last paragraph, etc., [of *Act of Faith and Other Stories*]) is that it is so easy to do.

The stilted simplicity of this style keeps Mr. Shaw's writing broadly popular, within reach of the people (who read the *New Yorker*); its underplaying of emotion enables him to convey his message without seeming to do so. Not that he is not forthright and outspoken; but as everything about him is forthright and outspoken, why distinguish his message from, say, his description of the juke box in a bar? Thus he can deliver a message without having to apologize for it—an old *New Yorker* trick, except that the method of delivery is already the most abject and groveling of apologies.

Another trait of Mr. Shaw's delivery is its pseudo-sophistication. He knows everything; that is to say, sex and liquor. He has had all these commodities, not without enjoyment, of course, but nevertheless with just that properly arch touch of weariness, lest anyone think him naive. Whatever one needs to keep well informed—a knowledge of Freud, politics, modern painting, and poetry—Shaw has it; his writing, so highly polished, reflects this knowledge at every turn. Never before has shallowness served sophistication so well. And what purpose does sophistication serve? It is the caste mark which the left-wing middle-brow, going down among the peasants, never forgets to paste above the bridge of his nose. Aware of the risk in condescending so low, our left-winger, by his smartness and his tone, assures himself of his place in the group a notch or two above the one for which he writes.

Such is the style of Mr. Shaw and his colleagues. Yet it is not for style alone that Mr. Shaw is noted, but for the moral attitude which the style embellishes. Here, again, some subtlety is necessary to criticism, for his attitude, as made clear by the title of this collection of stories, as well as by the stories themselves, is one of faith, and faith is something that no one is against. It is in all cases preferable to cynicism—except, I should say, in the present case.

Irwin Shaw has faith in the people, in democracy, in America, the future, etc.—all excellent things to have faith in. Yet the faith in these things that reason would approve (for we are not speaking of sacred mysteries) is not unacquainted with cynicism. Our experience of politics and our knowledge of Marxism, to name only two of the many possible sources of a rational attitude toward the world, have developed in us the skeptical sense. We know that the Declaration of Independence (or the Atlantic Charter or the Communist Manifesto, or any such statement of ends) is a fine thing; we also know, on the strength of experience, that any claim for a political event in the present world, such as "x is a perfect example of end y," is to be met with skepticism. Moreover, so far as certain claims go, claims, say, that might be made for platform promises in national elections, skepticism, while necessary, is far from sufficient; without a certain cynicism, one would be at the mercy of every party demagogue. (An excellent instance of the necessity of cynicism for understanding politics is afforded by the British Labour Party's campaign promises about the Jews.) Cynicism is of course deplorable; yet it is often justified by our common experience, and if not by common experience, certainly by extreme experience—the shock and destruction of war. Now what I hold against Mr. Shaw's kind of faith is not that it is faith, but that it is such a prissy and careful faith. Mr. Shaw's faith does have some apparent connection with cynicism; he does admit at least a reasonable doubt of some of the conventional articles of faith; what is objectionable is that he is so quick to quash it.

Thus in the title story, Seeger, the Jewish soldier-hero of "Act of Faith," wants to go on a spree with his Gentile buddies. They lack money. Seeger has in his possession a Lueger, taken from a German officer whom he killed. He can sell the gun for $65, enough to go to Paris. But he receives a letter from home in which his father tells him that his brother, discharged from the army on account of "combat fatigue," imagines that the streets are full of armed mobs out to get the Jews. Perhaps, adds the father, and Seeger shares his doubt, he is not so crazy after all. Perhaps it is we who go on as if nothing has happened, nothing were threatened, who are the real madmen. What shall Seeger do? Shall he hold on to his Lueger? Who knows, he may need it some day—not as a plugged memento, but as a weapon in self-defense. But America. . . . Realizing that he will have to trust his buddies on the streets at home far more than he ever relied on them in the battlefields, he decides to sell his gun and raise the money they need. "Forget it," says Seeger to his friends when they express their regret at seeing him part with his prized gun. "What could I use it for in America?"

The faith in America is admirable; it is the chance we all take, willingly, gladly, with our eyes open. But how much weight does Mr. Shaw really allow the alternative? It is presented through a ruined mind; the soldier who trembles in fear is, after all, psychotic. Yet what about the hypothesis that it is the rest of us, going about as though nothing had happened, who are the insane? Merely a gesture, not followed through.

It is here that the fault lies in this all too ready and too fluent faith: it shows no appetite for struggle, for doubt. But no faith today can be so certain as to call doubt madness. It is in fact the mark of all genuine faith that while the affirmative choice is made, the struggle toward it is great and uneven, and the adversary is not slighted. All the rest is complacence.

It is precisely such complacence that exposes the moral pretensions of the school and the movement to which Mr. Shaw belongs. The criticism of society which proceeds from this direction is self-undermined, for it is full of the images, the rhythms, the poses, the easy values of the successful middle layer, the middle competence, the middle-brow. Conscience is troubled—yet whose is not these days? For which reason it is so simple a matter to satisfy it—a story of five thousand words in which the hero strikes the posture of easy fortitude does the trick neatly.

The left-wing middle-brow obtains the flattery of action, the illusion that something has been done, for himself and his audience, among whom, to the greater detriment of American taste, complacence spreads like a yawn. What does it matter that our hero is not a human being to begin with, that all those bravely faked words are choked off by mashed potatoes, and that that guts-and-Dry Martini attitude toward life is the very thing we must avoid in the interest of what is truly liberal and free? What indeed does it matter? It is not taste, not art, not truth that shall save us, but that advanced sophisticated vulgarity, always carefully a notch or two above the people for whom the good fight is fought.

Commentary, November, 1946

ᵛᵛ Second Thoughts on Huxley's
Brave New World

WHATEVER ITS LITERARY MERITS, *Brave New World* in the fifteen years since it was first published has caught the popular imagination and become a sort of standard reference to the world of science and the future. By this test, which is not an exact one, it would seem that Huxley's satire is successful and that his images of the over-rationalized life—babies in bottles, the alpha, beta, gamma, delta plus and minus division of society, hypnopaedia and orgy-porgy—should rank, say, with Swift's images of irrationality.

Brave New World is, however, a partial satire, its scope taking in but a single aspect of contemporary life. There is in this, as in all of Huxley's novels, a preoccupation with biological theory, the philosophical antecedents of which are social Darwinism and evolutionary thought of the nineteenth century, and whose political connections with the present are perhaps best illustrated by fascism. But there is another strain of thought in modern life on which Huxley's satire does not comment, and that is what one might call the analytic, as opposed to the integrative, tradition, as reflected in some present-day philosophies of science, and which carries over the assumptions and the empiricism of democratic theory from its origins in the eighteenth century. These two traditions are so closely intertwined in the world that it is something of a wonder that Huxley has ignored the latter. There is as much movement in the direction of "individualism," with as much horror in the process, as Huxley, seeing the individual engorged by the group, at the mercy of its pressures, finds in the opposite direction. It seems to me that when Huxley declares in his introduction to this edition of the novel that the state of utopian affairs envisaged in *Brave New World* is now nearer realization than he would have thought at the time he wrote it, he is making an optimistic, however grisly, assumption. The nations, though on the brink of total destruction (our greatest theoretical convenience, the atom bomb), are still far from putting away their furious raging together to see what can be done by way of integrative group coercion of the folks at home. Moreover, the integrative process, thus far, and with no sign of letting up, has gone on in virtue of the coexistence of its opposite: *Gleichschaltung* required the Polish furnaces as much as Goebbels, and in Russia there is the NKVD as well as the charismatic leader cult. The same may be said of the color and race prejudices that infest both British imperialism and our own domestic democracy—one group is solidified at the expense of another. Whole societies are propagandized into cohesion while other whole societies are cut off, all their ties broken before the death that each man in them must face alone. There is therefore no evidence, for whatever comfort this is, that we are moving in a unilinear direction toward Huxley's dread Utopia.

This limits what one can say for the scope of Huxley's satire. Its quality is to be determined by literary considerations, the most important of which is that *Brave New World* is not a good novel. Satire is, of course, a special case, very often departing so far from the novel that it cannot be judged by its standards; but *Brave New World* has the form of a conventional novel and to a large extent its imaginative purpose. Much depends on the inner experience of the protagonists, and the psychological validity of that experience—states of disaffection, rebellion, and reversion to the social norm which mark the behavior of a number of the characters—becomes at times so important to the novel's structure that it occupies a crucial position in the story; the social satire, otherwise the whole bulk of the novel, diminishes at these points to the status of a background. Yet the characters cannot stand out against a background, for by the novelistic standards by which they must now be judged they are no more than paper-thin. Bernard Marx, the undersized Alpha-plus, who as a bottled embryo was mistakenly fed alcohol, puts forth the greatest claim to character in virtue of his defects. He is a possible source of conflict with society, a center of dissatisfaction and opposition out of which drama can arise. But his limitations are too severe—in part, as the result of what his character is within the novel, a necessary limitation, but also as the result of what his character is outside the novel, that is, simply in human terms, where the fault is the author's who tried to make his drama more engaging. Set against Bernard is the novel's true moral hero, the Savage, flown to utopian London from an American Indian reservation. He has in him all the virtues of natural man as well as a poetic remnant, by way of forbidden Shakespeare, of the old culture that once flourished on earth. The Savage is the extreme opposite of the utopian world, and makes the tragic attempt, ending in his suicide, to live as an individual human being in spite of progress. Though he is credible as a repository of the vanished human culture, he is rather hard to take as the mythological figure he is also meant to be. It seems to me that the opposition between artless nature and the utter artificiality of modern man which Huxley tried to establish through the Savage's character was itself utterly artificial. Huxley has by now dropped the Nature half of this opposition, having recognized it as a typically modern myth and therefore far from the unconditioned, fundamental thing he originally took it to be (I believe *Brave New World* is the last of his novels in which the Natural Man as such appears). But Ground, which has since taken the place of Nature, is no more satisfying from a fictional point of view. While representing a position of the utmost metaphysical generality, and therefore, perhaps, free of the specific cultural motives of our time that generated the nature myth, it lacks the latter's vividness in point of imagination and is even less suitable, in being so far removed from contemporary issues as to seem gratuitous, as a source of opposition to modern civilization. For fiction at any rate, opposition to the times is always best centered within the times—which gives the figure of the revolutionary the outright advantage over that of the savage or the mystic. Huxley's antagonists to the world have always lacked this central position; they have, moreover, suffered from the fact that they are clapped together out of convictions which, while undoubtedly sincere, have never proved themselves fictionally by submitting to the test that only detailed, dense, imaginative experience knows how to put to ideas.

Such reservations have to do with the quality of Huxley's fiction as a whole. Considered with respect to their timeliness, where *Brave New World* has the greatest strength, Huxley's novels have all the virtues of philosophy and journalism. As a satire of our present culture *Brave New World*, in spite of its limited scope, has at least the philosophical prestige of several well-thought-out criticisms; thus the criticism of the movies, and in general of our passive spectator roles in sport, play, and whatever enlivening rewards modern life has to offer—a criticism he has developed elsewhere—enters this novel in the unsurpassed image of the "feelies." The moral of withdrawal and rejection is on all such occasions very well founded both as philosophy and, for its imagistic value, as fiction. But the total withdrawal and rejection exhibit journalism's typical impudence. The confounding on one level in *Brave New World* of Henry Ford, Mussolini, Marx, Lenin, and Freud has no more to recommend its intelligence than a Hearst-press witch hunt, where similar modes of thought are employed.

Perhaps one reason why the social concern of Huxley's fiction is not so broad or so careful as it seems, or certainly as it ought to be, is that his bête noire is not the whole of modern social relations but mainly the sexual part. The real horror in *Brave New World* is sex, from the embryo bottle to the contraceptive belt, and the big thing, as in all his novels, is the seduction scene, meant to tie together all the themes and summarize his evaluation, but most fascinating on its own account. The sexual atmosphere in Huxley's books is always one of voluptuous or promiscuous or decadent or undignified, cold, or queasy fornication; and this atmosphere is so heavy that it stifles the moral that love is lacking. Huxley's attempt to give sex its due as a proper reward of life led to such unhappy results as Mark Rampion, the vulgar prude of *Point Counter Point,* who called Beethoven a eunuch, and made Huxley's nature myth as unnatural and inhibited a thing as his subsequent transcendence of nature is forced and old-mannish. Sex, as it seems to have obsessed him, and as it appears in *Brave New World* in transition between mythologies, is the pit in which lies waiting the two-backed beast of our perpetual embarrassment. It traps all with its promise of compensation; it is the escape from horror, from which in turn there is no escape, as the horror itself is deeply sexual. A man, he insists in *Brave New World,* has the right to be unhappy, alone, detached, free in his individuality; but while one endorses these precepts, it would seem that they would carry greater conviction, and the satire which surrounds them, greater weight, if the horror to which they represent the recoil had less to do with the sexual attachment. Yet satire is not without an item of ironic self-expense, in that its distortion, which is to shock the world back to sanity, is often itself the most insane thing; without its own disorder it would never call attention to the world's. Thus the distortion of sex, in Huxley's case, its predominance and overwrought horror to which one may attribute his lack of a wider social scope, may actually be responsible for such scope as he has.

Nation, October 19, 1946

❧ Isherwood's Master Theme

ISHERWOOD'S greatest accomplishments are his characters, the energy and vividness with which they are drawn. Mr. Norris, Sally Bowles, Frl. Schroeder, Schmidt, Kuno, the Nowaks, etc., and above all Bergmann—they comprise a sort of minor Dickens gallery. A Dickens, to be sure, in the more astringent terms of the present, with greater caution, less bounce, and less zeal. But the energy is still remarkable, at least for our time, and it is expended on characterizations in such a way that we find Mr. Isherwood daring even when he is most conventional. Mr. Norris's wig, for example. That wig is a hard thing to forget. In all truth, one might even resent it, resent the ease with which Isherwood appropriates such an old, obvious prop from the storeroom, the grace with which he carries it off. Or the expansive histrionics of Bergmann, the movie director in *Prater Violet*—again the surprise of the obvious, catching us, like a logician's example of novelty in the syllogism, at the point where we have ceased imagining that the self-evident can appear in new relations. Isherwood has the wisdom of the arch-sophisticate; he rushes in and fools, not himself, but us. There is, in fact, something of the movie director in him. He is not afraid or ashamed of using the crude stock gesture, for he knows vulgarity to be the underside of magnificence.

In addition to their vigor of characterization, Isherwood's stories have an excellent quality of contemporaneity. This quality does not derive entirely from the fact that his narratives are set in the present-day world and have immediate reference to political events. Were this the only source of his contemporaneity, as it is, I think, of Koestler's, we should have to consider him a superior journalist. But journalist he is not. Just as he can utilize the most obvious traits of characterization in the most subtle way, so Isherwood uses the materials of journalism to fashion what is always beyond the reach of journalism—an account of essential and representative current experience, felt as direct confrontation and emerging as literature.

What further distinguishes Isherwood's writing from journalism, though I don't mean to belabor this point, is the all-important minor role the narrator plays in his fiction. William Bradshaw of *The Last of Mr. Norris,* and the "I," the Christopher Isherwood, whom he calls "ventriloquist's dummy," of *Goodbye to Berlin* and *Prater Violet,* are not only sensitive reporters of the experience they are undergoing, but exemplars of it, embodying its meaning in what is at once a personal and objective sense. The narrator is always drawn rather narrowly, in contrast to the figures about him; he appears unhappy and repressed, though Mr. Norris credits him with great wit and Bergmann is stimulated by his presence. There is a silence about the "I," a weight almost of nonentity. He is at the heart of the recorded experience, and it is, after all, his experience, but he is withdrawn from it; he catches trick and detail, movement, gesture, motive, and personality; he gives the world its due and more than its due and does not regret his expenditure—but of himself and in himself he gives and reveals nothing. The "I" thus becomes symbol in addition to narrator: he is the alienated man, in whom alienation is embodied as the master theme.

Prater Violet is the story of a movie (I am assuming that the *Berlin Stories,* reprinted after several years, have been read and discussed widely enough not to be reviewed here in detail). Christopher Isherwood is offered a job as a script writer by Imperial Bulldog Pictures, an English movie company, and much against his inclinations he accepts. He is to work on "a show called 'Prater Violet,'" and to assist Friedrich Bergmann, the famous

director, in the preparation of the scenario. "Prater Violet"
is an abominable thing, laid in Vienna, about "a girl
named Toni, who sells violets. . . . As she wanders down
the alleys carrying her basket, lighthearted and fancy-
free, she comes face to face with a handsome boy in the
dress of a student. He tells her, truthfully, that his name
is Rudolph. But . . . he is really the Crown Prince of
Borodania." And so on. Bergmann charms him into under-
taking this impossible assignment: but then Bergmann
has a way with everyone. He is a man of irrepressible
spirits and undeniable gifts, a genius.

Friedrich Bergmann is the dominating figure of this
short novel, as he is of Isherwood's whole gallery of characters. Never before has the author been as close to a
character as he is to the man who, the "I" frankly admits, has become a father image for him. The portrayal
is a work of joy, and the result is sheer overflow.

The director is an Austrian Jewish refugee whose
vitality has withstood all disasters. There is even something comic in his strength; he is too great for the part he
must play in the production of the silly movie, he is too
great a companion for the weak English script writer
who still lives with his mother, and all the lesser people,
things, and circumstances about him set him off not only
in contrast but incongruity. He is a Samson, weakened
though unshorn by the conspiring small fry of movie producers and their underlings, and in the end it is Bergmann's very strength, his effort to right himself, that
makes him topple into absurd rationalization, if not defeat. He kisses a copy of *Mein Kampf* before throwing it
into the waste basket, saying of Hitler, "I love him!" with
a wry, comical face; meanwhile his family is in Vienna
under the Nazis and the war is coming on. And he gives
the same wry kiss of comical love to the movie script of
"Prater Violet" in an effort to dispose of it—the dilemma
of Crown Prince Rudolph becomes the "dilemma of the
would-be revolutionary writer or artist, all over Europe."
The left-wing intellectual is exactly in the position of the
Prince in that he remains bound to his own class while
flirting with the workers. Bergmann makes a great point

of this; it becomes an attack on the Oedipal, umbrella-carrying young English radicals. But meanwhile the show goes on, in all its cheapness and vulgarity.

At last their work is completed and Christopher Isherwood takes leave of Bergmann, walking with him, late at night, down a deserted street. Isherwood, relieved of the long, meaningless task on which he has been engaged, speculates on the nature of life, which is not unlike working on "Prater Violet."

> The telephone rings. You go off somewhere in a taxi. There is one's job. There are amusements. There are people. . . . It seemed to me that I had always done whatever people recommended. You were born; it was like entering a restaurant. The waiter came forward with a lot of suggestions. . . . The waiter had recommended teddy bears, football, cigarettes, motor bikes, whisky, Bach, poker, the culture of Classical Greece. Above all he had recommended Love: a very strange dish. . . .
> Love had been J. for the last month. . . .

But after J. would come K. and L. and M., right on down the alphabet. (The initials introduce an element of sexual ambiguity, which is both honest and discreet.) J. will pass, but the need will remain. The need of the sexual embrace, which expresses both the fear of death and the longing for death. Death and war, the bombs, the screams, the doomed cities, universal death, one's own death. "And behind them, most unspeakably terrible of all, the arch-fear: the fear of being afraid."

For a moment he catches a glimpse of another way, leading to safety, away from all fear. It is the midnight mystical flash, glacial and inhuman, the end of personality. But he knows he hasn't the courage to take this way, which is more terrible than bombs and having no lover. He prefers the human; though it be more absurd than "Prater Violet," and is glad of his love for Bergmann, glad of having found a father. Bergmann holds out his hand and says, "Good night, my child."

I have said that the "I" of Isherwood's novels represents the alienated man. This statement must now be qualified.

It is true that he carries the theme of alienation, and that he is the center of consciousness which implicitly judges and withdraws from the world about him. But he is divided in himself, and balks at either a full acceptance or a full rejection. The position in which he found himself while working on the movie "Prater Violet" exemplifies his general position in life: he knows better, and yet he is involved.

Simply as portrayal, there is greater justice and accuracy in such a treatment of the "I" than there is, say, in Albert Camus's *The Stranger*. The stranger Meursault, who is completely and unambiguously alienated from society, is much less a real person than Isherwood's "ventriloquist's dummy." But the reality that attaches itself to Isherwood's "I" does not have more than psychological validity; that is to say, it is true for the "I," and to that extent must also be true for as much of Isherwood as enters into the narrator, but it is not true morally or philosophically for what we know of Isherwood's full position, and does not represent him as well as Meursault represents Camus. (This discrepancy is a fault in the artist rather than the art, and since such criticism is necessarily *ad hominem* it does not affect Isherwood's novels as such or diminish them in aesthetic value. The Stalinist critics, who have had their innings with *Prater Violet*, condemned the novel for a lack of political responsibility, as they understand responsibility for the moment, as if all were lacking if the moisture of the right line were lacking.)

Prater Violet does indeed stand in an odd relationship to Isherwood's mysticism. Perhaps it is one that a mystic can explain without embarrassment by claiming that fiction, in so far as it represents the empirical self, does not come into conflict with the trans-empirical; the latter alone, he can say, is capable of resolving and removing the conflicts of the ego. This is all very well, and from the point of view of fiction one should, I suppose, be grateful that the empirical Christopher Isherwood is empirical enough to spurn the midnight revelation during his final walk with Bergmann. But there remain empirical conflicts which can be met empirically, and one is entitled to ask, what, short of Vedanta, gives the self strength to overcome (and at the same time, remain connected with) such things as Imperial Bulldog Pictures and Hollywood? What gives us the strength to see, not under the midnight flash, but in broad daylight? Some of that strength is in Bergmann, caught though he be in the net of illusion, and some of it is in the "I," to the extent of a partial alienation. But the recognition of illusion is a tricky matter, for we often continue to believe in a thing precisely because we are not taken in by it. This ironic justification brings together Vedanta and Hollywood, and while it does not otherwise detract from the brilliance of Isherwood's accomplishments in fiction, it does give him the right to be timid.

Kenyon Review, Summer, 1946

ᮠ Kenneth Burke's
A Grammar of Motives

KENNETH BURKE'S criticism, from *Permanence and Change* to the present volume, has been moving toward greater generality in form while remaining more or less static in content. He has been covering the same ground, but each time around the course has cut a deeper track. The subject has remained "motives," which, as Mr. Burke uses the term, means "situation," "situation involving attribution of motives," "statements about motives," "criticism of statements about motives," etc. The term has also designated a variety and complexity of things having to do with, among others, poetic, monetary, and political strategies and perspectives—the purpose of such "anatomizing" of motives being to inculcate an attitude of "linguistic skepticism" and to "purify war" by extending the area of rational intercourse. The means to this end have grown more specific; one can trace their development from the multitude of interlocking linguistic perspectives in *Permanence and Change,* through the extrapolation of dramatic or poetic perspectives as basic strategies, with the comic serving as *primus inter pares,* in *Attitudes Towards History,* to the present division of the dramatic perspective into five key terms: Scene, Act, Agent, Agency, and Purpose. The interrelationship of these key terms and their analytic function in varying ratios make up the text of *A Grammar of Motives.*

The use Mr. Burke makes of his pentad of terms and the significance he attaches to them call to mind Kant's deduction of the categories. The dream of philosophical criticism, as of critical philosophy, is the discovery of categories which are necessarily involved in all analysis. (Mr. Burke's shift from strict Kantianism is a characteristically modern one—from categories of the understanding to categories of linguistics—a transformation exemplifying what he would call a "conversion downwards.") The key terms, then, are said to figure necessarily in all discourse about motives; and their generating perspective must be "dramatist," as distinct from "scientist," for although statements about motives may be empirical, the subject of motivation is philosophical and can be adequately treated only from a perspective that transcends the limitations of science by resisting the reduction of *action* to *motion*.

The first problem with which Burke deals is that of placement. The characterization of an act, or of any other object, in whatever way, places it with reference to an environment or Scene. Here begins the domain of the term "scene" which appears in such relationships as "container and thing-contained," an action (in drama) as related to its scene or settting, etc. By use of this term, analysis discovers the particular meanings that accrue to an object when its environmental or material background is emphasized. Ratios arise in the overlapping of terms and create a range from purely scenic ways of placement to placement in mixed modes: scene-act, scene-agent, and so on.

A specifically linguistic way of placement is shown forth in definition. Here Burke analyzes what he calls the paradox of substance. A thing is defined in terms of what it is not, and as a definition sets up an equation between *definiens* and *definiendum,* we get the paradoxical result that a thing is said to be what it is not. This paradox can lead to great confusion, especially when a thing is reduced, as in science, to terms of a different or lower perspective. The greatest danger is that we may continue to speak of a thing substantively when we claim to be doing otherwise. But because substance characterizations persist even in fields that supposedly have dissolved substance, Burke, by a curious shift, makes the antinomies of definition stand as a reason for retaining the idea of substance. We will need it particularly, says he, for dramatist purposes, since substances call for analysis in terms of act or action. Science, however, in dissolving the terminology of substance also carries away the features essential to action, leaving in their place terms of mere motion. Burke's favorite example is that of the animal psychologist, with his poor rabbits and white mice, who transfers the results of animal motion, as studied under artificial conditions in the laboratory, to the human perspective and thus reduces the philosophical problem of man's complex motivational behavior to nonphilosophical terms. At this point Mr. Burke develops a lengthy critique of ways of reduction, showing the falsifications inherent in the use of simple, exclusive "God-terms." The proper study of man can be conducted only by maintaining a delicate balance of motives and meanings, sacrificing nothing to the strictures, however convenient for a limited purpose, of reductive analysis. It is the purpose of the pentad to detect such errors of reduction; and since everything that can be significantly said about motives, or about statements about motives, must be expressed in terms of the pentad, it stands guard against falsification by bringing to bear on the human scene the enlightening perspective of drama.

The second part of *A Grammar of Motives* is devoted to an interpretation of the philosophical schools with the aid of five key terms of dramatism. Thus, Hobbes, exemplar of materialism in general, represents in its purest form the predominance of the scenic in philosophy. The scenic elements of Spinozism are also analyzed, and it is shown how Spinoza, though a rationalist, stands at a crucial moment in the history of science, for his rationalism and his God-Substance-Nature equation provide the systemic groundwork for the logic of empirical science, once the metaphysical elements are cut away by the principle of Occam's razor.

Idealism features the term "Agent," because of its stress on the percipient subject. Berkeley, Hume, and Leibniz are examined with regard to Agent. Kant is shown to be dealing with a typical Agent problem in his concern with finding the grounds of freedom (action) in the world of science (motion). Hegel and Marx are also placed in the tradition of Agent-featuring, as is Santayana. The term "Act" is located in Aristotle and Aquinas, and in the nominalism-realism controversy of the Middle Ages. Pragmatism is shown to be the logical home of the term "Agency," and the Agency-Purpose ratio typical of James is investigated in some detail. Mysticism features Purpose, as established by its concentration on ends, union with the Divine, and disregard for the nature of means.

Part Three, On Dialectic, is concerned with the Dialectic of Constitutions as the most representative "anecdote" or case of the effect of men's interests and motives upon a linguistic structure, and with Dialectic in General, which returns to a development of the more abstract linguistic properties considered at the beginning of the *Grammar*.

However indispensable to the practice of criticism Mr. Burke may have found his five key terms to be, I do not see how he can maintain that they are logically necessary. The attractiveness of a Kantian deduction is obvious, and so are the advantages of possessing a set of concepts that are at once ultimately constitutive of a given part of nature and of the language in which all statements about this segment of nature must be expressed. Yet the very linguistic perspective which Mr. Burke has been developing should have guarded him against the erroneous ambition of claiming so much authority for his system. The logical necessity of the pentad holds only within Mr. Burke's language. That is to say, his terms are analytic, and their apparent necessity follows not from the nature of human motivation as such, but from motivation as defined within the dramatist perspective. Mr. Burke's own definition of his subject matter and the criterion of relevance whereby he selects its features constitute a reduction in scope, a particular, limited formulation. Since his selection, like every other possible one, is no more than partial, it follows that other selections can be made, that other perspectives can be framed, and that the dramatist perspective is not exhaustive. And just as inquiry into meanings, motivations and their linguistic reflections remains open in the material sense, allowing the isolation of other "substances," so, too, it remains open formally. Other terms may be chosen to do the work at present performed by our five; and the work which the new terms will do will reconstitute both the object of inquiry and the language in which it is carried on. Who shall say that other perspectives are impossible? Least of all a perspectivist. The reason Mr. Burke believes his pentad to be necessarily involved in the analysis of dramatic situations is that he has fixed its meaning in advance. Its logical necessity turns out to be purely tautological or formal; materially, it possesses no priority at all.

I also fail to see what is gained by clinging, as Burke does, to the notion of *substance*. It is strange that, after presenting in some detail the various arguments which have been advanced for discarding the substance concept, Mr. Burke should show such little curiosity about the truth of these arguments. He counters the arguments against substance by calling attention to the reductive perspectives in which they are formulated and showing their inadequacy from a dramatist point of view. But this merely begs the question. What, to begin with, is his ground for asserting truth within his own perspective, when his whole development of a theory of perspectives has been to establish that linguistic frameworks give a weighted deflection to assertions made within their confines? A general theory of perspectival translation would first be necessary, whereby statements in one perspective could be adequately examined in another. Lacking this, Mr. Burke's position is a kind of linguistic solipsism. Another step necessary for the justification of the truth claims he makes for his own perspective is the construction of a "grammar of truth," a statement of what is meant by "true" and a criterion of evidence for perspectival assertions. Such groundwork is not even attempted in this *Grammar*. Moreover, Mr. Burke's linguistic analysis of substance, like so much of his criticism, generally, is linguistic only in tone and terminology. It is actually no formal doctrine, no statement about language proceeding from the logical analysis that his program should require, but itself another bit of philosophy, a substance metaphysics. That a particular philosophical perspective requires a substance concept is no good reason for retaining "substance" as a term of linguistic analysis, especially when the truth of the perspective in which it occurs has not been independently demonstrated. There are, however, methods of linguistic analysis (of which I shall speak later) that are metaphysically neutral, that discard substance in the light of the very excellent reasons for so doing and that at the same time achieve clearer and better results than Mr. Burke's *Grammar*.

The damage Mr. Burke does his case by clinging to a nonrelational, substantival logic of language can be estimated linguistically, from the following passage:

> If we quizzically scrutinize the expression, "the motivating of an act," we note that it implicitly contains the paradox of substance. Grammatically, if a construction is active, it is not passive [and vice versa]. But to consider an *act* in terms of its *grounds* is to consider it in terms of what it is not, namely, in terms of motives that, in acting upon the active, would make it a passive. We could state the paradox another way by saying that the concept of activation implies a kind of passive-behind-the-passive; for an agent who is "motivated by his passions" would be "moved by his being movedness," or "acted upon by his state of being acted upon."

The whole "paradox" here rests in taking an act to be substantively other than its motive—hence the two can never get together again. Once the purely verbal nature of this difficulty is recognized, and it is seen that the word "other" does not generate a distinction in substance, the motive can very readily get into the act by way of an inference that selects one or more of a field of possible motives. Obviously, "motive" and "act" belong together—as Mr. Burke, up to this point, has confidently assumed; to argue that there is something suspect about their union is to reach that stage of subtlety which marks the evaporation of sense. And to insist on this paradox is all the more idle when techniques, no more recondite than the ordinary inferences of everyday life, exist for getting around it. "Inference," however, is a term that Mr. Burke zealously avoids. He clings to his paradoxes (which he converts into *recommendations* for substance!) on the ground, apparently, that to infer is to incur a loss in perspectival dignity. Inferences are for scientists (rat torturers) who would deprive man of his true essence by imprisoning him in the category of motion. Dramatism alone, faithful to action and substance, is the defender of freedom. Which seems to be little better than philosophical petulance.

As a general observation, I should say that the greatest fault with the *Grammar* is that it is not a grammar at all, but a mixture of formal and material elements comprising a metaphysics. That metaphysical methods are ill suited to the analysis of language should, I trust, be clear from the foregoing. It remains to be shown that linguistic analysis can be conducted nonmetaphysically and can attain greater generality and clarity when freed of the impediments with which Mr. Burke burdens it.

A Grammar of Motives, as a treatise on motivation, covers only one third of the ground open to linguistic analysis. (It is certainly time to remark that there is an ambiguity in the words "linguistic analysis." The expression can mean analysis of language, or analysis by way of language. Kenneth Burke engages in both.) In the Theory of Signs, a general theory of semiosis, as developed by Charles W. Morris, motivations fall under the heading of Pragmatics. Pragmatics is in turn defined as that dimension of sign-functioning (which, for present purposes we may restrict to language activity) that comprises the practical, or the expression of the practical: sentences in the form of evaluations, moral judgments, technological statements, imputations, etc. The two remaining dimensions of sign-functioning are Syntactics and Semantics. Syntactics investigates the relations of signs to each other, as in logic, mathematics, art, etc.; semantics is concerned with the relation of signs to the objects they refer to; and pragmatics studies the relation of signs to their users. The key terms are three in number: "implies" (syntactics); "designates" or "denotes" (semantics); and "expresses" (pragmatics).*

In this relatively simple framework, Mr. Morris has been able to work out a fully articulated system of analysis, of which linguistics forms only a part. The advantages of this system are its range and scope (the whole field of semiosis), its clarity, economy, and neutrality. The latter quality is particularly noteworthy; though Mr. Morris's theory is constructed on an antimetaphysical bias, it is of sufficient generality to cut under specific metaphysical issues. Moreover, the selection of key terms is neutral in that it proceeds from a consideration of semiosis in general, rather than, as with Burke, from a perspective that is metaphysically deflected to begin with. There is no reason, for instance, why a metaphysician should not be able to avail himself of the purely formal apparatus of the Theory of Signs for the analysis, development, and presentation of his own system. Burke, for one, could certainly profit from it; it would cut under a good deal of his unnecessary verbiage.

One may well ask how serious are objections of the sort I have been making. A book, like a good deed, is not necessarily invalidated by the mistakes which attend its execution. To dig for contradiction, to posit formal consistency or simplicity as the sole standard of merit is, in a manner of speaking, like divining with entrails: *Innerlichkeit* is falsely satisfied, and the bird does not have the worth of its own offal. It is a habit encouraged by linguistics, and whoever would undertake the improvement of linguistics must first dissociate himself from its narrow regulations and replace them by the criteria —"dramatist" or simply human—by which he would judge the more representative concerns of men in society at large.

Let us therefore preserve only the essential criticism, which, as is always the case, has to do with truth. If one may apply the term to matters of logic, Mr. Burke's theses, of which I have examined only two, the claim of

* Cf. Charles W. Morris, *Introduction to the Theory of Signs* (Encyclopedia of Unified Science). University of Chicago Press.

logical necessity and the doctrine of substance, both implying a critique of empirical science, are not true. But as even a false premise can lead to a true conclusion, one must now examine his conclusions in a broader way than heretofore.

The "purification of war," at which the *Grammar* aims, is the final public cause of all semantics, which, observing the verbal distortions caused by a clash of interests, believes that a technique of verbal clarification will serve also as a means of moderating the incompatibility of conflicting ends. I am not convinced that it can ever attain its objective; on the contrary, it seems to me that except in so far as given conflicts are *purely* verbal, semantics is a useless oil that does not affect the waters on which it is poured. Rival imperialisms, for example, will not call off their rivalries when deprived of the ideological disguise of their ambitions. Ideologies have a way of perpetuating themselves, if only because truth will also serve as a weapon of war, and ideologies (need one point out?) are sometimes true. When issues are real and important enough, when conditions of conflict are sufficiently desperate, men can even afford to be honest. At best, semantics can have only a symptomatic effect, for in overthrowing one ideology it but prepares the way for another. The cause of conflict, unaffected by purificatory rites, will continue to provide distortions. Burke's kind of semantics even becomes a technique of falsification; in its emphasis on the verbal aspects of conflict, it leads to the development of a perspective in which nonverbal causes are minimized, discounted, and forgotten. At best, his purification of war yields only greater exactitude of war, and though the area of reason is spread, war is not thereby diminished. Modern war, with its tremendous rationalizations of industry and society, its systematic planning and co-ordination—and especially as the Anglo-American allies fought the last one, with (comparatively speaking) a minimum of ideology ("As the war progresses, it becomes less and less ideological," said Churchill), and with the majority of our soldiers not even knowing "what it was all about"—

can even be called a triumph of reason. So much for a semantical peace.

Kenneth Burke's own gloomy prophecy, expressed in a single paragraph, of an age of bureaucracy that will exceed anything we have known to date and, presumably, deprive the world even of such freedom as survives our most recent war, outweighs, for sheer reality, the entire body of countermeasures that semantics can propose. How will an "attitude of linguistic skepticism" forestall the bureaucratization of the earth? It is the very political application of semantics, intended to lead criticism out of the closet, that in the end double-bars it there.

Which suggests that Burke's own criticism, at the height of its present confusion, has reached the "watershed" point. To remain meaningful, it must develop either in the direction of greater formal clarity, or greater material commitment, that is, toward pure linguistics, or a sociology of knowledge and a program of politics. Even as a work of "poetry," which, I suppose, is the justification that Mr. Burke would claim for his opus (A *Rhetoric* and a *Symbolic of Motives* are forthcoming), it lacks the commitment, the sheer espousal value, whether of essences or of doctrines, that poetry always embodies. The *Grammar* as a whole is "scenic"—it is without inwardness in its analysis of ideas. Not only does it fail, as in its treatment of empiricism, to get at the heart of an intellectual tradition and discover the structure or "meaning" of meaning contained therein, but it confines itself to the mere *logistics* of ideas (symbolically borne out by the fact that Burke first considered taking a railroad terminal as a representative case study for his section on dialectic). As such, it reduces intellectual history to matters of transformation, placement, and position— in short, to the very terms of motion that the five key dramatist terms were designed to prevent.

⋖§ *Approaches to Kafka*

THE PUBLICATION OF *Metamorphosis* and *The Great Wall of China* in American editions is a credit to the publishers; and it may be hoped that it will be of some benefit to criticism of Kafka, which, as the recently published critical books make clear, does not seem to know what Kafka is about. The malarial title of the New Directions volume indicates even better than its contents where criticism stands with respect to Kafka. Unfortunately, there is such a thing as "the Kafka problem." Taking criticism as a whole, the problem is whether or not Kafka was a religious writer; and its subsidiary aspects are whether he is to be understood solely or mainly as a psychoneurotic or psychotic personality, an allegorist, a dream-writer, a Jew, a rationalist, irrationalist or anti-rationalist, a thorough though perhaps unwitting chronicler of the basic social conflicts of his time, etc., etc.

In partial extenuation of the critics, it must be said that the interpretation of Kafka is always a difficult thing. But one cannot forgive the booming philistinism of some of the contributors to *The Kafka Problem* [a critical symposium, edited by Angel Flores] and the general confusion. Edwin Berry Burgum in his article, "The Bankruptcy of Faith," attains a level of idiocy that surpasses even the demands of Stalinism. He declares that the murder of K. in *The Trial* "symbolizes the final ascendancy of fascism," likens a scene in *Amerika* to "the promise of a Second Front in the recent war" and says of Karl Rossmann, the hero of *Amerika,* that "like Mr. [Herbert] Hoover or Mr. Westbrook Pegler, he fears the combined aggression of the working class, since he conceives of the individual worker as a selfish, illiterate brute and his labor union as the organization of racketeering to devour society"—all this in defiance of the first chapter and its dominating image of the stoker, with whom the young Karl identifies himself. Kafka's dilemma, "stated in political terms . . . was that he could not become a fascist. 'The Burrow' is a bad story because it has only one character in it. . . ." It is for such reasons that "the Kafka problem" lies mostly with the critics.

But there will inevitably be a conflict even of legitimate points of view in any consideration of Kafka's work. I should like to cite a passage from *Metamorphosis* in example of the many readings Kafka's text can bear. *Metamorphosis*, the story of a young man's transformation into "a monstrous kind of vermin," seems to give its greatest support to the writers who claim that Kafka must first of all be understood in relation to his father. In connection with this claim, one may read in "A Letter to My Father" (*A Franz Kafka Miscellany*) the words which Kafka puts into his father's mouth: ". . . And there is the struggle of vermin, which not only stings, but at the same time preserves itself by sucking the other's blood. . . . Such are you. You are not fit for life, but in order to live in comfort, without worry or self-reproach, you prove that I have taken away your fitness for life and put it all into my pocket." But the latent content of *Metamorphosis* cannot be arranged in such a simple and obvious pattern of Oedipal conflict. One complication is the presence of a death wish, for which some critics find evidence in Gregor Samsa's changing from a higher to a lower order of life, and finally to dead matter. While the restoration of the father to power and authority, a process that keeps pace with the further degradation of the transformed son, can be explained in terms of the father-son conflict, it seems to me that there are many aspects of the story, such as the young sister's sudden blossoming into womanhood, which require an independent explanation. The crucial episode is the sister's playing of the violin. Gregor, hearing her, crawls out of his room, to which he has been confined, and listens to the music.

> Could it be that he was only an animal, when music moved him so? It seemed to him to open a way toward that unknown nourishment he so longed for. He resolved to creep up to his sister and to pull at her dress, to make her understand that she must come with him, for no one here would appreciate her music as much as he. He would never let her out of his room—at least, while he lived—for once, his horrible shape would serve him some useful purpose; he would be at all doors at once, repulsing intruders with his raucous breath; but his sister would not be forced to stay there; she must live with him of her own accord; she would sit by him on the sofa, hearing what he had to say; then he would tell her in confidence that he had firmly intended to send her to the Conservatory. . . . His sister, moved by this explanation, would surely burst into tears, and Gregor, climbing up on her shoulder, would kiss her neck; this would be all the easier, for she had worn neither collar nor ribbon ever since she had been working in the shop.

This passage discloses further meanings in the metamorphosis. It is no longer merely the son's unfitness for life before the father, their conflict, the father's triumph and the original sin of the son's rebellion that are responsible for the degradation of Gregor. The sin, as is made clear by the roach's reaction to his sister's music, is generalized to represent man's whole fallen estate before God. The music moves Gregor so (he is not only an animal) because it is the sign of faith, which is "a way toward that unknown nourishment," or Grace, that he longs for. Now his horrible shape, or his sin, serves a useful purpose, for as a sinner who has been made to see his loathsomeness he can take heed of the way to salvation ("no one here would appreciate her music as much as he") and guard it ("repulsing intruders with his raucous breath"). His hope of attaining Grace is expressed in his desire to have his sister come and live with him; the music flows from her, hence the way leads to the state of Grace which she is in. But it is also a womanly grace that he desires of her, which opens a new interpretation of his sin. Now deflected from his father (and from his mother) his sin takes the form of an incestuous desire for his sister, which adds a further loathsomeness to his transformation. Not content with "kissing her neck," he would have her share his incestuousness by living with him of her own free will. The self-justification he would offer her by telling his sister that he had firmly intended to send her to the Conservatory is revealed as the rationalization and disguise of his unclean motive—which, moreover, was originally suspect in that it was always incestuous, and, insofar as it was related to the sister's welfare, was never carried out. Thus the sister, a symbol of Grace, becomes also a cause of Gregor's downfall; and by indicating his essential degradation she reveals what his true position in the family has always been. Her bare neck arouses his desire to kiss it, which is now all the easier as she has worn neither collar nor ribbon since she went to work in the shop. But she works in the shop because Gregor, transformed, can no longer support the family. He has sinned not only as a man before God, as a son and a brother, but also as a provider. His position in the family was all along compromised by his sinfulness, and, by extension, his whole position in life; and his sin was original in his entire being, in the good, hard-working commercial traveler that he was before his metamorphosis. Gregor's death, no less horrible than his life, is a universal release and expiation: it fulfills the will of God, restores to the father his power and his hope which were lost in shame, and liberates the sister, freeing her from the atmosphere of incest to grow sinless into a woman.

Thus we see that even if we begin with an explanation that seems to lead straight to the heart of the matter (the father-son relationship), we are at once led in other directions, ascending, by way of the father image, to the level of the divine, which is where the sister's music also leads us, as well as going down to the natural level by way of the family and the sibling relationship. The curious thing is that the critics should miss, not this direction or that, but the significance of the fact that there are so many directions to follow in the interpretation of Franz Kafka's writing.

Even at their best, the various commentaries on Kafka's work which analyze symbol after symbol in story after story fail to say anything about Kafka himself. Thus John Kelly who interprets *The Trial* in terms of Calvin, Kierkegaard, and Karl Barth—an interpretation which is illuminating as far as it goes—by neglecting the author's significance as an artist, pushes his analysis into such a narrow passage that only a ghostly, algebraic version of Kafka's symbolism can get through to the understanding. Ruling out other readings, he presents *The Trial* as a gloss on the theology of crisis, to the exclusion of such internal evidence as exists to the contrary. This does violence, for example, to the conclusion of *The Trial*, where Joseph K., at the moment the knife is thrust into his heart, exclaims, " 'Like a dog'; . . . as if he meant the shame of it to outlive him." Mr. Kelly paraphrases the Barthians who say that sin "is known only when it is forgiven. This is the source of Joseph K.'s final, overwhelming shame." But then why should Joseph K. *mean* the shame of it to outlive him? It seems to me that the shame can be attached only to the execution (he is *killed* "like a dog"), and not to the sin for which he is punished. Intent only on theological exegesis, Mr. Kelly does not allow Kafka his full richness of meaning; Joseph K., caught, in Claude-Edmonde Magny's phrase, in the "irreducibility of points of view," and, after all, a natural man, cannot help but protest the earthly injustice of his punishment even as he yields to Divine Justice. On the other hand, Miss Magny, who puts forth her interpretation as an alternative to a religious reading of Kafka, fails to see that the irreducibility of points of view, with which, she believes, Kafka was basically concerned, can very well reinforce a theological exegesis with its stress on the incommensurability of God and man. The partial character of such explanations—which are mistaken in thinking themselves mutually exclusive—is due to their neglect of Kafka as artist. The critics seem to assume that he is a great writer *because* his works require the attention of a theologian, a psychoanalyst, a sociologist, or a historian; but he might as well have been engaged in the construction of acrostics, for the kind of criticism he has received.

Necessary to any proper critical appraisal of Kafka is a consideration of his artistic accomplishment. And here the fact strikes one that so many of the apparently contrary meanings that have been read into his work are perfectly just in their claim of importance to the understanding of the whole. There is no other modern writer whose subject matter—for all that Kafka's talent has been called a narrow one—is so broad, or whose symbols, whatever their partial explanation, are so closely articulated in a statement that embraces and gives the quality of so much of modern experience. His two major works, *The Trial* and *The Castle*, must be regarded, in part, as allegories of Justice and Grace. But to regard them exclusively as allegories is to rob them of their reality, their natural beauty and power, and ultimately of their value as art. From which it follows—this is Albert Camus's finest insight in his contribution to *The Kafka Problem*— that it is to do Kafka an injustice even to regard his symbols primarily as symbols. They have a twofold character, one of which, the textual, can be determined only by the position and significance of the symbol in the narrative; but the other aspect of Kafka's symbolism, which one might call contextual, and whose context is to text as life is to letters, is the truly important one for understanding the unique art form of his writing.

The uniqueness of Kafka's work lies in its capacity for joining disparate traits of experience. In Kafka's scheme, man's struggle with God, for example, does not, as it does in theology, involve an abstraction from his natural condition; more generally speaking, his symbols must be understood to approach, rather than depart from, and to include, rather than exclude, the whole range of meaning that encloses an object. The symbol is, directly and inherently, all its range of meaning. One cannot therefore say that Kafka's art consists in a certain kind of symbolism, as if art were the limit of a symbolic system, reached by a summary of the steps taken in interpretation of that system; it is nearer the truth to say that Kafka's symbolism consists in a certain kind of art. It is a supremely conscious art, in which sensibility becomes, for once in modern writing, the direct medium of ideas. Ordinarily we distinguish, as in T. S. Eliot's epigram on Henry James ("He had a mind so fine that no idea could violate it"), between sensibility of nuance and detail and the philosophical order of expression. But with Kafka it is the function of sensibility to provide precisely the perception of generality. Like all perception, it is unified, it establishes the relationships of things. But these relationships have never before been perceived in such vastness, nor have their interpenetrations and identities been presented in such great structural detail. It was his genius to see the world's unity; even if we take a single aspect of his symbolism, say, man's struggle for Grace, it at once reveals something of the moral, psychological, social, and even political structure of the world in which man lives. The symbol, for Kafka, is itself a symbol, embodying the one and the many; the world is also such a symbol, as each part of it is part of a world—for which reason, Kafka's symbols are realities.

His art is therefore a kind of realism, in the logical sense, in that it finds relationships to be objective. But what distinguishes his art from the animated philosophy that so many critics take it to be is that the objective relationships of the world are perceived in and evoked by things. The world, as in a mystical system, becomes a visible legend. But Kafka's mysticism is secular, and strictly speaking it is no mysticism at all. Mysticism as we have known it is a vision of the world united in support of a faith; the demands of faith, exceeding reason, produce, through an extreme insistence, a proof in experience for transcendental belief. But there is no evidence that Kafka had such a faith (another respect in which the theological exegesis goes into error, on the simple assumption that he was a believer). The evidence of his vision is self-supporting. Kafka's art affords a kind of tautological proof of his vision of a world united against man.

A certain tautology is inevitable in symbolism. The artist's consciousness, in any work that takes a symbolic whole as its subject, returns upon itself, and his vision, though a vision of the world, is ultimately self-contained. Thus there is no direct empirical validation for the unity that Kafka perceived in the world's structure; to see it presupposes an acceptance of the world in terms of Kafka's symbolism. Yet there is historical evidence: for those who can read Kafka's work *only* as an ironic protest against bureaucracy, there is the record of the increasing bureaucratization of society to confirm his vision; for those who read him *only* as theologian, there is the fall of man, which is all history. And so on. But partial confirmation, like partial analysis, distorts his art. Kafka restored to writing the consciousness of the world as a whole, and it is to the whole expression of his sensibility that one must turn to confirm his perception and, ultimately, to understand his symbolism.

For this purpose it is necessary to take into consideration one of his last stories, "Investigations of a Dog" (*The Great Wall of China*). The story is of a dog who early in life began to examine *la condition canine*, and particularly the question, how do dogs obtain nourishment? There exists among dogs a kind of science which tells them that the watering and scratching of the earth, in which they all engage, enables the earth to produce food. Yet Kafka's dog is aware of the fact that food comes down from above. (The human agency is invisible to dogs, as, in the interpretation, is the divine agency to man. Here, as in the rest of the analysis of this story, I am following Philip Rahv's exegetical notes which provide an explanation—I believe a correct one— in terms of existential theology for the major symbols of some of the stories in *The Great Wall of China*.)

Kafka's dog undertakes an examination of canine belief, both in its scientific and religious aspect, and conducts an experiment to discover what relationship exists between science and the appearance of food. He will fast and not go near food and engage in none of the dogs' ritual to determine whether the production of nourishment obeys laws other than those which canine science has assigned to it. When he was still a puppy he encountered seven musical dogs whose music overwhelmed him and set him upon the inquiries which were to consume the best energies of his life. Now, while he is suffering the hardships of his fast, he again encounters a musical dog —a hound, hardly aware of the music he produces, whose music nevertheless expresses the necessity of faith. The fasting dog is driven out of his investigations; the music, which again overwhelms him, now restores him to the canine community. His inquiries, begun out of contact with music, or the science of the divine, are also ended by music. He regrets that he is so poorly instructed in music, and that his investigations must fail through his ignorance of its higher powers. And yet his failure is not altogether without reward, for if his scientific capacity is limited, it is because of an instinct that makes him "prize freedom higher than everything else. Freedom! Certainly such freedom as is possible today is a wretched business. But nevertheless freedom, nevertheless a possession."

Here, the generality of Kafka's subject may be seen at its most general, but also its most personal and poetic, expression. The subject is at once an inquiry into man's relation to God, the mystery of faith, the nature of theology and of empirical knowledge, the nature of the scientist's and the artist's task. The limitations of human knowledge are set down with a Kantian finality; the effort to transcend these limitations springs out of a sense of necessity even more urgent than in Kant—the necessity of freedom, not only that the moral order may be fulfilled, but that we may be free even in our own lives. It is for its final assertion of freedom that the story is most remarkable; and here lies its great importance to the ultimate analysis of Kafka's symbolism, to which it supplies the master key. It is to freedom as a final cause that the whole of Kafka's art has been moving (though "The Burrow," written at the same time, or somewhat earlier, is again a denial of freedom—as if an ending were a further beginning). Without it, his whole vision of the world, almost magical, almost mad, in its sense of identities, is as yet incomplete. Without acknowledgment of at least the possibility of freedom, his whole effort, in its extreme suffering and understanding, is not yet done. It is a freedom in spite of the world, in spite of the ultimate struggle, for which man has no capacity, in spite of the Law, which is incomprehensible, and God, who cannot be known. "Investigations of a Dog" acquires its final musical wisdom and beauty—as of Shakespeare's *Tempest*—in its assertion of a purely human freedom.

Only now, with a knowledge of the end, can the beginning, the first of Kafka's symbols, his first parable, be explained. The order of interpretation is circular: the tautology of art has been achieved, but also its truth, and the evidence in support of its truth—a complete description of the condition of man. Kafka begins, where he ends, with an understanding of the limitation of human freedom, and an effort to transcend that limitation to the achievement of as much peace as one can reach in mankind.

New Leader, April 12, 1947

⋽ *The Two Gides*

THE IMAGINATION IS THE MAN. Professor O'Brien, who says of Gide in his introduction to the *Journals* that "like Montaigne and Goethe, he is first a man and secondly a writer," provides ground for a possible disappointment in these notebooks, by leading us to expect a more intimate revelation of the man than the *Journals* have to offer. We are much too ready to believe that "intimate" writing—letters, diaries, journals—is somehow truer and more revealing of the writer than his imaginative work; we suppose, in this age of the overestimation of the biographical, that every man has a confession to make, that the confession is his supreme work and that everything else is ancillary. But the truth is the other way round; if not in every case, certainly so in Gide's. The *Journals*, at any rate, are bound to disappoint the usual expectation: that here is the man, laid bare of his fiction and his other disguises, to be seen for the first time as he really is. Gide has always been stripping himself clean, paring away the core; and there is more of the "intimate" man in his autobiography and his fictions (to respect his judgment that *The Counterfeiters* is his only novel), than in the *Journals*. Besides, the separation of man from writer, always questionable, is false in Gide, where the whole man is the interaction of a man and writer, and each of these elements of the self is the result of the other. And why maintain that any writer is first a man? Our idea of "man," "real" man, "essential" man, is through and through a literary one. "Character" is not something directly taken from nature which the imagination, if it be powerful, can approach as to the limit of its power. "Character," rather, is the work of imagination, whether in literature or in life. We would pay the debt which our sense of reality owes to fiction if we discarded the distinction between man and writer. But there remains the usual division into inner and outer man, private and public self; at least so much of everyday psychology is every day in order. I should like to see what relevance the usual placing of a "man" in relation to his "work" has to an understanding of Gide.

The first thing of use from *The Journals* is the picture Gide draws there—as he has drawn it everywhere—of himself as a divided man, his own actor and spectator. He speaks of having to constrain himself to throw off constraint, of forcing himself to joy. He complains of being ". . . merely a little boy having a good time"—compounded with a Protestant minister who bores him and writes, "Never a man, I shall never be anything but an aged child. I live with all the incoherence of a lyric poet, but two or three ideas, crosswise in my brain and rigid like parallel bars, crucify every joy; everything that would like to try its wings at random runs into them." (*Cf.* Edouard in *The Counterfeiters:* "I am constantly getting outside myself, and as I watch myself act I cannot understand how a person who acts is the same as the person watching him act, and who wonders in astonishment and doubt how he can be actor and watcher at the same moment.") Such statements may be said to show the personality structure of the writer and the problems, at the personal level, that Gide's awareness of himself puts before his mind. It is here that the analytic separation of man and writer appears most justified; but it is also from this point that Gide in his work begins to move toward self-integration.

The personality problem is repeated in the literary problem. We find it expressed in the *Journals,* at the higher, symbolic level of writing, in the vexation Gide feels at his inability to keep his journal rapidly written, spontaneous, uncomposed. (Why the vexation at all; hasn't composition its own spontaneities?) The *Journals*

are full of dissatisfaction: complaints at being trapped in
division, at inadequacies of mood, energy, vitality. . . .
Gide applies himself to the *ad hoc* solution of the problem
—he forces himself to be spontaneous, he sets himself
the task of working from nature, of recording, describing,
evoking the scene—a French seascape, a North African
landscape, a garden, a town—of rendering the qualities
of Italian sculpture and painting, etc. He looks everywhere for help, to conversation with friends, notes on
his reading, reflections on literature, music, and morals.
But everywhere his dissatisfaction remains: whether we
find it in the absence of positive felicity (in the writer—
the writing is felicitous in spite of him) or in the
presence of a curious publicity in the motive of the
Journals—the difficulty Gide has in hitting the truly
"intimate" tone, which shall not show itself to be compromised by the intention to publish what he writes "for
himself."

Another thing in the *Journals* which allows us to
maintain the division between man and writer is the
trouble Gide has with imaginative writing. One never
feels in reading his entries—as one does in reading say
Chekhov's *Notebooks*—that they are connected by an
ongoing imaginative activity, a continuous process in the
intercourse between writer and world. In Chekhov's
Notebooks the imagination converts the recorded objects
into personal symbols—in virtue of their objectivity.
Things stand by themselves; the writer need not present
himself. The whiskers, shoes, trousers, medals, and watch
fobs with which Chekhov loads his pages, the snatches
of dialogue and plot, the sometimes silly notations, answer
for the man. Imagination does the work for him of defining his relationship to the world. Whatever Chekhov
touches becomes his own object, and it is in the confidence
that he has left his mark that he absents himself with the
observation that a certain lady wears a lorgnette, a certain
gentleman, a fur collar. In Gide's *Journals,* however, there
is no such telling lightness of touch. We feel the pressure
of the hand that wants to leave its own impression; but

we are aware of its restraint—Gide knows the value of lightness. We get both the deliberate pressure and the deliberate withholding, but not the natural ease. In place of ease stands embarrassment; Edouard's perplexity at his own division into actor and spectator may be predicated also of Gide's consciousness wondering about its imaginative activity, and with that same wonder, inhibiting it. But here again, in the writing, is the "personality structure," the "man," typically modern in his overawareness, his overextension; the "writer" is never free of him. One might almost yield to the discomforts of the *Journals,* scrap the "writer" altogether, and grant the "man" mercy by conceding: there is value in this, the sum of value for our time. The *Journals* are of greater importance than the fictions. What we were accustomed to look for in the characters of novels, we must be content to find—as much of it as we can have—in the men of journals. Imagination is now impossible, the old value has been lost for good.

But precisely at the point of breakdown, where the "man" leaves us facing paralysis, literature comes to our assistance; it draws on a source of its own, converting separation into schematism, paralysis into equilibrium, personality into "character." "In art, what is merely stated," runs R. P. Blackmur's gloss on James, "is not presented, what is not presented is not vivid, what is not vivid is not represented, and what is not represented is not art." But the inhibition of this process can also be represented—Gide's discovery—and the breakdown celebrated instead of the safe arrival. The divisions of the self create in *The Counterfeiters* a novel of layers and levels. Edouard acts out Gide's crisis as actor-spectator; Edouard's Notebook acts out Edouard's crisis; the narrative in actual time acts out the Notebook, etc. The tension between the divided parts of the self is translated in *The Immoralist* into dramatic tension, and the theme of self-determination through the following-out of the homosexual impulse gives the story—and the author's personality structure—its unification. The personal derangement, the self's being at sixes and sevens, is never completely transcended; the "man" remains in the writer. But a new "man" is indicated; his emergence as a "character" at the upper symbolic levels of composition affects the self-divided man who remains below; the literary character becomes the unification of the actual personality. To the extent that a "solution of the problem" is possible by other than radical means—a complete break with literature, a surrender to psychology—Gide's imaginative writing "solves" both the personal and the literary problem.

The man-as-"character," at this point and from here on, takes precedence over the man-as-personality. We are left at last with the writer who has taken a hand in creating himself. And the advantage has passed over to the imagination—it is the created, artificial man, the literary character composed of parts of the real personality who reveals the "essential" man, and does so better, more fully, and more intimately than the man who writes the *Journals*. We are back at proper proportions. Confession, intimacy, personal writings always have an element of distortion. Inevitably so, as Paul Valéry made clear in his essay on Rousseau, for the self is naturally on guard, and to force down its guard is to violate its natural posture. But the imagination betrays the man; the more objective its work and the more distant from the personality, the smaller the suspicion with which it must contend and the greater the personal revelation. Edouard of *The Counterfeiters* has it all over the Gide of the *Journals*; thank God. And the humanity of *The Counterfeiters*, its earnest, didactic morality (which is also one of its weaknesses), its concern with the true way of love and the true way of life are the clarified expression of the self-complaint of the *Journals*.

The literary idea of "character" is primary to our understanding of human beings. We smuggle poetry into psychology and deal more with fictions than with facts. "Character" is a theme to be worked out, a pattern of emotional responses to be completed. In reality the

pattern is never completed and there is no final flourish
to the theme, which remains forever open. It is a pure
imposition of a literary idea on life to expect consistency
of character, the subordination of all impulses to the
dominant ones of theme. But the ambiguity of the idea
bestows a double advantage on the writer. The poetic
completeness of the imagined character completes his
own; but where, as in Gide, the character is not fully
imagined-off, where it remains open, owing its literary
reality to the fact that it may be said to represent the
actual loose, divided condition, then reality supplements
literature, and we find ourselves reversing the process,
and smuggling psychology into poetry. Gide owes his
"essential" nature to his poetic aspirations; and his characters, from which we derive and complete his own
figure for him—to the benefit of a doubt. The higher,
literary reality may, after all, be imperfect: a triumph of
naturalism in default of imagination. Here a deficiency
becomes a virtue. We reinforce our belief in the stature of
the artist precisely because it does fall short.

There is something impermanent about the present
estimation of Gide; with time it may settle to a lower
level. For all his pursuit and incorporation into his work
of the values of classicism, there is little of the classical
at the heart of his writing. Gide's famous clear style to
the contrary, much in his writing depends on illusion:
that the personal defect—the division, the wavering—
has been overcome. But the value of the personality is
enhanced by the same reservations. For though we admire and criticize the function of the personal element
in his work, when we consider the function it has fulfilled in his life, we can only admire it. Gide's good
influence on his time, his friendliness toward every new
or dissident impulse, his definition of the intellectual as
the man whose natural role it is to be heterodox, his
constant change and development have all been grounded
in the advantages of self-division. The honesty which we
celebrate in Gide is nothing accidental, nor is it a deliberately cultivated thing, as with a man who seeks out the
good by reputation. It is rather a constitutional virtue,

the reward in his life, as it is in his writing, of an irresolution that could never come to rest anywhere, and that kept him from acquiring, and favoring, vested interests in himself. Hence Gide's youthfulness, his frosty vitality. For as Edouard put it, "I am not far from thinking that in irresolution lies the secret of not growing old."

But doesn't this assert what was denied at the beginning, the supremacy of man over writer? Not really. Professor O'Brien's statement that Gide is first a man and secondly a writer is actually a judgment in literary criticism—and a severe one. It is because of shortcomings in the writer that we locate primary value in the man. But man and writer are one in Gide, and the judging of them belongs to literature. So also does the idea of self-revelation, which is all too readily appropriated for its own by the confessional predilections of our time. But the revealed man is revealed through the imagination, which we should restore not only to the man, Gide, but to our whole idea of what a man is, lest it be consumed in the mass of highly personal, irrelevant details on which the psychological sense gluts itself, to the impoverishment of understanding.

New Leader, January 3, 1948

✑§ Adam and Eve on
Delancey Street

It is months now that a crowd, several rows deep, has been gathering at the window of an East Side delicatessen store to watch Kosher Fry Beef come off the slicing machine. The process is simple and uninteresting. A flat chunk of meat is placed in the machine by one girl and received four feet away, at the end of a wire conveyor belt, by another girl, who wraps the slices in cellophane and stuffs them in a little cardboard box. The slicer is perfectly ordinary, the wire conveyor is not worth a second thought, and neither are the girls, both of whom look even more unattractive because of the blue waitress' uniforms, with beige collar and cuffs, that they wear. The chunks of meat are like gnarled pastramis, but resemble greasy driftwood much more than anything edible. Yet the crowd comes on and stands at the window oblivious of the burden of parcels, of errands, and of business; no comments are made, they stand in silence, not to interfere with one another's contemplation, as they follow the course of the slices, from the blade to the box. To be sure, some of the spectators may never have seen bacon or its kosher analogue. But what is there in bacon, kosher or *treif,* so to draw a crowd?

I spent I hate to admit how much of my own time in this study of Fry Beef, but learned only that it was a subject peculiarly designed for my own speculation; for I had already published a review in this magazine ("Kreplach," November 1948), showing that our old Jewish joke about the little boy who fears the sight of *kreplach* is related to our older preoccupation with the coming of the Messiah. Here was another mystery of food, to my taste; and I nursed it along, and had even written in my mind the first sentence of my essay, as it stands above. But the days went by, the crowd grew, and still the clue was lacking. I was attempting to locate the primal scene within the lifetime of the spectators, and I would long have continued in this mistake, looking for the appropriate infantile memory to account for the fascination of this spectacle, had it not occurred to me that it was not to the childhood of present adults that I must turn, but to the childhood of our people. Now I am prepared to say that this scene had its origin in Paradise.

When the Lord forbade Adam and Eve to eat of the Tree, He started something which has persisted throughout our history: the attachment of all sorts of forbidden meanings to food, and the use of food in a system of taboos which, though meant to regulate diet, have also had as their function—perhaps the primary one—the regulation of sexual conduct. With their first disobedience, Adam and Eve acquired knowledge of sex (woe to the prospects of clear thought on this subject, that even then this should have been called Knowledge of Good and Evil!). The first food taboo was a sex taboo. Since then we have been subjected, through Biblical and oral law, to an overwhelming number of injunctions against the eating of certain animals and certain parts of others, and have been forbidden to eat blood and enjoined to salt and soak meat, lest any blood remain. The simple act of eating has become for us a complicated ceremonial, from the preparatory phases of ritual slaughter, through *milchigs* and *fleishigs,* kosher and *treif,* to benedictions and postprandial prayers. It is for such reasons, among others, that the Jewish religion enjoys the reputation of being one of the most worldly and immanent, one of the most closely connected with daily life. What Sacred Communion is to Catholics, the everyday mealtime is to Orthodox Jews. He who eats, according to Law, Jewish cooking that has been prepared according to Law, becomes a communicant, in virtue of mere animal hunger, also with a mystical body; and while the Sabbath *chalah* is a special loaf, no consecrated wafer is necessary to this communion by way of the digestive tract. Daily rye or pumpernickel sufficiently embodies the Host.

There is great charm in a religion that can thus run coalesced along the two lines of sacred and secular without any apparent break; it avoids the usual dualism, the conflict in belief of realm against realm. No doubt, the faithful draw some advantage from this harmony, which perhaps can be observed in a balance of character, a sense of being at home in God's world. But dietary laws lead us more directly into the demerits of this system, the first of which is that any blemish in such a smooth course is hard to confine to a single spot and tends to spread over the whole. If our close and continuous touch with the world is anywhere spoiled, as it is, I should say, precisely in the respect of food, the trouble will affect, through the same parallel, anything in this world which our religion has linked with food, all along the line. As our food taboos are also sexually repressive, serious damage occurs.

With the Jewish taboo system in operation direct reference to sex is unnecessary. A well-regulated Jewish household, a Kosher Home, takes care of the matter unconsciously—and this is the most harmful method of repression. The direct *verbot* offers at least the advantage of naming the forbidden object; one can be aware of what is going on, and it is always possible to rebel. Where the repression is indirect, a gradual squelching and baffling of the natural impulse takes place; instead of rebellion, there is only perplexity. (An analogous technique, quite apart from any religious atmosphere, can be observed in some "progressive" nurseries. When teacher catches the children masturbating, instead of spanking or scolding them, she rushes up with an armful of dollies.) *Kashruth* should be permitted only to Hasidim. Where a natural enthusiasm and use for joy are lacking, the ideal of a Kosher Home becomes an insidious ruin of life. The food taboos are all that is needed.

It has been observed, I believe also in *Commentary,* that the hysterical mother who stuffs her infant with forced feedings (thereby laying in, all unwittingly, the foundation for ulcers, diabetes, and intestinal cancer with each spoonful she crams down the hatch) is motivated by a desire to give security to her child. Basic security being unavailable to Jews in a hostile world, food becomes a source of the satisfactions society withholds. The choice of food in this substitution is not accidental. Already a magical object, it is naturally selected to work wonders. The esteem in which this agency is held is shown in the number and prominence of eating establishments in Jewish neighborhoods. In the block of our delicatessen store there are also a restaurant and two lunch counters. Parked at the curb, stands a hot dog wagon bearing a beach umbrella, and next in line, a little metal stove on wheels where you buy baked sweet potatoes, and another for roast chestnuts. The ice cream cart, attended by a man in white uniform, is present every day, as are also several broken laundry baskets of salt stengels ("Why Go Hungry? 3 for 10¢"), with shabby old men and women in charge, and a knish wagon, potato and kasha. Every other day or two there appear on the same block a stall, carrying candies and nuts, and a tub, on a wheeled platform, filled with chick peas. All of which is to say nothing of the itinerant peddlers of fruits, vegetables, and ices. There is hardly room for the haberdasheries and men's and ladies' shoe stores, two of a kind, to squeeze in side by side; these have been overshadowed, for they sell stuff of lesser value in which a momentary security, or none at all, lies. Eat, eat, eat. Not that we are never sated: food is not food and it cannot satisfy a hunger that is not hunger.

Here at the delicatessen store the crowd stands in a sexual trance. For Kosher Fry Beef, "Jewish Bacon," is food in the form of the forbidden, an optical pun on kosher and *treif*. *Treifes* is of the whole world of forbidden sexuality, the sexuality of the *goyim,* and there all the delights are imagined to lie, with the *shiksas* and *shkotzim* who are unrestrained and not made kosher. (Pork, as you may learn from the street lore of children in Jewish neighborhoods, means the uncircumcised.) And the businessman stops in his rounds to look at kosher bacon, and the housewife stops at his side, and in their minds thoughts of the golden *shiksa,* wild and unrestrained, and the husky *shaigetz* do or do not appear; no matter, for in the popular sexual culture, where thoughts of the moment are not the issue, these emerge as eternal forms: *shaigetz* and *shiksa* are our yin and yang, the poles of sex. It is sad evidence of the sexual displacement in Jewish living that the sexual forms in the popular Jewish conception should derive not from the Song of Songs or any indigenous source within the presumably rich and close-textured contact with life Judaism maintains, but from a forbidden exogamy, symbolized in food taboos. And, worse, in the end, it is not merely the *shaigetz* and the *shiksa* who are taboo; the sexual object per se is *treif;* for within the culture it is overlaid by the all-nourishing mother, the authoritarian father, both under the incest ban. The sex object as lover, for the majority of us, is always out of bounds. (The counterpart of this complex, at the root of anti-Semitism, occurs in the popular sexual culture of the Gentiles in the form of a delusion about the sexual superiority of the Jews, who, represented as a lecherous people, are supposed to enjoy greater freedom from restraint. Our restraining rituals are held to be magical devices for bringing potency to Jews and injury to non-Jews.)

The complex centering in *kashruth* is not the only one that works on sex. There is also *milchigs* and *fleishigs;* and this, I think, is the arch taboo. My own Orthodox grandparents would tremble, as though some catastrophe had occurred, if *milchigs* and *fleishigs* ever came into contact with each other; and with good reason. This is the sexual taboo not only of exogamy, but of the sexuality of the tribe itself. It is the taboo of sex as such. *Milchigs*, having to do with milk, is feminine; *fleishigs*, meat, is masculine. Their junction in one meal, or within one vessel, is forbidden, for their union is the sexual act. (The Jewish joke about the man with cancer of the penis bears this out. He is advised by the doctor to soak his penis in hot water. His wife, finding him so engaged, cries out, "Cancer shmancer. *Dos iz a milchig teppel!*— Who cares about cancer? You're using a *milchig* pot.") The measures taken to make kosher again vessels that have come in contact with the opposite food-sex—boiling, burying in the ground—are surely suggestive of the sexual nature of the contamination. They recall the Biblical laws of purification—bathing, lying apart a certain number of hours—for one who has been sexually contaminated by, say, a woman in her period. It is hard to see how anyone could doubt the unconscious sexual quality of the *milchigs-fleishigs* ban in the minds of those who observe it. Otherwise how account for the zeal with which the law dividing *milchigs* from *fleishigs* is upheld by the faithful, and for their explosion into virtual terror at the least infringement? No one takes mere food so seriously.

Meanwhile the crowd gathers at the window where "Jewish Bacon" is cut and packaged, and stands entranced, devouring its totem in a moment of license that stretches out for five, ten, fifteen minutes of a hot, busy day. Reluctantly, still possessed, they tear themselves away, and recovering practical consciousness, rush down the street—to stop again at the corner, where they are lured from *fleishigs* by *das ewig Weibliche* in the form of an egg cream. There is time for a quickie, to try once more to satisfy this hunger which is not hunger, to drown this anxiety in the bottom of a paper cup.

Commentary, October, 1949

❧ Sensibility as Fiction

I. Charles Williams

I SHOULD DEFINE a minor novelist as a writer incapable of doing these two things at once—creating both art and life. Charles Williams is one of the best contemporary examples.

It is never a question of skill. Williams' skill as a writer is always evident in these two novels [*All Hallows' Eve* and *Descent into Hell*], as I imagine it must be in almost everything he wrote. Open either book at random, take any passage and you will find that the words hold up, they are never out of line or out of rhythm. Williams works with an orderly prose poetry in which there is even something thrifty, as when he makes old words yield new meanings. Moreover, he is always conscious of design, and here, too, random examples confirm his skill. Over and over again a word, a phrase, a group of sentences will strike an image which is both appropriate as a single part, and a reproduction in miniature of the image of the whole. This is mature craft.

By such simple, obvious, and yet most exacting tests —which are no different, it must be admitted, from the ones used to determine the quality of, say, a shipment of beans; the principle is that of the adequate sample— Williams is a good writer, an excellent writer. But so fine a writer deserves to be taken seriously; we cannot limit our response to praising his skillful use of words. He deserves, after a certain point of praise, to be ignored as a stylist and examined as a writer who has something to say. Here he breaks down as all minor novelists do.

In these two novels Williams is concerned with love.

As he is a religious writer, he at once separates love into its two cases, eros and agape. But this separation is never actually accomplished. Williams makes of both physical and divine love nothing more than a meaning; instead of two experiences, each intimately and mysteriously connected with and dependent on the other, he presents two meanings, one high, one low, neither of them felt. Now a meaning is not necessarily real; it can be attached to anything, and even an imaginary object can bear it. Thus these two novels of love are anything but love stories. They bulge with meaning, but are completely devoid of fact, and not a single passion, emotion, or anything even remotely felt occurs in them. The eros Williams concocts is something so bloodless and thin, there is only the name he gives it to tell us it is physical; and his agape gets lost among the chatter and teacups and polite English diction of its setting. How can one distinguish these two, when both are featureless? And when the great point of their identity has been lost?— the identity of both in sexual love.

The same grayness hangs over all the other aspects of these novels. The scene is limbo, raised to the surface in England, and the characters are either dead, or alive in such a way that again there is no real difference between them. In a word, they are all zombies. Now it is an author's privilege to write of zombies and even, if he pleases, of nothing but zombies. But it can hardly have been Williams' intention to do so; else why would he have needed two categories, the living and dead, when the single category of the zombie would have been sufficient? Once more we have a distinction without a difference, and neither spirit nor real wind, but fog.

Gross distinctions did not concern him. His was too fine a sensibility to be impressed by anything obvious, and so life and death achieved in his writing an impartial status, a kind of *ça m'est egal*. It was to the meeting and intermingling place of these two that he brought his attention, and a certain blurring of outline must be allowed. Both *All Hallows' Eve* and *Descent into Hell* maintain that the two worlds interpenetrate. There is contact and influence between living and dead, and this contact is established through love. Lester, the dead heroine of *All Hallows' Eve,* continues to develop spiritually as the love between her and her surviving husband, Richard, matures. The two of them, together with other material and immaterial characters, combine in a plot to frustrate the 300-year-old arch-spook and Cabalist, Simon the Clerk, in his plan to dominate both worlds. This villian, compounded of comic books, the occult, necrophilia, and anti-Semitism (the old stuff about world domination), means to send his own daughter Betty into the spirit world to do his bidding there; this, as the dead are already in his power, is all he needs to achieve his unholy goal. In a last-minute rescue, Betty is saved (she is half-English: it is worth the trouble), Simon is vanquished, Christian love prevails over the Jewish lust for power, and the living and dead go their separate, indistinguishable ways.

Descent into Hell is another theological thriller, featuring *Doppelgänger,* succubi, and medieval ghosts. Pauline Anstruther, still a virgin, has been running into her own image on the roads of suburban England and taking quite a fright. She is cured of this, without sex-life or psychiatry, when the good poet, Stanhope, teaches her the doctrine of substituted love, whereby we can all assume one another's burden. He promises to assume the burden of her fear, does so, and enables Pauline to run into herself late at night without batting an eye. She is not only reunited with her true self when this occurs, but freed to assume another's burden, that of an old ancestor of hers who had been burned at the stake as a heretic some centuries before, and had died crying out triumphantly, "I see the Salvation of my Lord!" This he does again when Pauline meets his ghost, in period costume, and gives him her blessing. Time runs both ways; the living ancestor, in the moment of agony and triumph, had foreseen this event, which, now accomplished, allows the good zombies to live, or rest, in peace. The bad, meanwhile, get theirs. Lawrence Wentworth, who has been having his pleasure of a local girl,

Adela, in the form of a succubus, is finally lowered into hell (the sections dealing with their intercourse, in which "He had no need of the devices against fertility which, wisely or unwisely, the terrible dilemmas of men drive them to use," make up one of the sourest and most self-damning tirades against sexual love in all of modern fiction); and the aged, unsuspected Lily Sammile turns out to have been Lilith all along.

Presented in such bare outline, both novels sound silly; yet they are entirely serious, religious, and grave. So much a minor art can do. But these novels *are* silly! (to say nothing of the sickness of life at their core). For the one thing a minor art cannot do is to create a sense of life out of its own aesthetic resources. Where a prior contact with reality and a deep grasp of nature are lacking, the only possible virtues art can have are those of style.

The reason for Williams' breakdown into silliness must lie somewhere along the line of his religious contact with life (it was his only commitment); and it seems to me that his religious sensibility was, like his aesthetic, also a minor one. The extension of life into death which these novels document is a flat presupposition, more bourgeois than religious, deriving, as with Kant, from a desire to insure the perfectibility of the moral order, rather than an absolute need, a passion of heart and soul, for immortality. Such gray survival is a far cry from "Yet in the flesh shall I see God." It is an insurance policy, written to give its beneficiary, the Church of England, a little more scope.

The failure is of passion, as it has been in every English novelist of recent years, with the one exception of D. H. Lawrence. There is a great religious cunning in Williams' art, a knowing use of symbolism, a textured cross-reference in word and image to Christian themes. But his writing is religious in a way that even Christianity is not. The Incarnation is an affair of flesh, after all.

Kenyon Review, Summer, 1949

II. Henry Green

THE OVEREVALUATION OF Henry Green in some of
our literary circles is a typical American relapse into
provincialism, an instance of our tendency to credit a
work as a great achievement on the insufficient ground
that its sensibility is finer than our own. The same mistake, in reverse, is now occurring in France, where the
predilection is toward the rude manner. Wherever it
occurs, this is provincialism: it is the elevation of *manner* to the highest rank.

Perhaps Green's advance reputation had something to
do with this; he was known, for a period of several years
before his publication here, to only a few in this country,
who regarded his work as though it held the last light of
truth in the modern novel. This is a disadvantage to all
but the truly great. Of Green it must now be said, what
there would otherwise have been no need to say, that he
is not a major novelist, that he does not have a major
sensibility, and that his work, granting its excellence, is
nevertheless quite small. He is another English writer in
the tradition which has become dominant since the death
of D. H. Lawrence—the tradition of sensibility, manners,
and the brilliant image, at the expense of everything
else in the novel. He has, like most of these writers, a
considerable liveliness of language. His originality within
this tradition (it helps cancel his debt to E. M. Forster
and Virginia Woolf and raises him a little out of their
shadow) consists in a unique range over the social classes,
including an intimate knowledge of industry, and a free
choice of subject matter within this range. In these
qualities there may even lie the chance that Green will
some day achieve the stature which is already claimed
for him. But this would call for a big revision in his writing, the greatest energy of which, at present, is spent
on the maintenance of a sensibility that ties him to the
minor scale.

Nothing, which Green himself does not seem to rate

very high, is as he describes it, "a frivolous comedy of manners," simultaneously occupied with the sexual adventures of three generations of Londoners under the Labour Government. The point of it appears to be that the elders, John Pomfret, a widower of forty-five, and Jane Weatherby, a widow and his former mistress, have it all over their children, Mary Pomfret and Philip Weatherby, when it comes to enjoying life and love; and that the youngest generation, represented by the little girl, Penelope Weatherby, is well nigh hopeless, for Penny has all the neurotic anxieties one might have expected the parents to show. Mary and Philip stay chaste during their courtship and engagement, while the parents go to bed with their lovers and finally, after breaking up the engagement, with each other again, to marry in place of their children. If the novel may be read as an indictment of the time for the dying out of vigorous youth, it may also be understood as a condemnation of the parents for having raised their children to this death. The point is deliberately left vague, for the novel demands an ambiguous interplay of attitude; nothing so indelicate as a stand may be taken, lest the fun be spoiled. The fun consists in skipping lightly over the accumulated horrors underground. These are sexual in nature or closely allied: the horror of sexual knowledge, approaching the point of madness in the young Penelope, moderated to neurotic in Mary and Philip, and disguised by sophistication to appear as glee in Jane and John; this is the most fully developed theme. Beside it stand strong suggestions of incest, pedophilia, and homosexuality, and for good measure one of the characters dies of gangrene. These themes are threaded together by double-dealing and malicious gossip, to the whole of which one need only add paranoia and voyeurism, present in the other novels, in particular, *Back* and *Concluding*, respectively, to obtain a fairly complete inventory of Green's underground. Yet he is by reputation a pastoral novelist.

He has gained this reputation from his style, which is poetic and oblique. The poetry is mostly early Auden, with the tiresome omission of articles, under a shower of rose petals. The obliquity is achieved by keeping the reader at a steady lag of ten pages or so behind the explanation of the action, and by presenting the action, whenever possible, through sketchy descriptions which the conversation must fill in. This trick of keeping ahead of the reader creates the effect of motion. But the motion does not always lie in the action of the story, for frequently, as the conversation develops, the characters are at a standstill in the progress of their own affairs; you meet them, for the hundredth time, pouring tea, sitting down to dinner, taking an unnecessary walk, or simply treading water while they tease and delay to the snapping point an exposition that might have been given in a short paragraph. The effect of motion is obtained from the reader's scramble to overtake the glancing allusion that will explain what has come before. Meanwhile, Green pipes at ease, shepherding his images; the time he has gained by stealing a march on the reader he puts to the leisurely uses of poetry.

The images are all that matter. He may be of all novelists writing today the one most preoccupied with the eye. But his eye seldom rests on objects in more than a cursory way; its faculty is reserved for the image suggested by the object, and this is what becomes visible. Thus, in *Caught*:

> At that instant, in great haste, on leave, and for only the second time, Richard tumbled into bed with Hilly. The relief he experienced when their bodies met was like the crack, on a snow silent day, of a branch that breaks to fall under a weight of snow, as his hands went like two owls in daylight over the hills, moors, and wooded valleys, over the fat white winter of her body.

You see owls flying in a winter landscape, not a man making love to a woman. *In great haste, tumbled into bed,* the only definite description of the action, is perfunctory, and conveys even a certain disdain. *Hills, moors, and wooded valleys, the fat white winter of her body,* combine to suggest nakedness, but it is the nakedness of the countryside that dominates the image, not of the female body. *Two owls in daylight* carries the connotation of a fumbling, nervous haste, but again the image takes precedence over the object, for while a branch falling loaded with snow and the sight of owls flying are perfectly consistent visually, the sexual relief which the fall is supposed to express is negated by the predatory connotation of owls. The owl, a hunter, has the value of a mounting tension, not of relief; the owl in daylight, borrowing a little blindness from the bat, carries the tension, in the sexual context, near hysteria. Again the relief in question, which is the gratitude of contact—this the image does not express at all—is sacrificed to the word-picture, though it is presumably the purpose of the image to make vivid this sense of relief. Moreover, the structure of the image is roundabout; it dominates the object to such an extent that it makes its own values primary, as though sexual relief were attractive to us because it called to mind the presumably more primitive, vivid, and pleasureful response to a falling branch. Animal experience is denied its natural primacy, and a mere verbal congruence is read into nature, to give the poetry a spacious base. This is an old trap of the language-bound: where words come first, they can never point beyond words—which is what communication means. The presence of a lively sensibility can do nothing to spring this trap, for the very condition on which Green's sensibility operates makes it respond to being only secondarily, only after, and in terms of, its response to words. This cuts off the sensibility from any effective communication of nonverbal experience, the sensations of pleasure (or any other feeling) as they occur in nature to the living animal, the communication of which is an act of humility on the part of language, a mute, and in the poetic case, awed, pointing to that which lies beyond its reach. The above passage, accordingly, has no use for the actuality which it is supposed to represent; it is embarrassed by the man and woman making love and it covers their nakedness with snow.

This passage is not exceptional; it is the usual case

with Green, who takes every occasion for the use of the eye to celebrate his own sensibility. His intention, on these occasions, is not to re-create the experience, to heighten its vividness and make it live through being shared. His intention, it seems to me inescapable, is to have you admire his prose.

Green's work is incomplete, it is full of tensions that are never resolved, gaps that are never filled. Sensibility is again at fault, because Green plays his like a solo instrument, scoring everything else as a supporting part. The sensibility is not particularly apt at conveying intellectual nuances; there are therefore no ideas as such in his novels. The sensibility is cold, it is incapable of sympathy; the characters are never shown in direct possession of a feeling. The sensibility has only a limited competence in integrating the materials of the novel at the image level; the underground, the gallery of horrors, is therefore never treated as anything more than a spectacle, an inhuman one besides, and we pass through it as through a freak show, possibly shaken, but never seriously engaged by its themes. Evil is reduced to wickedness, nature to landscape, object to image. Whatever the aesthetic gain, the price is too great. The loss becomes all the more apparent because of the occasional moments of breakthrough that Green does achieve, as in the closing pages of *Back*, where all the force that has been locked in words suddenly comes free, and there is a direct passage, rare in its strength for him, where the need of love, the submerged tears, the anxiety, the fear, the loneliness burst to the surface of a man's relationship to a woman in a surrender of sensibility to life. If only this force were more often available!

Kenyon Review, Summer, 1950

⊷ Terror Beyond Evil

WE STILL DON'T understand what happened to the Jews of Europe, and perhaps we never will. There have been books, magazine and newspaper articles, eyewitness accounts, letters, diaries, documents certified by the highest authorities on the life in ghettos and concentration camps, slave factories and extermination centers under the Germans. By now we know all there is to know. But it hasn't helped; we still don't understand. It is too painful for the majority—besides, who wants to understand? Even those who can carry willingness far enough to yield to such facts—even for them it is a dead end, as there is no response great enough to equal the facts that provoke it. There is nothing but numbness, and in the respect of numbness we, the innocent and the indignant, the relatives and coreligionists or friends of the victims, liberals all of us, who want anything from a reasonable settlement and a forgetting to outright revenge—when it comes to numbness we are no different from the murderers who went ahead and did their business and paid no attention to the screams. Here is a field dug with ditches and alongside the ditches stand hundreds, thousands of Jews, young and old, who are all going to be shot and buried where they fall. It is understandable that appeals to reason won't work, or appeals to mercy or compassion for the children. Everything has failed, the attempt to organize resistance, to escape, to hide, to outwit the Nazis. It is understandable that everything should fail. But at the zero moment, when there is nothing left but screaming—it is incomprehensible that

197

the screams also should have failed. How is this possible?
How can such things be?

It is questions such as these that Jacob Pat's book
raises, and though it does not answer them, nor even
try, the fact that it reduces the terror to such simplicity
makes it one of the studies that come near an answer,
that is, to the edge of the incomprehensible. Not because
Ashes and Fire gives the facts. David Rousset's book,
The Other Kingdom, also did that; but it was practically
worthless. It told us nothing because it left undisturbed
the usual assumption that there will come an answer,
this all lies within the realm of the explainable, the
workable, the preventable; let us only see that the right
people take over and put our world in order. Pat does
the opposite—actually, he does nothing at all; he merely
sets down what he has seen and heard on a visit to
Poland's surviving Jews. He encourages them to talk,
"Speak on, friends, tell me. . . . I want to know every
detail." He relates their stories and he tells what work
the survivors have done to re-establish Jewish communities and start life over again. But for this reason his is
so valuable and so good a book; it has the courage, together with, say, *The Black Book,* to stay near the thing
itself and not cast about for the usual reassurance. Next
to Bruno Bettelheim's *Behavior in Extreme Situations,*
it is the most enlightening study that we have of the
terror; in one sense, even more enlightening—in that it
is properly speaking no study at all.

This is the terror. Anything that stops short of presenting it in full leads nowhere, bogs down in the
wilderness with our usual assumptions—the wilderness
of good and evil, of ethics and morality, of reason, science, method, history, sympathy and mercy, the whole
human world, or what was, until now, human. All this
has been annihilated; or it will still do, but only for
controlled or normal or abnormal situations. But here is
the "extreme" situation, beyond all extremes—incomprehensible, unattainable to reason, and yet the one, the
only one, that constitutes the reality of our daily reality.

The terror is absolute. No extension of anything we have known until now will reach it, penetrate it, even though it lies so close to hand. All that is yesterday, it is compromise, a refusal to recognize what the absolute is, a sliding off the fact; at best it is nostalgia for the old morality of good and evil. There is no more good and evil—if there were, the screams would have been heard. There is only the terror.

How shall we, living in comfort, we American Jews and Gentiles, with brotherhood and interfaith meetings —and in an election year!—understand that there are only two principles?—terror and joy. Our old evil does not comprehend the terror, which begins, far beyond the point—already outside the human world—where our old evil left off. Our old good, which we continue to practice, sending food, clothing, and politics to the survivors, will do no good. Terror beyond evil and joy beyond good: that is all there is to work with, whether we are to understand what has happened, or to begin all over again.

New Leader, February, 1948

THE PAIN caused by stones in the gall bladder or the kidney can be the most excruciating known to human beings. But one may tell the sufferer he ought to consider himself lucky it's not cancer. It is in this sense that the Russian concentration camps are milder than the German. The two basic methods of totalitarian coercion are terror and privation: the Soviets have had much less to do than the Nazis with the former. But this is merely to say that they know how to make privation do the job; the fact that it's usually a different job, a political one, and that the Russians are not out to exterminate whole populations as such or practice torture for the fun of it, is not a great advantage to the prisoner, to whom all that such magnanimity means is that he shall be executed for political reasons or be worked to death. Concretely, how much better off were Ehrlich and Alter for being murdered because they were socialists and not because they were Jews?

Jerzy Gliksman was the half brother of Victor Alter, the Polish-Jewish *Bund* leader. He was arrested in Russian-occupied Poland in October, 1939; after the NKVD failed to obtain from Gliksman a confession that would incriminate his brother and his friends, he was released in the hope that he would lead a Soviet tail to his comrades. He shook off the NKVD agent by escaping to another city but was rearrested in March of the following year while attempting to steal across the border into Lithuania. Until August, 1941, he was a political prisoner of the Soviet Union; together with thousands of Russian and Polish nationals he was detained in cellars and jails, transported by cattle car to the transfer camp, Kotlas, and finally shipped to the "Corrective Labor Camp," UKHTIZHMLAG, in the northeastern, subarctic Republic of Komi, where he began serving a five-year sentence by felling trees in weather as cold as −50° F., and was employed, when his health was seriously impaired, at various other, though lighter, corrective tasks, until a Soviet decree freed the Poles two months after Hitler's invasion of Russia.

This is one of the few firsthand accounts we have of life in Soviet prisons and slave-labor camps. Gliksman makes no observations on Russian politics; his book is concerned merely with reliving an injurious experience— it does so often in extremely painful detail—that we may know what it was like for him and what it is like to the present day for millions of other prisoners. But *Tell the West*, as do all reports of its kind, provides a fundamental text of modern politics. It is from such sources that we learn what is in fact the dominion of government: the extent of the state and of its penetration into the lives of its subjects, its power *over* them and *in* them.

On the day of his first arrest, Gliksman was kept waiting in the corridor of NKVD headquarters in Kovel.

> The hours passed, but I was still not without hope that I would be freed. It seemed that my optimism was justified by logical considerations. Although I well knew that the NKVD organization was harsh and pitiless; although I knew of the Moscow Trials, of death sentences, deportations, terror, and so forth, still, I thought, people were not arrested, even in Russia, for no reason whatever. And, anyhow, what could they possibly have against me? I had been a Socialist all my life, and I had never shown any enmity towards the Soviet Union. And right here, around me, on the corridor walls, there hung pictures of the theorists of Socialism—Karl Marx and Friedrich Engels—whose writings I cherished so dearly. Well-known slogans, in which I, too, had believed since my early youth, screamed from posters and

red inscriptions on the walls. "Workers of the World, Unite!" I read in large letters right above my head. I could not believe that these did not mean what they said, and I became heartened.

The Soviet Union is fortunate in having in its service the myth of its ultimate, however small, generosity to the spirit of socialism. There is a "still," an "after all," that works in its favor, even among people who know of the Moscow Trials, etc.; thus it obtains representation in the hearts of those whose heads know better. The victims continue to hope; their hope is worthless, it is perhaps worse than none at all, for so long as the myth and the hope based on it continue to work, the totalitarian state continues to have power *in* the men who are at its mercy. A family tie, an incestuous bond. The fact that there is so little rebellion in the prison camps may not only be due to the harshness and efficiency of repressive measures; there is also the authority of the socialist myth among socialists. Their humiliation is all the greater for coming from so close a source.

But one is vulnerable merely in virtue of having had a childhood. Prison—and camp—regime breaks down the prisoner's morale by attacking precisely those habits, formed in childhood, on which the dignity, decency, and self-respect of the subsequent character have been based. Personal cleanliness in body, linens, and toilet, the discipline of controlling and satisfying the appetite in a regular way, the belief in one's right to a certain amount of privacy and the accompanying respect for the same right in others, and the satisfaction we are encouraged to feel in our ability to meet the standard social requirements at all the levels, from sphincter control and hygiene up through the ethical and intellectual formations, fair play, justice, etc.—all this is systematically violated in jail and camp by the rotten and inadequate food, the starvation, the repulsive facilities, the filth, the overcrowding in living and sleeping quarters (planks, arranged in tiers, on which so many sleep pressed together in rows that it is impossible for the sleepers to turn over, one at a time, when their sides are cramped; several times a night one of the jailed gives the command and all the rows turn simultaneously), the killing pace at which work is exacted and the murderous, impossible quotas, the bribing and thieving and informing, the constant subjection to ruthless and arbitrary treatment by the guards for the least (or suspected or falsely rumored) infraction or to bullying by the criminal element, whose brutality is condoned or encouraged by the camp authorities. Few men who have been brought up according to civilized standards can withstand such treatment without breaking down, without surrendering the integrity and self-respect which is the legitimate pride of us all. And what is true of the jailed is true of the jailers. A totalitarian society is one in which the mass of men is forced to recapitulate the early terrors, as in a waking nightmare, a nightmare from which one cannot awake because it is the reality. A prison camp is a kindergarten in a slaughterhouse, in which the penned must go round and round in a forced march to childhood, regressing to what they never were (the vacated possibilities between the first elements and the later formations of character realized, and the realized possibilities, which gave the mature person his amplitude, wiped out) that there may remain no interval of time or reflection between the word of authority and the obedience. And there is no redress, as to a righteous politics, a justice in the minds and wills of others, which was available even in the Tsars' days. This *is* Soviet politics; it is also the level and the limit to which all politics today can move.

So much we know. But we must be careful in reading this appeal to the West, not to make too much of our westernness; it is not synonymous with democracy—Germany is also West—and in itself it is proof against nothing. The character of an American and the values— "We hold these truths to be self-evident"—to which it conforms can be altered by the same methods. In fact, the immediate quality of American life has often impressed observers, our own and from foreign countries, with its violence and brutality, far more violent than the Germany which, by this impression, should have been a safe bet against succumbing to terror before our own country. It won't hurt to rehearse this; we have grown so used to the thicker layers of our atmosphere, we sometimes forget what we breathe. The South; but what about race riots in the North, and the brutality of American cops, urban and rural, the whole country over, and detention camps for Japanese and CO's and anti-Semitism and xenophobia and vigilantism and witch-hunts and the insane hatred that one can see mounting, holding back, growing into the subacute intelligence of sadism with its dead-right instinct for producing the crisis and explosion it means to produce?

Our democratic government holds (thank God or history) these forces checked, the democratic system relieves some pressures, exerts a counterpressure against others, and we have a tradition of due process of law, of equality, and a humane laissez faire, all of which has thus far been our protection. But it is impossible to believe, from what politics has already disclosed about itself, that a constitutional warrant is sure; it is no more than surface. The strength of any political surface depends on the deeper forces that attach themselves to it from the under side, by growing up to meet it and support it. Ultimately, the safety of a system demands the widespread existence among the people of a character structure which conforms, in impulse, values, in the basic orientation and training, to the values that are asserted at the surface. Our surface is cracked, our character structure, split. The totalitarian countries, on the other hand, have shown that such conformity between value and character is more than a theoretical possibility for tyrannous regimes. Our citizens, too, were once children, trained to potty, knife and fork, to good manners and respect for authority. They, too, can be demolished. What stands in the way of demolition is a system of politics which in turn draws its strength from the character of its people—a circle which is liable to become vicious. The "West" is no sure thing.

But by all means tell the West. It is as much for our own good as for theirs, the slaves lingering in their subarctic *lager* who made this request of Gliksman when his freedom was restored, that the truth about Soviet labor camps must be told. The West defends itself against such knowledge (an extreme but common form of defense, observable among fellow travelers, is to run in the direction of the threat, to be absorbed by it and thus to pass from its view). The West does not want to hear such things. This is bad. What is worse is that when the West is forced to hear, it reacts only with horror. It is a first horror, a horror of feigned innocence, whose real recoil is not from the thing revealed but from the excitement that the revelation produces, the unconscious recognition that we ourselves are capable of suffering and inflicting the same agony. This is dangerous, it can lead directly to the creation of the evil. We must be made to release our first horror, to come to the awareness that yes, of course, we too are capable and susceptible, all of existing humanity is susceptible. The admission thus wrenched from conscience leaves a place for knowledge to fill—the truth about today's politics in the extreme, that its scope is unlimited, that it has entered and possessed every inch of the private person, that it has nothing left to do with the pieties of the surface formulations. We will be better off for being thus disabused; and then there will be more point in telling the West. Even so, we will have a long stretch to cover. The full distance—a politics in which such things as in the Soviet Union not only do not occur, but are impossible. But this is as much as to say, a new humanity: a society and a human character structure, proof against outrage. Which is what was once meant by socialism. It is a long way off, further than ever, but we may at least know we're on the right track when we no longer need defend ourselves against the horror of contemporary politics, because our own brutal susceptibility will have diminished; and when we begin to feel, to our surprise, less and less horror and more and more of mere contempt (nothing else will be necessary) for men who do such violence—and at last, any violence—to other men.

Partisan Review, August, 1948

❧ The Meaning of Terror

I WILL SET DOWN a few propositions under two headings, though the argument can be expanded in all directions.

1. The Main Reality

All pleasure is innocent. We, the hedonists, are innocent, even though we now find no pleasure in life. Pleasure does not strike deep, it can exist in the mere absence of pain; like our virtues, it is the shadow cast by its opposite, and is not itself the real substance. But joy, said Nietzsche, wants "deep, profound eternity." Pleasure is not joy; it wants nothing of eternity, it is modest, there is no need to be alarmed at it. Yet most of the world fears pleasure. How much greater a fear we must have of joy, how much greater an incapacity to experience it! Refusing pleasure, we make pain the reality. Incapable of joy, we have only its opposite, which is terror.

Terror is today the main reality, because it is the model reality. The concentration camp is the model educational system and the model form of government. War is the model enterprise and the model form of communality. These are abstract propositions, but even so they are obvious; when we fill them in with experience, they are overwhelming. Unfortunately, there is nothing else into which we can fit our experience—traditions are broken and culture is unavailable. A culture is dead when the experience of men has no place in it. Our culture is an empty form, standing for a continuity of experience which is now discontinued, for the reality and inviolability of human values that are everywhere violated and denied. The common premise has always been: *still, there is mankind,* in virtue of which even the lowest of peasants and the most ignorant could be a man of deep culture. Today the cultured man is isolated; he may still exist, but his humanity is his own. He cannot share it with anyone (apart from his own exertions) because the cultural form that conveyed humanity and assured the transaction from one man to the next has been destroyed.

Men of culture are the first and the last to understand what has taken place. We know what has happened— and even this sets us apart; the majority do not know, in the sense, at least, of a knowledge that is more than information. The story has been printed in the papers— but the papers are full of lies. There have been films of the concentration camps, crematoriums, and gas chambers—but the films are only a public dream. What the people see in the movies, they are rendered incapable of experiencing directly. Hollywood is the good dream, and Buchenwald, the bad. Neither represents a reality. We saw the images of terror a long way off, far in advance of journalism and photography. Nevertheless, we, who know, still ask, "How is this possible?" How is it possible that thousands of men, women, children, and infants should be lined up in a field, to be shot before an open ditch, and that their screams should not be heard? That furnaces should be stuffed with human beings? That thousands should be marched into air-tight chambers, to be gassed or steamed to death, their naked bodies stuck together by the pressure and the heat? The death-schedules are possible: efficiency; the salvaged hair, gold fillings, and wedding bands: industry. But that no one should hear the screams? We cannot understand, we are as numb as the perpetrators of the crime. Our knowledge should shock us, it should stir us deeply, it should make our old life impossible, subjectively, as it is impossible in fact. But we are the true conservatives, who conserve values. The light is doused—we keep the afterimage alive; the wires are cut—we hold private conversations. But everyone is now a pragmatist (great gain); knowledge is only for action, as ours, too, must be, even if it be only to overcome the numbness that hinders our understanding of what has happened to the old world, and our participation in the new—decently, of course. But that goes without saying. We have our decency. What we need is necessity.

2. *The End of Alienation*

We are so sensitive that we cannot feel any more. When the moment comes to respond, our response is all spent in the anticipation. Hence our famous "alienation" —an alienation from the world we saw coming. Few of us realize that we are no longer alienated, now that this world has come. Woe to the prophet, the prophecy has come true! Hence the attack on intellectuals, the irresponsibles, the decadents (would that everyone were as decadent as we). But at least we are at home in this world. It is they, taken unprepared by the reality, who are alienated from it. We are the guides through the museum of dead culture—or if we, too, have lost our humanity, we are at least the nimble goats who can pick their way among the ruins.

Still we hear it said all around us that we are in a worse position than before—granted, but it is not the same position!—that we have nothing to say, and that even if we have, and our message be more precious than ever, we lack the language to express it and the audience to hear it. This merely describes the old alienation, when we saw what was coming and the rest of the world did not. But the rest of the world has caught up. The conditions have been established, by way of the common experience of the terror, for a universal communication. We can communicate the following.

Our old culture in which humanity transmitted its common life from one generation to the next was a moral culture, and the ethical was supreme: no greater good than good, no greater evil than evil. The death of our old culture came about when the evil greater than evil occurred—which is the terror. The good greater than good does not yet exist on earth: it is joy, which wants eternity. Together with terror, joy must replace the old pair of opposites, the old limits, which are now surpassed. Joy beyond good and terror beyond evil—the only principles. Everything else is privation.

But joy exists only in the minds of a few poets, though all men, unaware, may yearn for it. Its real existence will require a new character of mankind, which is also to say, a new culture. What will we have to take joy in? How can there be pleasures after the terror? But let us not speak of pleasure, we have no more innocence. (And how well we know, though we dare not admit the secret, that even the innocent pleasures were too much for us.) Our joy will be in love and restoration, in the sensing of humanity as the concrete thing, the datum of our cultural existence. It will lie in the creation of a new capacity, proof against terror, to experience our natural life to the full. What has once been transcended cannot be repeated; already we live without morality, though hypocrites study the old deceits. Men will go on to seek the good life in the direction of what is joyous; they know what is terrible. May the knowledge of joy come to them, and the knowledge of terror never leave!

So who is alienated? We are the prophets and inheritors of the present world and the only men who are at home in it, apart from the tyrannous bureaucrats—and even they regard us as their real enemies. It is impossible to live, to think, to create without bearing witness against the terror. But once we do so—behold, our great theme and occupation, our role, our language, our tone, and our audience—for what else is worth hearing today? This is the ground we have to defend against the terror, and on which we may hope to make joy come alive.

Partisan Review, January, 1949

Mind, Body, Spirit: The Road to the Castle

MAGISTER LUDI is a book of wonders. As far as I know, this is the first time that speculative intelligence has been given freedom in a work of fiction. It therefore has nothing in common with the theatrical philosophizing which, in all writers but Dostoevsky, has made up the so-called "novel of ideas." Hesse does not try to deduce characters from ideas, or vice versa, but dispenses with characterization altogether. Joseph Knecht, the hero, has the kind of existence that is given to philosophers by historians of culture: he stands at a point of intersection or convergence of lines of thought. Hesse absolutely commits himself to this conception of character; I was unable to believe it. I kept waiting throughout the novel for something "to happen," the usual conversion of character into drama. "Nothing happens"; and that which does not happen turns out to be a departure from the conventional novel, at a slow pace, creeping at times and even standing dead still, that goes at least as far as *Ulysses* though not, unfortunately, in as interesting a way.

The scene is somewhere in Europe, some time in the future, after the Age of the Digest, our own, which had all but destroyed culture, and whose wars had devastated the earth. To preserve the humane tradition, a number of scholars have joined together to found Castalia, a realm separate from the ordinary world, but dependent on it for subsistence. No one in Castalia works at practical things. The life, which with the exception of a period in youth is chaste and unworldly, is completely given over to a study of the various cultural traditions, including the Chinese, and of the development of the forms in music, poetry, mathematics, philosophy, etc. The work is scholarly, never creative. Its highest expression is achieved in the Bead Game, which lends itself to a refinement in subtlety as profound as chess, though it is played not with pieces (there are however beads to manipulate as well as hieroglyphics and other symbols) but with concepts. A theme, of music, poetry, science, or any such field is stated and elaborated, through meditation and in accordance with the rules of the game, to embrace other themes, until the game throws a net of formal relations over the whole history of culture. Joseph Knecht reaches proficiency in this game, becoming a Magister Ludi. The story of his life is the story of his intellectual adventures which Hesse, writing in the person of a Castalian, relates with few biographical details. The suggestion of an eventual breakthrough of repressed sexuality and worldliness is faintly established at the beginning; and though Hesse goes so far as to refer to Knecht's secret inner life as one of *Sturm und Drang,* he remains faithful to the Castalian tone in which one speaks only of mind, and does not exploit the opportunity for drama. Instead of drama we are given the Bead Game, and its marvelously happy symbolism is worked through over and over again to present the life of the mind. Fiction is thrown away in the process; but to say so is not a judgment on this novel, which makes no attempts at fiction.

But the breakthrough comes, and at that point Hesse, who has been writing in the tradition of Kafka (a qualification will follow), leans on Thomas Mann. Joseph Knecht, at the top of his career, leaves Castalia and enters the world as the tutor of the young son of his half-Castalian friend, Plinio Designori. He meets death, as does Aschenbach, in the form of the-young-boy-in-the-water. But here again, the dramatic theme is not developed, and the homosexual meaning not given openly.

Here Hesse's restraint appears as disdain: as though drama were somehow not quite nice, and ordinary psychology not pure enough to appear at the death of the mind.

Call this a weakness. But *Magister Ludi* has an extraordinary intellectual strength and simplicity. Its greatest quality is an implict literary criticism, a program, as it were, for writers to follow. Apparently acknowledging the tradition of Kafka as supreme for our time (for he takes his initial premise of the world from the same perspective), Hesse makes an adaptation of it that amounts to a radical transvaluation. It is not by accident that his hero is named Joseph Knecht (Joseph K.) and that his world is called Castalia. But there is no difficulty in arriving at Castalia, it is an accessible part of the world: the doors of the Castle stand wide open. *The Castle* has been rewritten from the interior point of view, the terror of God vanishes, and all suggestion of anything obscene in the exercise of His will, anything incommensurate with man's. A vocation exists always with reference to a world ordered by Law and prepared to fulfill it, and though the Law is still oppressive, it is fundamentally rational. It can be understood, mastered; as one rises in the understanding of it one becomes no longer a plaything but a member of the bureaucracy. One's bondage to the Law increases with this mastery (*Knecht* means servant, slave), but the entrance to the Law affords a two-way passage; Hesse, taking literally Kafka's fable in *The Trial* about the door to the Law which stands open the whole of a man's life, answers it with the charmingly simple-minded observation that one can also walk out. Joseph Knecht leaves Castalia with no more trouble than he entered. *Magister Ludi* is a translation of Kafka into the tradition of philosophical naturalism. And while this is done ironically— the scholars and bureaucrats of this well-lighted Castle are after all concerned only with a game—Hesse's irony, it seems to me, is not meant to detract from his optimistic recommendation in the spirit of enlightenment: enter the Castle, make yourselves at home.

Moravia's novel *The Woman of Rome* starts at the other end of the scale, taking its metaphor from the body. The Woman of Rome is Adriana, who finds her vocation in being a whore. She has a great natural capacity for it, and is the only character in this novel, as well as any other recent one I can think of, who is able to love. The drama of her life is not, as in Knecht's, unachieved by the author; but it is unnecessary, as are also the self-conscious intellectual insights Moravia never rests from trying to add to it: an existentialist sense of being alive, which as it is a tenuous sense, is ludicrously out of place in a full-bodied woman. Moravia lacks the courage of his sensuality, he does not let it stand as such, a poem, its own being, self-augmenting. He worries Adriana, constantly intervening, in his own voice spoken through her mouth, to school her sensibility. Yet if she has love's capacity, if in the sexual embrace she holds all of life, what need has she to sound like Sartre?

Adriana is sheer overflow, the novel cannot hold her. Moravia, hurriedly throwing up action to keep her in the story, only makes her nature seem so much the more tide-like, "undramatic." He leads her into an entanglement with a schizoid student, Mino, whom she loves and a brutal murderer, Sonzogno, who, of all her lovers, is the only man to possess her completely. Left to herself Adriana, I have the feeling, would not have stood these men; she would have rejected the humiliation Mino imposed on her, and as for Sonzogno, far from being fascinated by his horrible depravity and by the thought of being owned by it, she would have laughed in his face, for he is a pretentious idiot. Overevaluation of the murderer is a mistake, not of the lover, but of the serious novelist who raises the scent of the dramatic moment: meanings must spill out like blood. But love can afford to be lighthearted, it can do without these meanings. To add an existential dimension to Adriana, whose tragedy is not sickness of life but health, is to diminish and insult her, to throw up to her the fact that she's a whore.

Both these novels are clear in their ruling metaphors of mind and body. Neither succeeds in extending the metaphor dramatically to the point of including the other —*Magister Ludi* is sexless and *The Woman of Rome* falls under an extraneous philosophy. It is to the achievement of such a synthesis, one that may be called spirit, that Georges Bernanos devotes himself in *Under the Sun of Satan*, the story of a provincial priest, Father Donissan, who attains sainthood. The saint presumably stands at the height of spirit in virtue of his struggles in and with the flesh; the intellectual issues are furnished by the tradition of Christianity with its uneasy equilibrium of faith and reason, set aquiver in each fresh act of faith. But the issues at either side of spirit, at least in the context of this novel, are mediocre when not false. Father Donissan's spirituality reduces itself, rather shamefacedly, to the fact that he needs a woman—for which we are expected to admire him, and also for the fact that he mortifies himself, with hairshirt and chain. His intellectual commitments, mostly scraps, are supplied by the author, for Donissan is an ignorant peasant, and consist in a disdain of "neurophysiology"—which would call his behavior by its right name—and a belief in the reality of the devil, who appears to him in the flesh. His struggles are the usual circular agony of pride: mortification, leading to greater pride, requiring a greater mortification, etc., *ad inf*. This mess Bernanos calls holiness. I shall forego the obvious psychological objection; the literary objection is just as strong. There is a vindictive philistinism in this glorification of perversions and absurdities. *Credo quia absurdum est* has come to mean, to hell with science, to hell with learning, to hell with truth—I believe! There is no cheaper way of buying saintliness, but its pride is appalling. Little wonder that one after another Catholic novelists are reviving Lucifer—I presume, for moral support.

But here is a paradox. *Magister Ludi* and *The Woman of Rome* are well grounded in reasonable conceptions, their metaphors of mind and body are controlled with skill, taste, sophistication, both are good books—Hesse's is even a great book—but they are inferior as novels. *Under the Sun of Satan* is an abuse of intelligence, its issues are stale, its conception of spirit, perverse—but it is superior as dramatic fiction. As though a novelist cannot afford to be too sure of his ground. This may be the case, for Bernanos seems to thrive on a lack of confidence. He patterns his conflicts after Dostoevsky even to the detail of hoping to arrive at and sustain a faith which will justify his perversity. Meanwhile, he lacks the ultimate faith to which he has committed himself, and because he is always slipping and falling down in his pursuit of it, he must grasp at anything that will steady him. He takes hold with greater force than a writer who has a matter well in hand; and so he clutches at scene, word, monologue, everything is pressed to the limit, and dramatic effectiveness is implicit in the very pressure of the act of writing. But is it worth it? Mere fiction cannot justify this deliberate poverty of spirit, a bore, a nuisance, and ultimately a vicious thing.

But Hesse's invasion of the Castle, as a mere stroke of imagination, even if it fails, Moravia's single creation of a real woman of flesh, have a greater dramatic potential than Bernanos' fever and delirium. Health, naturalism, the joy of love, the preservation of secular culture, these small and still very shy little devotions to enlightenment shall have to provide the dominant movement of fiction if drama is to mean a real adventure, not a crack-up, of spirit. The road, let us say, has been opened to the Castle. The way is long (even if one does simply walk in, as with Hesse), and who knows what can happen on the way? And picture the excitement—it will be the greatest dramatic moment in literature—if one finds on opening the door that Adriana has already moved in and lies there waiting on her sacred couch.

Partisan Review, November, 1949

Religion and Naturalism: A Personal Statement

[EDITOR'S NOTE: Early in 1950 the editors of *Partisan Review* asked a number of intellectuals (among them A. J. Ayer, R. P. Blackmur, Sidney Hook, Alfred Kazin, and Paul Tillich) to contribute to a symposium eventually published in several issues as "Religion and the Intellectuals." Isaac Rosenfeld's response refers to the editors' queries, which are therefore given here in brief form:

1. What do you think are the causes of the present revival of religion? Is it due to the worldwide failure and defeat of a real radical movement in politics? To a renunciation of hopes for any fundamental social improvement? Or to some kind of breakdown in the organization of modern society, to which religion would seem to supply a remedy?

2. What has happened to make religion more credible than it formerly was to the modern mind?

3. Can culture exist without a positive religion?

4. The revival of religion has perhaps been most noticeable in the literary world. Does this imply some special dependence of the literary imagination upon religious feeling and ideas?

5. Certain writers have attempted to separate the religious consciousness (as an attitude toward man and human life) from religious beliefs. Is this separation possible? Is there a valuable religious consciousness that can be maintained without an explicit credo postulating the supernatural? Assuming that in the past religions nourished certain vital human values, can these values now be maintained without a widespread belief in the supernatural?]

THE REASON I cannot accept any of the current religious philosophies is that they are all crazy in one very basic respect—their denial of nature and attempt to push man out of nature. It may be that I have not read enough theology to find the exception. But the theologians I have read—Kierkegaard, Berdyaev, Niebuhr, Maritain—all agree in claiming man's true nature, his essential being, his humanity, his freedom, or whatever else they choose to call it, to lie outside historical time and the world of nature. Miguel de Unamuno with his longing for immortality "in this flesh and in these bones" may have been a real exception, but his Catholicism makes me doubt it. Moreover, as there cannot be revealed religion without the supernatural, all such religions must regard man's occupancy of nature as something of a comedown or at best a temporary condition, as though he were only slumming in this world. I call this crazy. This longing to clear out is not represented metaphorically as an extension, say, of the desire to find a new apartment or visit foreign countries, but literally—as though there really were someplace else to go. One might as well say of fish that their real life lies in a realm outside water.

I am a naturalist. This doesn't mean much, for in modern philosophy the term covers too many positions to stand for anything very definite. But it presents at least one issue clearly: there is no realm outside nature and everything must be found within this world.

1. Yes. The social, political, and economic conditions you list in your questions have all contributed to the religious trend. But you fail to mention any specific psychological causes. The mass neuroses of modern society are probably the most important.

2. Since convictions are not independent of circumstantial influences, the above should answer for the gain in credibility to the modern mind of certain religious ideas. But here naturalism, or at least its reputation, is also to blame. I imagine that for many intellectuals naturalism has come to mean something like Chatauqua or single-tax, a lot of lost ideas, about as helpful as cupping the dead. Helpful is the important word—also consoling.

Naturalism won't help or console anyone, it isn't meant to, its business being solely to present truth; but in the course of doing so it must touch on living concerns. But the way naturalistic philosophies are taught in many of our schools, making them a matter exclusively of professional technicalities with no end of words about methodology in which nothing gets said, the subject loses all significance. I don't blame people for objecting to this. It shows that they have more life than the professors.

Meanwhile, religious doctrines, which are all consolatory, score their gains. They have an emotional appeal, the issues, as presented, are of love, salvation, brotherhood, humility, sacrifice—and these themes, for a great variety of reasons, not all of them neurotic, exert a tremendous drawing force. If a man stands in need of consolation (practically, this means nearly every man almost all the time), he will much sooner be reached by a doctrine in which such themes are heavily represented than by one in which they are scattered or absent. Religion, furthermore, can be given an urgent tone, it can be made to appear a matter of life or death. The consolations of religion, in other words, offer themselves soothingly or melodramatically, and there is as much solace in the latter, possibly even more, as in the former. Religious existentialism is a case in point. It stresses absurdity, the incommensurability of man and God, human loneliness, the difficulties of communication—it is, on the face of it, a "realistic" philosophy, and it consoles men by allowing them to believe that they are not seeking consolation, by letting them think that they are brave. Unfortunately for some present-day versions of naturalism, there is more emotional immediacy in this than in an abstract aping of physical science, in method-chopping, in endless talk about values without a single assertion. I would blame our educational system for this, or whatever it is that had reduced a great philosopher and aesthetician like John Dewey to the dismal common denominator of School of Ed., and the whole of naturalism to something dreary and toneless.

3., 4., and 5. Culture can certainly exist without a positive religion. This is true both in the limited sense of art, and in the broader anthropological definition. One of the best modern examples of both, unfortunately little known, is the secular Yiddish culture that grew up round Y. L. Peretz in Warsaw at the turn of the century. Both secular and religious cultures have flourished and degenerated—and this is of course a truism, but it seems to have escaped the notice of those who call for a return to religion, as though religion of its own accord bestows viability. On the contrary, the existence of such a call is usually a sign of the degeneracy of the culture in which it is issued. Ours is a degenerating mixed culture of sacred and secular elements. That religion has contributed to the degeneration of this culture is obvious even to the religious who have not lost the capacity of blushing for their beliefs. Consider the average sermon or the reactionary role that the various churches—in particular the Catholic—have played in politics, in the perpetuation of authoritarian superstitions, and in obstructing measures even remotely approaching reasonableness in matters of sex. The position of the Catholic Church on sex is one of the very worst features—secular or religious—of our entire culture; unfortunately it happens to be both secular and religious, and the damage the Church does in supporting the general cretinism that marks our cultural attitude toward sex is thereby doubled. One may argue that these are the faults of the institution, not of the underlying religious beliefs. This argument is false for two reasons: the doctrines of all present-day religions, as understood and observed throughout the world, justify most of the institutional practices which one might call upon them to correct; and secondly, it is impossible to separate the beliefs from the institutions in which they are formalized in any way which would be significant for culture. So far as the culture is concerned, religion is the sum of religious institutions. Besides, a culture in which religious institutions disappeared would inevitably become purely secular; in time it must become the culture of the remaining institutions. Religion being what it is today, this leads me to believe that it is impossible to build a flourishing culture on religious foundations.

Even if it were somehow possible to separate religious beliefs from institutions, it would still not be necessary to maintain the former as the condition of culture. The argument that one cannot understand, appreciate, or otherwise participate in a culture without sharing its religious beliefs is obviously nonsense in the case of Classical culture. It should follow from this that participation in the Medieval synthesis by way of direct belief is unnecessary to the appreciation of Dante (and probably harmful, so far as any modern perspective is concerned), but for some reason this argument, though a true one, is never advanced. One can very well understand Dante's faith (or anyone else's) in his own terms and appreciate its part in the creation of his poetry, without sharing it in the least. Otherwise one should have to argue that atheists cannot be cultured men, and that the religious can have no contact with cultures whose religious traditions are different from their own. To the degree that the religious beliefs are incompatible with one another, a true love of Dante, in terms of this argument, should limit one to at best a partial understanding of Dostoevsky and a complete incapacity and actual antipathy for Chinese poetry—all of which is absurd. But the contrary is true—the less one shares the religious beliefs of a given period, the better does his position with regard to the culture become. This holds even in religion, as in Bible study; for the general tendency in the development of any culture is away from fundamentalism and toward the granting of greater autonomy to the aesthetic and historical construction of doctrine. This shift, which takes place in all cultures, is an implicit recognition of naturalism and an admission that the naturalistic basis is sufficient for culture. All that need be preserved in going from a sacred to a secular tradition is a feeling for the religion, as distinct from belief, and this is available to a normal act of empathy. It is no greater mystery than any act of insight in any social context. There are some that have it and some that don't. No amount of religious

exercise will help those who are unable to establish contact with the feelings of another; for as a rule they are out
of touch with their own religion, and in general with
their own emotional milieus. If a man is incapable of
understanding the work of a religious poet, look to his
sensibility rather than his baptismal certificate. Religion
is no cure for stupidity. And since there are great non-
religious figures and great secular cultures, religion is no
more a qualification creatively than it is in criticism.

The argument that religion is necessary for culture is
sometimes advanced in the limited but familiar form of
"the tragic sense of life." Only the religious point of view
can raise the vision of life to the grandeur of tragedy. The
naturalistic perspective brings life into focus only as a
blind, meaningless, or mediocre transaction, a vision
lacking in dignity or value and therefore in everything
that makes life worth while in the specifically human
sense. This argument is utterly cockeyed, and is advanced
only because of the widespread prejudice against naturalism. Actually, the very opposite is true. For if man is
not wholly of nature, if he has one foot planted in some
better, higher realm, what is tragic about death or any
other predicament of the natural world? What meaning
has any natural frustration, in terms of this argument,
except as a prelude to supernatural fulfillment? I fail to
see how anyone can have even a suspicion of the tragic
sense of life unless he is already deeply committed to
naturalism; unless death and frustration have a finality,
an irreducible meaning for him—which only naturalism
allows. It follows from this that naturalism is implicated
in any genuine religious philosophy. Everything else is
pie in the sky.

Human values must be derived from nature as the
sufficient ground. There is no other derivation, and even
the most unworldly religions fall back ultimately on some
connection with life, though this is often so weak it is
hard to recognize. The natural derivation of value is no
academic issue, a matter of premise and conclusion with
a theory hanging between the two. It must be experienced
directly, the dependence of everything on nature must

be felt concretely within one's own life, before naturalism can be anything more than an attitude, and a superficial one at that. But there can be no naturalistic dogma,
for our sense of nature, our ability to experience it, does
not remain fixed, and the true intellectual expression
must retain something of the character of dialogue. (But
here I can speak only for myself.) An example from
Berdyaev is relevant.

In *Slavery and Freedom* Berdyaev opposes to all the
modes of slavery into which man can fall the personalistic ideal of freedom, found not in this world or any part
of nature, but in the higher realm of personality, which
is independent of time, and strictly speaking, religious.
Now though I stated at the outset that I find all such
separations of man from nature repugnant, at times I am
myself drawn to this view. It is such a perfect refuge
from the encroachment of the world, that is to say, from
politics. The tyranny of the state, when I fear it most,
seems to call for such a separation. There is the sense of
the state closing in, confusing innocence and guilt, good
and evil, devouring the world and the little space in it in
which I have hoped to lodge my personal independence,
and hoped that my children will be able to secure theirs.
At such times this position is very attractive, I feel the
urge to cry, "I am not wholly of this world."

But at other times, when the fear is gone, I see that
what I have regarded as refuge is merely uplift, and that
I have no refuge apart from the satisfaction of my desires—and this is no refuge but an open, vulnerable
commitment to life. But I have an urge to live and I come
alive, my work goes well, I feel love, and this little space
of personal freedom fills the world. Now this is no more
a solution to the problem of the state than Berdyaev's
separation from nature; politics is politics, no matter
where you stand. But it does seem to me to solve problems of religion. To the extent that my own life is un-
impeded in the satisfaction of desire (I am not speaking
of a happy life, only of a deep one), to that extent the
formulations of religion fall away, with the need for
refuge and consolation, and I am not religious. The exact

motion is that of a seesaw, and its only honest representation in words is through dialogue. But halt the ascent
of the seesaw at its highest point—what I find then is
the ideal which I would oppose to the personalistic ideal,
or any other that demands separation from nature. It is
the ideal of natural fulfillment, of the self-regulative or-
dering of values (in societies as well as individuals) where
values offer themselves of their own accord in the experience of life, without residuum in some other world.
Call this ideal, if you must, religious. But then to all the
intellectuals who are crying, back to religion! you must
say, "O ye of little faith."

Naturalism is meaningless without such direct experiencing of values; it is meaningless so long as the religious
definition of value, involving separation from nature, has
meaning. All the extensions of religion into other spheres,
into morality, the regulation of conduct, the sanctioning
of standards, the preservation of culture, spring from the
failure at the core of naturalism to experience life directly.
For those who are dead to it, nature offers no evidence
of values, and these must be imported from abroad. But
this merely continues to lower the repute in which spontaneous manifestations of nature—especially the sexual
—are held in our society, and it obstructs recognition of
the fact that the humane values are natural functions of
love. And above all, the cost of this religious importation
is too great; we must pay for it in the dying out of the
sense of life, in a doom of submission to a world ruled
by dead men who, because they can no longer feel love,
can no longer feel anything, not even the terror of the
concentration camp, let alone sympathy and brotherhood
for other men.

Partisan Review, March, 1950

৺ Gandhi: Self-Realization Through Politics

THERE HAS probably never been another "great man" —that vast, vague, abstract personage which we celebrate in human terms but conceive as a stuffed shirt—who has written so simple and direct a book as Gandhi's *Autobiography* (Public Affairs Press, Washington, D.C., 1948). In the name of Truth, and for the purpose of describing his experiments with Truth, he tells us about his character, detail by detail, with a directness and completeness that is astonishing and shocking and that may appear irrelevant even after we have grasped the connection. But irrelevant these minutiae are not; Gandhi merely understood the facts of life better than the rest of us.

This Great Soul, Latter-day Avatar, Architect of India's Freedom, as he was called, reveals to us his early attitudes toward parents and teachers, his sexual practices, his relations with his wife, his theories on the subjects of diet, medicine, and cleanliness, and his various experiments in these fields; he describes himself ironing collars with the same underlying seriousness and attachment to moral significance as when he tells of nursing the sick and the dying. Often one must laugh, our sophistication demands it; to withhold the ridicule this self-confessed quack frequently deserves is to refuse to honor the simpleton in him, the plain *nudnik,* and to violate his unity. He was all of a piece, the man whose desire was "to wipe away every tear from every Indian eye," the neurotic who regarded sexual intercourse without intent of producing children as a grave crime, the submissive

224

rebel who spent his days confounding authority and meanwhile kept his eye open for a vegetable substitute for cow's milk. It was all one with him.

Nehru said of this man: "People who do not know Gandhi personally and have only read his writings are apt to think that he is a priestly type, extremely puritanical, long-faced, Calvinistic, and a kill-joy. . . . But his writings do him an injustice; he is far greater than what he writes, and it is not quite fair to quote what he has written and to criticize it. He is the very opposite of the Calvinistic priestly type. His smile is delightful, his laughter infectious, and he radiates lightheartedness. There is something childlike about him which is full of charm. When he enters a room he brings a breath of fresh air . . . which lightens the atmosphere. He is an extraordinary paradox."

All this appears in the autobiography—the smile as well as the long face. The paradox lies not so much in the conjunction of opposite qualities (this is common enough, and it can be explained) as in the peculiar exception he provides to the rule of reaping what one sows. He emerged uncrippled from the crippling inner life he made himself lead; almost as though he had never led it, and more natural than many a man who is pledged to accommodate the instincts.

"What I want to achieve," he declared, ". . . is self-realization, to see God face to face, to attain *Moksha* [salvation, freedom from birth and death; it was "an unbroken torture" to him that he was still so far from this]. All that I do . . . and all my ventures in the political field, are directed to this same end." To understand him, one must understand, as he did, the connections among chastity, self-realization in politics, and the belief that a man's diet should consist only of fruit and nuts.

Gandhi was an extremely shy child. He adored his mother (her strict observance of fasts and of the most rigorous religious vows are of significance for his later life) and loved his father not so well (he speaks of him as short-tempered and "To a certain extent he might have been

given to carnal pleasures. For he married for the fourth
time when he was over forty." Gandhi was born of this
last marriage). His schools days were lonely, "books and
lessons" were often his "only companions." He was punc-
tilious in attendance, but would run home the moment
the bell rang, afraid to play with his schoolmates lest
anyone poke fun at him. Of his classroom experiences
he remembers "nothing more . . . than having learnt, in
company with other boys, to call our teacher all kinds of
names. . . . [This] would strongly suggest that my intellect must have been sluggish and my memory raw." It
suggests even more strongly that his teachers were no
good, but of this, not a word. It was not like Gandhi
to criticize authority. Of a later period in his life, when
he still considered British rule beneficial to India, he
said, "Hardly ever have I known anyone to cherish such
loyalty as I did to the British Constitution." But by that
time he was already learning the technique, unavailable
to the merely submissive child, of taking a stand against
authority and simultaneously assuaging his guilt feelings.
The method consisted in inflicting on himself, for every
act of insubordination, some hardship, most frequently in
religious form—a vow to abstain from certain foods, to
give up certain pleasures—as though in punishment for
a fault greater than the one he must condemn in the
authorities.

At the age of thirteen he married Kasturbai, who was
illiterate. For a number of years Gandhi was very jealous
and suspicious of her, and he made her miserable by
watching her every move and imposing severe restrictions
on her social life. He wanted to make her an ideal wife.
"My ambition was to *make* her live a pure life, learn
what I learnt, and identify her life and thought with
mine" (italics his). But he was "passionately fond of
her," and lust prevented him from devoting himself to
her education. She remained poorly educated to the end,
having profited so little from his instruction that she
could do no better than write with difficulty "simple
letters and understand simple Gujarati. I am sure that had
my love for her been absolutely untainted by lust, she

would be a learned lady today; for I could then have *conquered* her dislike for studies. I know that *nothing is impossible for pure love*" (italics mine; this is one of the many indications that pure love, for Gandhi, was often like a pile driver).

Gandhi's memories of his early life are distorted in the direction typical of ascetics, who endow that past with an extravagance of error and sin. The motive, one must suppose, is to make the rectitude of the present life appear so much the nobler and, in its unconscious part, to quicken the pleasure-starved heart with at least an imagined lust. The excesses of which he speaks are perfectly innocent: smoking, a minor theft, the eating of meat; and the rest are attributable, if they are excesses at all, to adolescent sexuality enjoying its first fling, thanks to the institution of child marriage.

But an event of this period—in Gandhi's system a terrible sin—which confirmed the guilt feelings about sex that he must already have had and proved crucial for his later attitudes, occurred with the death of his father when Gandhi was sixteen. Kaba Gandhi had long been ill and his son Mohandas took turns with other members of the family in nursing him. On the night of his father's death young Gandhi, relieved by his uncle, went straight to his bedroom to have intercourse with his wife, who, to his "double shame," was pregnant with their first child. Father Gandhi died while they were having intercourse. Gandhi never forgave himself for this, and all his life remembered that it was sexual desire which prevented him from being at his father's bedside when he died; he also assumed the guilt for the death of his first child, born of this pregnancy. Taking into account the attitudes toward sex that he later developed—for example, the extreme agitation he showed when a young man and woman of his *ashrama* (religious order) broke their vow of chastity, and the fast he undertook to punish them—as well as the latent hostility he must have felt for his father, one must suppose that he considered himself a murderer, and the sexual act a murderous one.

At the age of eighteen he underwent a "long and

healthy spell of separation" from his wife; he sailed to London to study law. There had been opposition in the family to his going, and technically, Gandhi was outcaste all his life for breaking the prohibition of overseas travel; but he obtained his mother's consent by taking a vow not to touch wine, women, or meat while abroad. He stuck to his vow and led a poor, lonely, grinding life in England for four years; despite the gentlemanly airs he assumed, silk gloves and top hat, he remained shy and awkward and most of his contacts were with vegetarians. Gandhi's shyness stood in the way of his legal career on his return to India. He was too bashful and frightened to speak up in court; and also too much the egotist. But that egotism can lie behind failure too, Gandhi never recognized. He was aware of his egotism only on the level of direct contact with the world, never suspecting that the measures he adopted to hold himself back might also have been motivated by it. He was already a perfectionist; and it was the high standard that he set for himself, along with the fear that his performance might not overwhelm the world, that stopped his tongue. Later, when he had mastered the way of satisfying both his extreme egotism and his passion for humility, he proved himself a moving speaker.

The first step toward the resolution of his lifelong conflict over egotism he took in South Africa, where he had gone to make another attempt at the practice of law. He found that a certain measure of satisfaction could come to him through service to others. The more he denied himself the immediate satisfaction of acting on his own behalf and in the interest of his growing family, the more capable he became. The usual income of rewards in fame and money he had always checked because of guilt—a guilt, precisely, over the demands he made of the world; these were his true "excesses." He learned to detach himself from his ambitions, to ask, while serving others, less and less for himself, letting the rewards accumulate to the credit of his public self (it was his greatest private pleasure to disclaim gratification in his public self). His egotism, which had cut him off from contact with the world, thus

diverted, brought him into a growing contact with the
world, as he denied himself profit in direct returns. This
became the basic operation of his personality.

It was a powerful operation, and as he came to perfect
it, he established himself as its foremost entrepreneur.
He exploited the world's conscience as ruthlessly as any
exploiter, but with the significant qualification that he
never spared himself. In fact, he had to drive himself always harder, always one step further than he drove the
world, for the essence of his power lay in a clear conscience. "I have the right," ran his justification, "to demand this of you. Look—I myself have given more!" But
asceticism not only gave him contact with the world; it
enabled him to conquer. Suffering as much as he did to
gain humility, he could overlook the power aspects of his
drive; his empire, he could well believe, was not of the
world, but of the inner world of his own instincts.

There is a swindle here, which, from the fact that
Gandhi conspired in it all his life, suggests that a man
can support an exacting conscience on hardly any self-
insight at all. The ordinary dishonest man, the good
average citizen who meets all the requirements but does
so imperfectly, is much more fearful of conscience than
the saint. He assigns himself a limit, beyond which he
will not go, and he knows his limit (the saint does not);
this knowledge seals his mediocrity, it does not allow him
to persist beyond it. Yet the ascetic's hunger for power
presupposes a conscience, and an active one; else why
should he have to work so hard? Each blow he directs
against himself falls to his credit, and this being a gain, it
requires another blow, and so on in an infinite regress of
pride-in-humility. But somewhere in the course the organism is enfeebled, and when it can endure no more, conscience is satisfied to call a halt. What is saintly in every
case, and certainly in Gandhi's, is that the process is halted
at a point which for most men would be well beyond
death. Thus the saint enters a real immortality, even in
his lifetime.

Such was the mechanism of Gandhi's powerful fasts.

The nearer he approached death, the greater his power became; the nation would beg him to stop and promise to be good and obey. The fear of the Indians may not only have been due to the great guilt of parricide he stirred up in them ("We have killed Bapu!"); at a deeper level it may have been a fear that the basic moral contradiction of the saint's hunger for, and use of, power would break through to recognition. This would have meant not only the death of "Bapu," the father, but of "Mahatmaji," the honored Great Soul, and with him of the whole system of ideals that his moral strategies had created in the New India. It is noteworthy that Gandhi was assassinated not by Moslems, Communists, or any religious or secular out-group, but by a member of the Hindu Mahasabha, a fanatical orthodox society and the only one in India that could claim sanctity greater than his own.

A man who wields such power does not come by it overnight. Before he left South Africa he had completed the work on the foundations of his character, which included *Brahmacharya*, "control of the senses in word, thought and deed." (*In thought*—one of his great naive insights was the statement: mind is the root of sensuality.) This meant absolute chastity; he would live with his wife as with a sister, and regard all women as the equals and companions of men, and no longer as objects of lust. (Since sexual intercourse must have seemed to him an act of murderous violence, the ban he imposed on himself with *Brahmacharya* was the symbolic climax to the taboos on eating, destroying, or otherwise injuring flesh.) "Before taking the vow I had been open to being overcome by temptation at any moment. Now the vow was a sure shield against any temptation." He speaks of the joy *Brahmacharya* brought him, for all that it was hard work. Having mastered it, he was secure, he had built the last barrier in a system of defenses against the world, which system, at the next remove, was a defense against his own impulses toward the world, and which was finally to give him command of the world. *Brahmacharya* was a joy because it was the ultimate maneuver in the negotiation of this treaty (such a man must have a genius for politics); it brought the last straggling impulse of life under control, halted the conflict between sexuality and self, and put an end to the struggle between public and private ego. These conflicts, so long as they raged, represented a possible return to direct satisfactions ("temptations"). He was now beyond temptation, and the full price he had asked for the assumption of power, he had himself paid out. Gandhi was now ready to turn his power operation directly on the world with the work of *Satyagraha,* his self-realization in politics.

Examination of the self that Gandhi sought to realize can lead one to think that the ascetic need not invent a sinful past; he need only attribute to the past the sins of the present, which the process of acquiring sainthood brings him to commit. Much of him is merely absurd, and this amuses us and endears the great man to us. But much of him is overbearing, insensitive, and even brutal. Our original question—"How can he have emerged uncrippled from the crippling life he led?" becomes, "How can he have been so crippled, seeing that he emerged whole?"

The simpleton in him, wanting to save money, decided to launder his own shirts. "So I equipped myself with a washing outfit. . . . I bought a book on washing, studied the art and taught it also to my wife. This no doubt added to my work, but its novelty made it a pleasure." He describes the first collar he laundered. He had used too much starch and pressed it with an iron that was not hot enough. "The superfluous starch continually dropped off it." All the same, he wore the collar to court, to the amusement of his colleagues. He was impervious to ridicule (at the cost of being ridiculous—but that's actually a saving to a Don Quixote) and was glad of the chance to provide his friends with some fun at his expense. But even here, charming as this incident is, he was far from innocent, for Gandhi was still engaged in scoring his characteristic point. He wears his collar with a straight face as an example of the "beauty of self-help," and must feel an increment of humility trickling to his credit. His whole character is here reproduced in miniature.

One frequently finds him buying a book on some household subject, mastering it, and then teaching it to his wife—for this, one must be a Gandhi. He instinctively believes that the world is authoritarian, run on principles as solemn as his own, and it is respect for authority and desire to conform that make him humble himself in a way that only an idiot or a nobleman can afford. In these small, simple things (as also, for example, with his opinions on handwriting, where he expresses his regret, at the height of his career, that he had neglected to improve his penmanship, and adds, "Let every young man and woman be warned by my example and understand that good handwriting is a necessary part of education") he surprises us by betraying the kind of mentality at which the self-help ads in the pulp magazines are aimed.

It is otherwise when a moral issue is involved. Then this spendthrift of good name who prospers on ridicule cannot resist a proud show: the temptation to act on principle is the one thing his vanity is not armored against. I imagine him interrupting his practice of sweetness and gentle humility; his favorite prayer to Rama goes dead on his lips, the spinning wheel is abandoned. Still with a sweet smile—which now has the tension of a bird dog on the point—he turns to his old friend and disciple, Kallenbach, during an ocean voyage to London, to persuade him that possession is evil, and that Kallenbach, accordingly, ought to get rid of "the pair or two" of expensive binoculars he brought with him on the trip. The discussion goes on for several days; at last Kallenbach throws the binoculars overboard to put an end to Gandhi's nagging. And Gandhi is himself persuaded that the power of pure love has again prevailed.

Or the presents that the Indian community of South Africa has given to him and his wife when the Gandhis are about to return to their native land. Gandhi, who as a public servant will accept no reward for his work, returns his own present and argues that Kasturbai is bound to do the same. Her present, some expensive jewelry, has been given not for her work but in recognition of his; her acceptance would therefore constitute his taking payment for his services. Kasturbai replies, with very good reason, that without her toiling and moiling for him, his public work would have been impossible. Besides, she does not want the jewels for herself, but for her sons, who will some day marry; let them have the jewels as a wedding present for their wives. His sons, answers Gandhi, shall not want to marry girls who care for ornaments—"Will you, boys?" The boys, of course, agree with papa, Kasturbai is overwhelmed, the jewels are cashed, and the money derived from them is put aside in a trust fund for the Indians of South Africa. Which is no doubt a noble action —but all the same, poor Kasturbai.

Or when his ten-year-old son, Manilal, lies dying of typhoid and pneumonia (the same incident is repeated whenever a member of the family is very ill, and several times with Kasturbai). The doctor, a Parsee, advises Gandhi that medicine can do the boy little good; the only hope is to sustain his strength by giving him nourishing food, which means eggs and chicken broth. Gandhi replies that he is a vegetarian and that his religion does not permit him to use meat or eggs. Had Manilal been of age, Gandhi would have consulted his wishes; but as he has to decide for him, he will not allow his son this sacrilege. He is conscious of the risk; but it is precisely at times like this that a man's faith is put on trial, and Gandhi prefers to place his faith in God and not compromise his honor. He gives Manilal hydropathic treatments, with hip-baths, and keeps him on orange juice diluted with water. But the boy's fever rises to 104 degrees, with delirium at night. "I began to get anxious. What would people say of me? What would my elder brother think? . . . What right had parents to inflict their fads on their children?" But Gandhi comforts himself with the thought that God must surely be pleased with his faith. He continues his own kind of treatment and Manilal, such being his father's luck, recovers. Gandhi rejoices that he has not had to compromise his principles, and fails to observe that he was willing to sacrifice his son's life to vain honor. This is the same brave man, all of a piece, whom the threat of violence never deterred, and who lived by the Sermon on the Mount.

Satyagraha or "truth-force" is the nonviolent form of struggle to gain an objective without injuring flesh or compromising the truth. Truth, for Gandhi, had a curious connotation; it meant what it means for all, but it was also the name he gave to his own life-process, the conversion of self-denial into power. *Satyagraha* is the same conversion turned outward, with public objects standing in place of the inner life. It was an act of genius on his part to recognize that politics need be nothing more than the simple extension of psychic economy. Away with governments, legislatures, police; the regime a man follows in conducting his own life is the sufficient model for society. Gandhi's anarchism is obscured by the stress he placed on moral authority; nevertheless, he always acknowledged his debt to Thoreau and Tolstoy.

That his own character was the model for his politics can be seen from the many parallels between his life-process and his social principles. His famous preference for primitive household and village economies over centralized modes of production, his love of the spinning wheel and hatred of modern machine industry, are symbolic continuations of his inner denial of direct power impulses; and they impose the ascetic form upon society. His opposition to science is of the same order; he saw in it a rationalization of power that threatened his own. From his masochistic identification with the lowest of the low, one may derive his campaign for the abolition of untouchability; and so on, the list could be extended over his whole career. There was hardly a position he held, a gesture he made, which was not the logical outcome of his character structure. And while his actual politics may have been, at times, as inconsistent as any politician's, it is a blessing to deal with someone like Gandhi, for you know the man is not improvising. The mode is love: he gives himself. So also with the instrument of struggle he

made out of truth in *Satyagraha*; it was the highest paradox of his nonviolence, the achievement of force without
force.

His softness of approach was deceiving. It concealed,
as his violent death made clear, a dangerous force in
and about him, for which the British, in their own terms,
were quite right to keep Gandhi so many years of his life
in jail. While Gandhi meant by *Satyagraha*, literally, the
force of truth, to the British, and even to the masses who
followed him, it was more the other way round. The civil
disobedience movement had a thrilling, crackling atmosphere of thunderstorm; without this high potential of
violence, pacifism is mere church. Yet this force was
generated by the same methods that had led, in his own
case, to peaceful self-rule. With the peace he had won
by repressing all violence in himself, he must have developed a partial blindness; his attitude on the occasions when
he called off the civil disobedience movement because of
the sporadic bloodshed it caused would suggest that he
was not all along aware that he was handling fire.

For his own part, Gandhi relied on the power of truth
alone, and he did so neither in sentimentality nor naïveté.
He came to it experienced and assured. He had already
achieved by these means empire over his instincts—an
empire to which nothing military can compare; and round
this empire he had built an unbreachable defense in depth
—vegetarianism, nonviolence, dietary and medical quack-
ery (the word is his own; it is the most charming aspect
of his defense that he can laugh at it, to make it appear
light), self-control in word, thought, and deed, over-
towering it all with *Brahmacharya*. Only then did this
empire turn its might outward to bring the world under
its sway.

The war of *Satyagraha* began, which he was to wage
the rest of his life against war itself, British rule, the
subjugation of India by poverty, disease, color and religious prejudice, untouchability. The public self that
commanded this war fought joyously, and at the public
level we see only the ego's armament, forged and beaten
and polished to shine like love—it is light and mobile, it

suggests nothing of the pain and fear and self-abuse of the deprivations, the sickness of life that attended its manufacture. We are amazed that so much satisfaction should lie in war. And the greatest achievement of this emperor is that this was a real satisfaction to him, one that called out a natural smile and laugh. When the world offered itself, surrendering its egotism, its pride and lust, he received it as a child does a toy.

He had long been prepared for the gift of India, having anticipated the surrender by making its masses part of himself, by living and dressing like them, sharing and outdoing their poverty and starvation and religious observances (fortified in these ordeals, especially in the later years, by some of India's greatest millionaires. A photograph of the entire estate Gandhi left behind at his death —it serves as a frontispiece to the autobiography—shows a spittoon, a prayer book, a pair of eyeglasses, two pairs of sandals, a watch, some eating implements, and a statuette of the three monkeys, "Say No Evil, See No Evil, Hear No Evil"; he was living at the time in Birla Mansion). Now politics, like diet, sex, and medicine, was brought down to the level where he could attack it directly, as empirical a matter as a woman's cooking. It became an issue, like any other, of character—and as simple. What truth is there in the opponent's words and in his life? How does he live? How can he be persuaded? How shamed into obedience of the spirit of his own words? How forced into taking advantage of India's willingness to endure suffering until he himself is worn down by the hardships he imposes? The enemy in this war was an empire, but Gandhi refused to recognize armies, battleships, and parliaments, official ranks and dignities. He persisted in fighting it, exasperatingly, man to man: I, Mohandas Gandhi, am a man, and you, Lord Viceroy, are a man. Over and over again he extended his smiling, patient, eager invitation to the battle, until many a representative of abstract power learned in panic that one could take no abstract measures against so concrete a human being.

Satyagraha worked. For all that might be said in qualification—that the British Empire conspired in its success, having been vulnerable to opinion, or that it yielded not to *Satyagraha* but to its own internal pressures; that *Satyagraha* might have worked better without Gandhi who, on at least two occasions, called off the movement, as it was reaching full effectiveness, in punishment for minor infractions of the rule against violence; that Gandhi neither aided nor interfered with the historical outcome, the events of which took place on their own level, without reference to his values—all the same, *Satyagraha* worked. In a country so deviceless as India, this poor device must appear an inspiration; it converted every weakness—ignorance, disease, religious fear, and superstition—into a national resource. And much of the credit for its success, however qualified, belongs to Gandhi's shrewdness as a politician. He had the insight to incorporate a material demand in every one of his spiritual principles (whether in the handy strategy of the Khadar movement for the wearing of homespun cloth, or the heroic "March to the Sea" to break the British salt laws, in principle, the whole struggle for *Swaraj*, self-rule, had long before been privately carried out by Gandhi); and this was not so much politics as nature, for he had always practiced a kind of materialism in relating his spiritual experiments to daily life. Moreover, the moral success of *Satyagraha* was assured at the outset. Self-realization through politics—with this desire, Gandhi brought life into a field that stinks of death. For this alone, may the God whom he never succeeded in seeing face to face keep his name alive.

But who ever heard of such a thing? Politicians have hobbies, they paint, collect stamps; they "go in" for self-realization in the manner of the middle class, home from the office. The self does not exist on the job.

Political realities and the realities of the self are absolutely opposed. From the perspective of the self, politics is unreal, and the more closely it approaches the level of *Realpolitik*, the more it becomes an illusion. Gandhi's politics had less than any other man's to do with bureaucracies, papers, and laws; it consisted of personal realities. Still, this unique practice did not succeed. Politics was not the way of self-realization; it was Gandhi's defense against knowing himself.

It is remarkable that someone with so high an ego-ideal, and so unsparing of himself as Gandhi, should have remained so blind to the most obvious traits of his own character. But if he had discovered, say, the power aspects of his asceticism, he would have been paralyzed. This must not happen, and to prevent it, he turned to politics. In politics one can always claim objective necessity for the personal act; it is a refuge from introspection and from too much truth. Now a man like Gandhi, committed to self-realization, but in no position to afford complete knowledge of himself, must have had some such reason (among others) for entering politics—to keep intact, and out of consciousness, the power of his ego regime. Self-realization, in the sense of knowledge, is impossible in politics.

But what is self-realization? *Gnothi seauton* ("know thyself") has given the West an extraordinary philosophical conceit. Self-realization must concern our deepest desire, and who will say this is to know ourselves? Gandhi, on the sly, bypassed Socrates; and even when he was clear of him, he tried to cover, through faith, a deficiency of knowledge. Politics was for him a branch of religion, and actually in religion he found self-realization, though it was characteristic of him to seek it in every part of life. But before speaking of his religious life, we must consider our psychological assumptions.

Thus far we have been examining in Gandhi's case the operation of a psychological system whose purpose was the aggrandizement of the ego by indirect means, which it achieved by converting self-denial into power. One could go on indefinitely showing the articulation of this system without gaining any new insight. The psychology of the ego has its limits, and once it has demonstrated the particular principle by which experience is made to serve the self, its work is done. Such analysis is exhaustive only when, in the given subject's life, there is nothing beyond the self and the self-regarding values.

It would be a mistake to argue that Gandhi, or any other man with mystical and religious impulses as deep as his, was such a thoroughgoing egotist. It is far simpler to grant some autonomy to the religious life, freeing it, to that extent, from service to power, and to admit that some of the things a man gives to God may have no strings attached. The difficulty in trying to make the whole world revolve about the ego with its power impulses (the so-called "will-to-power" philosophies) is that, as in Ptolemaic astronomy, too many complicated epicycles become necessary to account for apparent motion in other directions (e.g., an endless play upon selfless acts to show their selfish motivation, for nothing in this system, not even joy in natural beauty, can be selfless). A new center of explanation is needed if the religious life and related phenomena which do not easily fit the power system are to have any reality of their own; and here it is precisely the psychoanalytic perspective that would release the spiritual from subservience to the practical, by basing it on independent ground in sexuality.

I shall assume that Gandhi's sexual energy, which found no direct expression after he had taken the vow of *Brahmacharya* in his middle thirties, did not entirely go to work for his ego. (To assume, with the concept of sublimation, that it did so go to work, is to land once more among the epicycles of ego psychology. Other reasons for discarding the concept in Gandhi's case, I shall mention later.) Some part of his sexuality must have remained free, and it was this free energy which found mystical expression in his religious life. Here one must follow Freud and Reich in their interpretation of the dominant mystical symbolism, the yearning for union with God, as a sign of sexual longing.

In this hunger for instinctual satisfaction lies the genuine capacity for self-realization beyond the ego, beyond the power principle; the sexual drive is anyway deeper than the ego's and in some part independent of it—the more so with the ascetic, who has all along given it no place among the activities of the self. But there must be a "descent into hell" in every such life; shamed, despised, and avoided, sex becomes the condition of salvation. Only when denied sexuality breaks through in religious form is it possible for the ascetic to achieve self-transcendence. In posing the mystical ideal of *Moksha,* for union with God, he has already established contact, albeit round-about, with the sexual forces. So much of life is restored to him; and as the long repressed sexual desire grows, so grows also its conscious, and only possible, representation: the desire for dissolving union with the divine. Both "hell" and "heaven" have this in common—that there, and only there, is the dissolution of the self accomplished; in the sexual orgasm, and in the standing face to face with God.

The depth of Gandhi's religious feeling must not be underestimated. Without his religious life, without his submerged sexuality deeply at work, he would indeed have been life-hater and crank, the mere eccentric. But he had his center, the same center round which India's serious spiritual experiments have always turned. It was his long-ing for sexual gratification represented by *Moksha* that connected him with life, and the form this longing took that placed him, whether or not he wanted the honor, among the saints.

It is necessary to remember that Gandhi was a per-fectly centered man, directly in the heart of a spiritual tradition. Only so can we rid ourselves of the notion that, in spite of what his contemporaries say, he must have been flinty and severe. His irreducible severities, the arrogant humility, the failure to feel for others stand, and are not to be explained away. But what requires explanation now, as a final contradiction restores to the man all the joy of life he would seem to have sacrificed to the ego-ideal, is the fact with which we began: the delightful smile, the infectious laugh, the radiation of lightheartedness. How does a man who followed such a difficult way of priva-tion and suffering, so far from the course of sexual satis-faction our psychology must prescribe, attain this peace? I take it for granted the smile is genuine, not a mask of bitterness. He could not, wearing a mask, bring a breath of fresh air with him and lighten the atmosphere when he entered a room, nor could he suggest anything child-like and full of charm.

Gandhi's centrality brings to mind one answer: he did not go his way alone as the neurotics do who deny themselves without reason in an increasing ignorance, misery, and loneliness; he had the Indian solidarity to draw on, of martyrs and religious men, among whom he found a precedent and a reason for each intimate detail of his conduct of life. The smile thus acquires the joy of an accomplished work, a work which has dignity and social value. But how is this acquisition made; how does any way of life in accord with an ideal, and opposed to nature, so secure its values as to seem natural?

This question seems to me the most difficult of all, for it leads us into a direct confrontation with the whole man, Gandhi, with the theme, so to speak, of his life, instead of the partial phrases that are comparatively easy to follow. Every life has a theme, and the theme of the great life raises questions, to answer which one must advance the actual frontiers of knowledge. It is a simple enough matter to follow anyone's career in the broad, rough encounters with the world that make up the province of egotism; even to go one step further and find in sexuality a principle beyond the ego, applicable to the understanding of the religious life, is no very original accomplishment, as the course had been marked by Freud and in recent years gone over repeatedly. But to go beyond that, in analysis as in life, is as hard as it is rare. It is precisely this in which Gandhi's greatness lies, and in which he has few peers: that he performed a basic operation on life, converting everything natural to the ideal with such success that in his case one must almost create a special category—this life of artifice and regulation by the will represents a new species of nature. It need not come to this, for the measure of other such wonderful things has always, in time, been found. But we stand too close to Gandhi, and perhaps the knowledge on which we must rely is also too young an instrument. For all the work that has been done in psychology and the various departments of social science, a clear theory of culture and character in their influence upon each other is still lacking. But every day in works of art, particularly in the symbolism of religious productions, and more commonly, in our ordinary intercourse with people we love, we see this connection, a streaming into each other of life and value in a single experience. No hypothesis of social science has yet been worth (perhaps never will be) a single moment of the experience in which this connection is found, however vaguely.

We are bound to look for the contribution a man's culture makes to his life; and let us suppose a closer continuity between character and culture than has hitherto been imagined, an actual *physical* contact, in the hope of understanding Gandhi. That India has traditionally been the home of the great ascetics, the fakirs and saints, is platitude, but a fresh truth can be forced out of it. Let us suppose that a special environment can, somehow (but *how?*), raise man's pretense to the life of pure spirit to a higher degree of reality (to the degree, at least, that the usual skepticism of spiritual claims as a system of deceits and rationalizations must be abandoned). Now spirituality may have a neurotic as well as a hypocritical connotation; the latter falls away in our supposition, the former remains. Neurotic is neurotic the world over, even where it represents standard behavior: it is a way of life (Gandhi's is the supreme example) in which sexual satisfaction is impossible. In a culture like our own an unequivocal value cannot be assigned to neurosis, for the culture itself is contradictory with respect to sex, urging its members on in a riot of stimulations, while it upholds conventional and moral restraints and taboos. But in the India at least of Gandhi's childhood and youth a homogeneous accretion of value to neurosis must have been possible. The mere existence of such a thing in India as Yoga (not that Gandhi was a Yogi, though he may have practiced some of its exercises), and the fact that Yoga enjoyed prestige, was enough to give security to the ascetic's task and absorb his neurosis into the religious atmosphere.

This relationship between man and culture is not a haphazard one. In India it has worked itself out in a startlingly detailed and organized way, as an illustration from the Yoga system of breathing may show. It has been noted that a disturbance of breathing, with the chest held in a high, fixed, inspiratory position, failing to move with exhalation, is typical of many neurotics (cf. Wilhelm Reich, *Character Analysis, The Function of the Orgasm*). The purpose of this is apparently to deaden bodily feelings, a convenient unconscious device in a society where natural sex behavior meets disapproval. Now in Yoga the same mechanism is consciously developed, for the same purpose—to deaden bodily feelings and prepare the way for disembodiment of spirit, the so-called "perception of immateriality." The exercises of Yoga would seem to be a training of the nervous system to complete the process of withdrawal from life which every neurotic unconsciously carries out on his own. It is a comment on the culture as a whole that a religious discipline should have such deep insight into the problem of psychophysical unity, and strike on such an effective way of establishing its values within its adherents. The contact between character and culture is so much more intimate than it is in the West, with our traditional dualism, which has been almost wholly determined by religion.

The significant point toward the solution of the problem raised by Gandhi's life is that a culture whose values can find direct, physical representation can be counted on to provide a rerouting of the repressed sexual energies through some form other than mere neurotic symptom formation. Nothing can make a man feel so much at home in the world as to realize that not only the role he has created for himself has value for his time, but that his very being, his whole underground, unconscious, instinctual life also belongs, in its most private aspect, without shame, to the universe of man. There is bound to be joy in this, and an end of the usual loneliness.

Obviously, we are dealing with something far beyond

the reach of sublimation; this mechanism would at best account for the appearance of sexual energy in some substitute form or activity, but not for its spontaneous emergence as the joy of life. In Gandhi's case we may have to consider the possibility of "transublimation," a sublimation that does return to the original goal—and though this shifts to the second word the difficulty of the first, the suggestion of transcendence is relevant. One may expect that somehow in the life he led, extraordinarily integrated with his culture, the cultural forms— singularly concrete things of body and nerve and sexual representation—poured back into him the energy he spent in quest of *Moksha.* Certainly this energy undergoes a transfusion as the man becomes one with his ideal; the principles take on life and flow through his veins; the ideal world is conquered by an act of submission, a complete surrender in the body to the claims of spirit. But the remarkable thing is that this energy also remained unchanged. From its first transformation into a spiritual value it ascended through a curving hierarchy to come back to itself: what began with nature returned to nature. This should be sufficient for *Moksha.*

And perhaps Gandhi did achieve *Moksha* after all. Part of the definition he somewhere gave of this term was that of a state in which the distinction between action and contemplation disappears; a man who has achieved it and contains all in himself, the contradictions resolved, need only contemplate, and from the contemplation the action will flow of itself. Gandhi's contemplation was active, it had a tremendous attractive force; so much so, that it may not be stretching a point too far to say he attained the kind of mythical existence the great characters of literature enjoy, whose essence is their whole existence.

But there is time for the myth. The actual man, the physical Gandhi, still confronts us, and his example is strongly persuasive. But of what? Can culture really become nature? How does a man go against life and return to it, distorted but whole, with the satisfactions that failed in the beginning marvelously restored? There is something mythical, nevertheless, about this journey; I cannot explain it; the last step in the transaction between character and culture is missing, at least in my own understanding. What we cannot explain is a mystery. This, the living, childlike smile, so unlike the smile of the Sphinx, and yet of the same enormous silence, is for me the mystery of Gandhi.

Commentary, August, 1950

✑Reflections on Orwell

I. Gentleman George

IT IS STRANGE that the fair, bland, decent, fresh-butter wholesome Orwell of the essays should have been such a terror in his fiction. One after another, the heroes of his novels come in for a thorough shellacking, a savage going-over hideous to behold; such, at least, is the lot of the central characters of *Burmese Days*, *Coming Up for Air*, *1984*, and *Keep the Aspidistra Flying*. This violence is quite uncalled for; his Florys, George Bowlings, Winstons, and Gordons are ordinary men, neither conspicuously noble nor *sale type*. As far as I can see, his only grievance against them was that they did not measure up to the old-school definition of a gentleman. This remark may seem a bit unfair, as Orwell was always riding charges against old-school stuffiness—not in the manner of a St. George, but in a casual and unpretentious way, flying only the colors of human decency.

But he was ahead of his age in being conservative, and this quality of his went largely unnoticed during his lifetime; he combined the gentlemanly with the democratic, an oxymoron typical of conservatism. Orwell detested the snobbery and class ground on which the definition of the gentleman stood, but the concept itself was a different matter, and in the greater part of his literary career he behaved in perfect accordance with it. Hence the fairness, the unassuming and disarming honesty of the writing, which we have come to regard as characteristic. Nor was the gentlemanly, as Orwell entertained it, such a narrow notion. The gentleman was for him the private citizen and irreducible unit of social life, more or less as John Stuart Mill thought of him, the free man of free mind and cultivation, whose continued existence was essential to the health of a democracy. Taken in this large sense, the idea was by no means inconsistent with Orwell's socialism.

In *Keep the Aspidistra Flying*, Gordon Comstock, thirtyish, a poet with a "slim volume" to his credit entitled *Mice* (good press, bad sales, soon remaindered), chooses the life of poverty and failure in preference to a career in copywriting (for which, unfortunately, he has more talent than for poetry). He makes this choice for the sake of his writing, to keep himself free of the success drive, but in so doing he also stages the usual young man's rebellion against the middle-class expectations of his family. To his disgust, he discovers that it was all in vain. If success is a swindle, so is failure.

Living in furnished bedrooms, under nosy landladies, working at miserable jobs in dusty bookstores, he is too demoralized, too tired and lonely at night to do his writing, and too poor for beer and cigarettes, let alone amusements. His life is in no way more liberal than that of his drab, dull, penny-pinching family, and the same gloom hangs over him as hangs over his self-sacrificing spinster sister, off whom he sponges. Short on principles, he makes himself a martyr for his living conditions, and blames all his misfortunes on money. The literary world snubs him because he is a pauper, women are indifferent for the same reason, and if his own girl, Rosemary, has been holding out on him for years—for what other reason can she refuse him than his poverty? When she finally does sleep with him, it is out of pity and disgust for the hopelessly roach-ridden, torn-shirt, dirty-neck, who-gives-a-damn condition into which he has fallen. But as the result of this single act (and him too poor to buy contraceptives!) she becomes pregnant. Then Gordon, backed into a corner, takes the job in the advertising agency and does right by the girl. But his first official step as a husband is to buy an aspidistra. This house plant had always been to him the abhorrent symbol of middle-class domesticity—as much as to say, "He loved Big Brother."

I have heard it said that this is a false interpretation; that Gordon, far from being the sniveler and weakling I take him to be, must be understood as something of a hero of our time. At the last moment, just as he is teetering on the brink of the inane, with the cliff crumbling away at his feet, he rights himself, comes to his senses, puts away childish things and chooses life, responsibility, and maturity. This is an attractive interpretation, and I am tempted to agree with it because it fits so well my own point about the conservative element in Orwell. Moreover, one of the central symbols of the novel, Rosemary's pregnancy, does yield up such a meaning (among other meanings, however). But the reasons for withholding consent seem to me too strong to allow such a reading. The preliminary indictment of Gordon is too heavy, and the evidence against him is presented without mercy. We see him in every last, sickening detail of his folly, without a single ambiguous touch that one might interpret to his credit. Nor does Rosemary's pregnancy carry much hope for him. He does the right thing, but his decision is not the result of right thinking—he never has, and never acquires, the courage or intelligence to understand himself. His style of living will improve, he will wear clean shirts and eat well-balanced meals, but the regenerative meaning cannot reach him. He has been presented as the sort of creature who not only invites but deserves his misfortunes; it is too late to save him. The pattern is so well established that the life symbol of the pregnancy is wasted on him—the child is the final springing of the trap. Not only success, not only failure, life itself is a swindle.

I return to my first observation, that Orwell was always mauling his characters. Here, I believe, lay his failure as a novelist; not that he was brutal, but that he did not justify his brutality in fictional terms. There is no good reason for walloping Gordon, or Flory, or the others. Their only offense, as far as I can see, is that they were not gentlemen. They lacked the grace, strength, resourcefulness, dignity, good sense, and clear understanding; neither nature nor society would bend to them or receive them among the elect. Modern fiction is full of such types, but Orwell, evidently, was unable to leave the shabby, poor bloke alone; I suspect he felt put on the spot when he confronted him. The reminiscences which Orwell's friends have published show him forever struggling with, and striving to kill off, his own gentlemanly ideal. The contradiction in himself is matched in the characters. He deliberately chose the bloke, the sniveler, the man who cannot make it, and to hell with the gentleman—and then punished them cruelly for not being gentlemen.

But why pick on Gordon? Many a dead horse has been flayed, this one was skinless to begin with. Because he makes all the better a carcass for his author's self-destructive appetite to feed upon.

Because such a procedure is unjustified in fiction, Orwell soon leads us out of bounds; and I, for one, could never resist speculating on his self-destructiveness. I know very little about him, and I can't say how accurate my impression is, but under the bland, fair, mild, empirical, and fair-minded manner which he perfected in the essays, I feel he was full of self-hatred, rage, spite, and contempt. This is no reason for disapproving of a novelist, so long as the personal motive is well covered. In Orwell it was usually uncovered, it showed through the devices of his fiction and called attention to himself when he should have been most in control to direct attention to his characters. Their undoing became an obvious substitute for his own, and one smarted and felt uncomfortable—a relationship to an author which it is hard to pass off as literary.

Even so, this would not have mattered—and in *1984*

it was of little importance—if only he had been able, more often, to find an appropriate fictional object to stand in for himself and receive the assault. For there are ways of conducting the flagellation so that the ego, to all appearances, is spared; one can, for instance, turn the self inside out and convert it into a world, or find cause, among public objects, for one's secret discontent. This he succeeded in doing in *1984*, where a world is present; Winston goes down, but the totalitarian mystique goes with him. In the other novels, too little of the world is involved in the destruction of the hero. And in *Keep the Aspidistra Flying* he drags down the drain with him nothing more than a few dried pips and peels of a somewhat off-center antibourgeois tirade: a desiccated family, a spinsterish sister, a sisterish girl friend, and a wealthy and therefore uneasy socialist and literary patron, one Ravelston, who befriends Gordon and makes him feel all the more disgusted with himself. It is Gordon all the way, and therefore Orwell all the way. And wherever Gordon can't quite completely symbolize his author's *Selbstmord* (after all, Orwell *was* a gentleman, and no Gordon by a long shot), Ravelston fills in for him. Anything that won't fit Gordon will slip easily and without pinch onto Ravelston's foot.

Now this is nonsense, and terribly dated, like the old adolescent rebellion against shoe polish. In a much sounder and more honest investigation of poverty, *Down and Out in Paris and London,* Orwell told the truth about the self in the middle-class world, how one lives in it under the threat of starvation and resorts to devices to outwit the wolf—devices, more often than not, shameful and desperate, but still part of the dirty business of staying alive in a dirty world. He did not have to wear a stinking shirt by way of a Gordon in false pride, and even falser self-punishment, for his ability to come to terms with this world (this is, however, an accurate touch in the characterization of Gordon, since nothing galls the writer in advertising more than the recognition that he's good at it). No, he would have loved a clean shirt, clean linen, a bath, a decent living, and a circle of his peers. But in *Down and Out* Orwell was writing in his characteristic mien of fairness to all, himself included, and he made no bones about his reasonableness. He condoned his own failure to be a gentleman or—it comes to the same thing—managed to forgive himself for being one.

Commentary, June, 1956

II. Decency and Death

IN AN ARTICLE ON Arthur Koestler, written in 1944, George Orwell complained that no Englishman had as yet published a worthwhile novel on the theme of totalitarian politics—nothing to equal *Darkness at Noon* —"Because there is almost no English writer to whom it has happened to see totalitarianism from the inside." Five years later, with the publication of *1984* he had become the one exception. He had not in the interval gained any more intimate an acquaintance with the subject; the year he spent fighting with the POUM in the Spanish Civil War was his closest approach to it. The success of *1984* must therefore be attributed to his imagination. But this is precisely the quality in which all his previous work had been weakest.

Orwell was fair, honest, unassuming, and reliable in everything he wrote. These qualities, though desirable in every writer, are specifically the virtues of journalism; and Orwell, it seems to me, had always been at his best, not in the novels or political articles, but in casual pieces of the kind he wrote for the *London Tribune* in his column, "As I Please." He was a writer in a small way—a different matter from the minor writer, to whose virtuosity and finesse he never aspired. This lack of literary manner enabled him to give himself directly, if sometimes feebly, to the reader; he held back his feelings (even in his account of the Stalinists' responsibility for the Barcelona street fighting in *Homage to Catalonia,* his anger does not rise above the note of "You don't do such things!")

but only in the manner of restraint, and there was nothing hypocritical or false about him. He had all the traditional English virtues, of which he made the traditional compression into one: decency. When he died, I felt as many of his readers who never knew him must have done, that this was a friend gone.

Down and Out in Paris and London, one of his earlier books, is the steady Orwell who underwent no apparent development. Recorded here are some of the worst days of his life when he was unemployed, broke, and starving. But the tone is substantially the same as that of the article on boys' weeklies in *Dickens, Dali & Others.* The Eton graduate and former Burma policeman accepts dishwashers and tramps as his fellow men without condescension and with only a little squeamishness at the filth of his surroundings. He makes no effort to bend his prose to the sounding of lower depths, and he was to feel no need to make a special adjustment to the language and problems of political journalism when he returned to England to gain some recognition as a writer. Detached yet close observation, dryness, a stamping out of whatever may once have been the snob in him (yet never at the expense of the Englishman) and the correlated stubborn attachment to common sense, to which he sometimes sacrificed his insight—this made up his basic journalistic style, unchanged through the years.

In *Burmese Days,* first published a year later in 1934, there is considerable bitterness as Orwell expresses his disgust with the Indian Civil Service. This is hardly the same man writing. For once he is full of contempt, especially toward his hero, John Flory, though the latter happens to be the only "decent" character in the novel— he is not bigoted as the rest of the whites, he does not have the Imperial attitude, he is humane toward the natives. Yet he is a weakling, he gives way to alcoholism and the unrelieved colonial ennui, and he is incapable of withstanding the corrupt moral pressure of his colleagues; Orwell cannot forgive him this. His attitude toward this character—in whom there must have been a good deal of himself—is neither completely personal nor detached, and here Orwell betrays a fault which, until 1984, was to remain his greatest as a novelist, a fault of imagination, in not knowing what to do with a character, once the main traits and the setting have been provided. (The Burmese jungle, the character of the natives, their attitude toward the swinish pukka sahibs, the dances and festivals, the pidgin and official English were all excellently reported.) Flory, for all the significance a socialist writer might have given such a characterization, falls into the useless, unimaginative category of the weak liberal—anybody's whipping boy. The only interesting thing in his treatment of him is that it is so thoroughly bad-mannered; the mild Orwell makes not the slightest effort to spare his contempt for the man and ends by having him commit suicide, and the masochistic suggestion which this carries links Flory, however vaguely, with the ultimate characterization of the political hero (Winston Smith) as he who undergoes infinite degradation. Otherwise one is still unprepared for *1984*.

Coming Up for Air, written in 1938, reverts to the journalistic style of ease and understatement, the disquietude of *Burmese Days* worked out of it. But this does not do the novel much good, as it fails to catch the anxiety of the prewar days. The hero, George Bowling, running out on his job and family for a breather before the war which he knows is coming, refers to himself as a typical middle-aged suburban bloke, and Orwell, for the greater part of the book, is satisfied to treat him at this level. But his concern with politics had apparently been getting ahead of his style. Where Orwell's sense of politics in *Burmese Days* was of little more than incidental value, in *Coming Up for Air* it has become the source of the whole book. This, together with the continuing weakness of the novelist's imagination, accounts for such passages as the one in which Bowling, inspecting the shot motor of his car, compares it to the Austro-Hungarian Empire. Moreover, Orwell's politics suddenly appears to be out of joint. (A pity that it had not been more so. It is sometimes an advantage for a political writer to lose his grasp of politics, for the unreality of his observations brings him so much nearer to experience. But this, too, had to wait till *1984*.) Bowling's holiday consists in a return to his boyhood village, which he finds unrecognizably overgrown with factories and ugly housing developments. The values of his youth, Bowling realizes, have vanished for good. But this feeling is presented in such strength, it subverts the politics to a conservative tone. The decency which Orwell had linked, at one level, with the Socialist movement, in which he saw its only chance of surviving, now seems to belong entirely to the laissez-faire days preceding the first World War with their unshaken social traditions, the slower pace, the less highly developed technology. This again may be merely a failure of imagination, Orwell at as great a loss to know what to do with a theme as with a character; but it also suggests that the failure came of a division deep in him. He was a radical in politics and a conservative in feeling.

Though he continued to write his political articles and casual pieces in the same informal and disarming style, as though nothing were happening, his feelings were getting the better of him. This, though I have no evidence for it, I must suppose to be the case on the strength of the fact that he was for many years a sick, and during the writing of *1984*, a dying, man. His style, the character of the man, did not allow conflicts to appear at the surface, which had to remain undisturbed. He kept on writing in the easy manner that disarmed the reader of any suspicion of conflict, remaining empirical and optimistic all the time that he was turning over a metaphysics of evil.

A dying man, one may expect, will find consistency his last concern. Death exempts him from his own habits as much as it does from responsibility to others. Life being what it is in our world, the onset of death is often the first taste a man gets of freedom. At last the imagination can come into its own, and as a man yields to it his emotions take on a surprising depth and intensity. The extreme situation in which Orwell found himself as the

rapid downhill course of tuberculosis approached enabled him for the first time to go from one extreme to
the other: from his own sickness to the world's. His
imagination, set free, was able to confirm the identity of
the two extremes, turning sickness into art.

The torture scenes in *1984* have been compared with
The Legend of the Grand Inquisitor. The comparison
seems to me forced; a better one, it applies to the novel
as a whole, is with Ippolit's "Essential Explanation" in
The Idiot. The torturer O'Brien's words to Winston
Smith as he is re-educating him, "The objective of power
is power," are the equivalent, in what they reveal to
Smith of a politics stripped bare of morality, of Ippolit's
nightmare of the monstrous insect, representing the world
of nature without God. That the objective of power is
power may long have been obvious to some men, but
for the restrained writer who had muffled the terror and
disgust politics produced in him, who had held onto a
socialist rationale and let out his antipathies in an exaggerated idyll of the conservative past—for him such
words had a deeper meaning. They mark the end of
decency. Decency, meaning precisely the reserve of Orwell's own character, the constitutional intolerance of
the extreme course, has failed him. Now he is dying.
What good has this withholding done? He turns, like
Ippolit, against himself, with the cry, not of glad tears
of release, but of the jealousy of life, "I have been
cheated!" And now the decent man, Winston Smith, is
unremittingly punished for the loss. He is given neither
an opportunity for redemption nor even the small comfort
of dying with his inner life intact. His end must be beyond the last extreme, a species of pure diabolism: it is
to the embrace of Big Brother that Orwell steers him,
one of the most hideous moments of revenge in literature.

It is beside the point to argue that this revenge is the
Party's, which will not allow its victims to die un-
repentant, or that Orwell was merely following the "confessions" of the Stalinist trials. These arguments are
true, but it is also true that Winston (named, if uncon-

sciously, to honor his conservative principle) was too close to Orwell for his torturer to be an entire stranger. So close a vengeance is always taken on oneself.

The significant point is that Winston yields. The force to which he is subjected is overwhelming, any man would crack. Yet in novels all actions are willed; the force that seems to break the will is in reality the rationalization of its action. Winston's breakdown covers a multiple suicide. There is first of all Orwell's own suicide, committed, according to the reports one hears, in the course of writing the novel and in the year that followed, when he neglected his health and remained active, though with two best-sellers he must have had the means for a change of climate and complete rest. Winston's yielding is reminiscent also of Ippolit's suicide, which the consumptive bungled only that his death might occur as so much the greater an indignity. There is defiance in this indignity, deliberately sought. Both Winston and Ippolit rebel against a world in which everything is possible, in which 2+2 no longer equal 4—by yielding. The defiance is marked by the extent of the yielding. Though Winston hasn't even a squeak of defiance left, so much the more defiant is it, as though he were to say, "Take away my last shred of decency, will you? Then here—take everything. Here's lungs and liver, mind and heart and soul!" Everything goes, nothing is saved. "He loved Big Brother."

This is Orwell finally yielding up the life-long image, the character and style and habits of reason and restraint. I cannot conceive of a greater despair, and if it falls short of the magnificent it is only because Orwell was not a genius. But the mild journalist had at last attained art, expressing the totalitarian agony out of his own, as no English writer had done. He encompassed the world's sickness in his own: in this way, too, it may happen to a man to see totalitarianism "from inside." Whether Orwell's vision was true or false, consistent or not, or even adequate to reality, is a separate question, and not, it seems to me, very important in his case. All that matters is the force of the passion with which the man, who began as a writer in a small way, at last came through. The force with which he ended is the one with which greatness begins. This force, it will be observed, was enough to kill a man.

~ A Farewell to Hemingway

IT IS NOT ENOUGH to say that *Across the River and Into the Trees* is a bad novel, which nearly everyone has said (the fact is, a good deal of it is trash), or to ascribe its failure to Hemingway's playing Hemingway. Such judgments fail to go deep; they make an artificial separation between the man and the artist, and attribute to the former, as though these were superficial mistakes, shortcomings which are the very essence of Hemingway's art. It seems to me that no writer of comparable stature has ever expressed in his work so false an attitude toward life. Now this is more than a matter of temperament, though the pompous boasting, the sounding off on life, love, and literature in baseball, prize-ring, and military metaphors (the purpose of which is to demonstrate that Hemingway is so great a literary figure that he is primarily an athlete, a hunter, a soldier, a lover of fine wines and women—anything but a writer; this is what I consider trash) that run all through this book do help to create the impression that Hemingway has gone on a bender and deserted his art. But these monkeyshines are defenses, and to ignore the serious principle while criticizing Hemingway's legend of himself is to succumb to the strategy: at the expense of the man, to flatter the art.

It is easy to understand how Hemingway took hold of our imagination. The characters he created of the lost generation gave us an image of ourselves which we were glad to accept; it was a true image, and in the long run, ennobling. With considerable courage, he continued the work of realism in judging an old social order whose wars were not of our making, and for the wreck of whose values we were not responsible. Jake and his friends did not run out on life, they were pushed out; the separate peace which Frederic Henry concluded was the only sensible thing to do, and only the reactionary and the philistine would blame him for it. These characters, in their main outlines, were seen as the result of external force; the action of the world on them was recorded in the form of a wound. They were helpless. The drinking and the promiscuity were not to their liking. They were Puritan (which is to say, American) enough to hate themselves for it, and too Puritan to burn out the self-hatred. It was only on holiday—from the war, from their life in Paris after the war—that they had the chance to take their real pleasures, the few that weren't spoiled for them. These were simple pleasures after all—in *A Farewell to Arms,* a love affair, and in *The Sun Also Rises,* fishing, a trip to Spain. It is especially in the Spanish passages, celebrating Basque landscape and character, that Hemingway restores to his heroes a sense of value and participation in life, and he does so even with warmth, which, considering his fear of sentiment, makes this evocation of the might-have-been a generous thing for him. The rituals of the bullfight have only private meaning; nevertheless, Hemingway derived from them the good news he had to give his generation, the virtue of grace under pressure. The only plea he made for his characters—the argument is implicit in the action —is that they have or at least once had the capacity to give themselves; if they no longer do so, it is because they have been wounded.

It was only natural that a whole generation should seize on the wound in justification of itself. The success myth, as the not yet successful Hemingway had the insight to observe, was overthrown, and nothing besides the wound had offered itself. He had no false comfort to give and he told, as far as it went, the truth. It was not the time to examine this argument closely; to do so would have seemed like compromising with society. It passed unnoticed that Hemingway himself was offering a compromise; not the kind the world desired or which it even recognized. All the same, in the character structure which he gave his heroes—an entity by itself, which we now call "the Hemingway character"—the old values were never seriously questioned, and such clichés as manliness, courage, and self-reliance remained unchanged. There is no objection to these values as such; the objection is to the meaning society has given them. Hemingway never examined their social meaning; he merely cut the traditional world of application out from under these values and put something unexpected in its place. He did not tell the lost generation to go out and in the name of these values sell, conquer, succeed, or otherwise overwhelm the world. He did tell it, in so many words, in his books and in the concomitant legend of himself, to attack and refashion itself in character, to be, precisely, self-reliant, courageous, and manly—in a word, hard. It is here that he has been a misleading influence on a whole generation of American writers and their audience; and while he is not to be blamed for the army of imitators that has followed him or made (not without his example) an alliance, through the hard-boiled tradition, with bad taste, he is to be judged for what he himself has done. He has created his own subsection of the Myth of the American Male, supporting everything in this myth which is lifeless, vicious, and false—the contempt for women and for every tender feeling, as for something effeminate and corrupt, the apotheosis of the purely forceful, tense, and thrusting component of maleness as a phallic bludgeon to beat the female principle into submission, the perpetual adolescence of the emotions with its compensatory heroics to cover a fear, and consequent hatred, of sexual love; and this, not as a lapse from his art, but in its best practice.

In Hemingway's work there has always been a great lag between characterization and expression; the lives and characters of his heroes are set down to mean one thing, but they express something entirely different, frequently the opposite. Hemingway's men are hard, they contain their emotions; so runs their title to manliness. They contain their emotions because of a natural dignity and restraint, and this restraint becomes all the more appropriate as the strength of the emotion increases; it is only the trivial feeling that one can afford to let out freely. This creates an expectation for the reader, of a piece with the strong silent types of popular fiction—"still waters run deep," and similar overevaluations of standard Anglo-Saxon behavior. The repetitious monosyllables of the dialogue, the closed self-sufficient gestures, are transformed by this dialectic into symbols of a heavy, pressing force, barely held back from explosion. A great passion, such as Frederic Henry presumably feels for Catherine, is indicated as follows (my italics):

> I could remember Catherine *but I knew I would get crazy if I thought about her when I was not sure yet I would see her, so I would not think about her, only about her a little,* only about her with the car going slowly and clickingly, and some light through the canvas and my lying with Catherine on the floor of the car.

Instead of the actual feeling for Catherine, this presents us with a blank; a blank which the reader obligingly fills in. So good are the credentials of this style, we honor it with our whole experience. But when it is read for itself, without the usual expectations, what this passage expresses (as does the tone in which Hemingway always writes of love) is not a man's longing for a woman— where a man really would "get crazy" and not "only . . . a little"—but his conscious suppression of that longing, which cannot have been very strong. Moreover, this suppression is made within a context of unconscious repressions, which show a fear of women, and defenses against sexuality and love.

The unconscious repression is expressed very clearly in an earlier passage of *A Farewell to Arms*. Frederic is about to risk an operation on his knee, which will either shorten his recuperation or leave him a cripple. Catherine spends the night with him in his hospital room.

That night a bat flew into the room through the open door that led onto the balcony and through which we watched the night over the roofs of the town. It was dark in our room except for the small light of the night over the town and the bat was not frightened but hunted in the room as though he had been outside. We lay and watched him and I do not think he saw us because we lay so still. After he went out we saw a searchlight come on and watched the beam move across the sky and then go off and it was dark again. A breeze came in the night and we heard the men of the anti-aircraft gun on the next roof talking . . . Once in the night we went to sleep and when I woke she was not there but I heard her coming along the hall and the door opened and she came back to the bed and said it was all right she had been downstairs and they were all asleep . . . She brought crackers and we ate them and drank some vermouth . . .

The expectation is that there will be a desperate tenderness in their love-making, that they will try to give each other what reassurance they can in face of the present anxiety; this expectation may color even a second reading of the passage. But all affects are eliminated. The scene expresses infantile fear of the dark, with the bat symbolizing the castration anxiety. (The superstition is that bats get in the hair and can be removed only by cutting off the hair. This maintains the castration anxiety centered in the wounded leg.) The conversation and the light from outside are expressive again at the infantile level, representing the comfort the child takes, in his lonely room, to feel the presence of grownups about the house. The whole passage expresses loneliness, though the lovers are with each other. Catherine's presence is not felt, and it is not her part as mistress in the love-making that provides reassurance, but rather her re-entrance in the guise of mother, bringing food in the night, when the child wakes alone.

If this reading seems at all farfetched, it is no more so than the presence in the room, at a time like this, of the bat itself. How else did the bat get into the room? Moreover, this reading is borne out by the conversation between Catherine and Frederic on the following morning (it is the same conversation whenever "Hemingway characters" try to express their tenderest feelings); they tinkle at each other, "Didn't we have a lovely time, darling? Didn't we have a lovely night?" There is never real contact between Hemingway's lovers; there is chatter, eating, drinking, and a lonely lying together. Nothing is deeply felt.

The style covers up this starvation with the honorific leanness. Dividing its skill between the suppression of feeling and the presentation of the clear, clean impression for which Hemingway is famous, it becomes a paraphrase of his philosophy, which considers emotion a disgraceful epiphenomenon, and holds a man to be most human when he is most like wood. This always happens. What was meant to be a full engagement with life turns out to be a fear of life. All the softer emotions having been eliminated from the character structure of his heroes, the capacity for love and surrender vanish for good, leaving no counterpart in the outer world. Reality is to be read only in terms of violent action, the only kind of which his characters are capable; the world is that which answers to a man's capacity for dealing a blow. The only possible contact in such a world is that of devouring, the only yielding, death. Behaviorism is the only psychology, sickness, the only norm. There is nothing in this scheme to allow for growth, development, education of the feelings, since these do not exist. Hemingway is therefore one of the most static of novelists. His characters either learn nothing or, like Harry Morgan and Robert Jordan with their great discovery that there is some connection between man and man, reach, at the very end, the usual starting point of the novel. Without this education, which is one of the basic patterns of life, there can be neither a great form nor a great subject in the novel. But in behaviorism there is nothing more to learn; once the reflex is conditioned, it is fixed.

If this were no more than a false philosophy and psychology, it would still be possible for Hemingway's art to succeed, in virtue of its own insight, unacknowledged in the doctrine. But this philosophy—as with all such anti-intellectualisms—is irrefutable. It has no theory, which one can correct by drawing the example from the practice; this is the practice. The philosophy is but another way of expressing the limitation and the falsehood of the art. It is only when Hemingway's style is freed of its defensive obligations that it reaches its best level, as when he writes of landscape and machines; there are no emotions to fend off with the latter, and with the former, the emotions are not suspect, since they have only symbolic reference to the feminine.

There is a critical problem in the disparity between Hemingway's direct treatment and his unintentional expression of character. What credit is he to receive for the compulsive masculinity, the guard raised against sentiment and all deep emotion, with the inevitable admission of sentimentality, which his characters show? I find this hard to answer. Even if we argue that these traits are not actually present in the characterization, but merely inferred from the behavior, the writer must still be given credit for presenting the material from which the inference is made. But when the author denies the inference, when he considers it vilification? It is a perfect irony to see Hemingway fight off the meanings which his critical audience attributes to him, the very meanings which give one reason to take his work seriously. He is as blind as Oedipus, but his blindness must also be taken seriously. This leaves criticism in a hopelessly ambiguous position. It is no better when we offer to divide the credit between the writer and audience. This is a bad precedent. It makes the writer so incomplete that his work must be supplemented from without, over his dead knowledge. The artist no longer leads the response; he is determined by it. He presents a blank, which his more sophisticated audience returns to him, filled with insight. But we cannot afford to have artists so heavily in debt to their audience. It destroys literature, reducing it to anagrams and doctors' theses. But isn't this substantially the case with Hemingway? This is only one respect in which

Hemingway, in his own work and through his imitators, has been a pernicious influence. For all these reasons, it seems to me that his reputation must soon decline, and while the excellent aspects of his style, at least in the earlier novels and some of the stories, the clear, clean writing that he does at his best, will retain their value, the deep moral significance that some critics (e.g., Cowley) have found or pretended to find in his attitude toward life has already begun to look like a hoax.

The curious thing about *Across the River* is that while it is his worst novel, in one respect—but only in this respect—it is an improvement over all the earlier work. For once the severed halves of the characterization are joined, and the conscious and unconscious images of the hero closely resemble each other.

Richard Cantwell, Col., Infantry, U.S.A., who has come to Venice for several days to see his mistress and shoot ducks, is a man of fifty with a weak heart. He has the same structure as the earlier characters, with the same ascription of the inner anxiety to external causes, and the same discharge of that anxiety through substitutive behavior. He exists for the most part in conversation. Hemingway's clipped dialogue, which had always served the purpose of direct characterization (and of reflecting the unintentional characterization by keeping affect to a minimum), has now been loosened somewhat; it has a more complicated function—that of reducing the character to an even further simplicity. The gap between consciousness and behavior is now completely closed; at least, there is no language left to express it, as the displacement of tension through physical behavior (in Cantwell's case, battle) has been read back into the character, where it becomes the basic language: ". . . his ruined hand searched for the island in the great river with the high steep banks . . . 'Just hold me tight and hold the high ground, too (this is the girl speaking) . . . Please attack gently and with the same attack as before.'" But now, though the hero is still meant to exemplify Hemingway's attitude toward life, he is presented as a sick man; he swallows pills all through the action, he must avoid excitement and strain, and he dies of a heart attack. (His mistress, the nineteen-year-old Italian countess Renata, a beautiful, wealthy, and adoring pot of duck soup, has also been carried a step further in an even more disastrous simplification. The Hemingway heroine has always been pure bitch, pure pal, or like Brett Ashley, two in one. With Renata, the bitch has been dropped, and the great effort of the pal to please her man, all for him, is now no effort at all; it comes naturally, as it would to a doll. The result is something like one of the waxworks in Villiers de l'Isle-Adam.) Cantwell has also a touch of the Shriner. He plays a game with the headwaiter of his hotel, complete with Secret Order, passwords, etc., and gladly interrupts his conversations with Renata, in which he treats her to encyclopedic pontifications, for a mystical pass or two with the *Gran Maestro*.

This may be a serious disintegration in the conception of character, a boring and pathetic attempt in and out of character to play the great man, but it is not a total loss. For once the hero, a man of the same cut and cloth as all the rest, is identified for what he is. The claims to universality are abandoned: Cantwell is not a figure of the lost generation, he is not the representative of something going on in our time, he is not learning through fatal experience what everyone with natural feeling knows to begin with, that no man is an island. He is a man on his own, lonely, grown old, demoted from the rank of General to nobody, in love or persuaded he is in love (there can never have been much difference for him) with a girl who may or may not exist (again no difference), prattling of war, of the good life and the true love with an unfeeling, monotonous, heartsick narcissism, not yet having learned what he is doing, having learned nothing from life, nothing beyond the one thing he knows now—that he is about to die. The defenses are down, the myth is overthrown. This is a poor sick bum, giving himself airs; as sick as all his brothers have been, and like them empty, compulsive, and deluded, incapable of love. But for once Hemingway knows his man and for once it is possible to believe in his hero for what he is. He has come home, ruined, to something like humanity, the humanity, at least, of self-betrayal. What he acts out and what he expresses in his action, for once, are one.

This is the most touching thing Hemingway has done. For all the trash and foolishness of this book, perhaps even because of it, because he let himself be lulled and dulled by the fable of himself, he gave away some of his usual caution and let a little grief, more than ordinarily and not all of it stuck in the throat, come through his careful style. A little of the real terror of life in himself, with no defenses handy, not even a propitiatory bull to offer in sacrifice, nothing to kill but the hero. And a little real courage, more than it takes to shoot lions in Africa, the courage to confess, even if it be only through self-betrayal, the sickness and fear and sad wreck of life behind the myth. Wish him luck.

Kenyon Review, Winter, 1951

❧ Faulkner's Two Styles

FAULKNER'S *Collected Stories* form a continuous commentary on the whole of his work. They do not make as clear a design as the excerpts in the Viking *Portable Faulkner,* but because there are more constants—locale, family, historical themes, character—in Faulkner's writing than in that of any other American novelist, a collection of his stories assembled on any principle is bound to give a fairly exact impression of the range and quality of his work. You have here the old Indian South, the South of the Civil War and earlier, the present-day South, and a few excursions Faulkner has made to other American regions and to Europe. The range of character is just as large, from the Indian chiefs, through his main Southern families, to the pilots and stunt fliers and students on a walking tour. Some of the stories bear a direct relation to the novels, in which they appear as episodes. Others are connected with the body of his work only through similarities of style. But whatever the degree of connection, this is, in all but one respect, the essential Faulkner whose work grows out of, turns round, and always comes back to, the basic themes of blood, land, and the fusion of the two in human character. The only aspect of his writing of which this collection does not give an adequate impression is the legend of the South that he has constructed, over and beyond the Southern reality—and it is to this legend that I should like to devote the space I have in this review to deal with Faulkner.

The paradox of William Faulkner is that the element

of greatness in his work is inseparable from his Southern qualities, but he does not write well in his main concern with the South, its history and legend. The virtues and defects of his writing are co-ordinate with two styles, which are almost always mixed. One is simple and full of references to nature; there is nothing to equal it in American writing today. It is in this style that he creates the plodding, patient, modest indestructible vitality of his Dilseys and Lena Groves, his perfect images. They owe their perfection to his love of them, and of the principle of life which they embody: their goodness is their profound submissiveness. Whatever you may think of this as a principle (I myself don't like it), it is necessary to concede the depth to which Faulkner carries it in his characterizations. (At times it virtually takes him out of American literature and into the nineteenth-century literary and political legend of the Russian peasant.) So also with his villains, the Popeyes and Jasons and Joe Christmases, whose villainy is a denial of this principle. The worst thing he can find to say about them is *depth-less*. They are the stiff-necked, the cheap, the mechanical, the cheats of life, which they think they can escape by refusing the rituals of yielding which the good folk perform daily. In this love and in this hatred, there is no one more open than Faulkner. He is unashamedly touching and simple, and he would certainly be a homiletic writer were it not for the fact that he is pointing up no trite morality. There is no morality at all in his sense of character; he constructs a good and evil without it, by-passing morality in his immediate feeling for life.

In illustration of this style, I present one of its best moments, a passage from *The Wild Palms* in the counter-pointed narrative, "Old Man," which describes the Mississippi in flood:

> It was as if the water itself were in three strata, separate and distinct, the bland and unhurried surface . . . screening as though by vicious calculation the rush and fury of the flood itself, and beneath this in turn the original stream, trickle, murmuring along in the oppo-

site direction, following undisturbed and unaware its appointed course. . . .

This is not only a description of flood; it is so excellent an analysis of nature that it contains also a schematism of human character structure, one which he has followed in all his work. Most likely Faulkner is unaware that this scheme corresponds exactly to that of Freud and Reich; as he may also be unaware of the original Lao-Tse who saw in water the symbol of the Tao. In Faulkner, also, but purely as instinct, the Tao and the Teh—the way of nature and of human character—are one. This is the element of greatness in his work.

In his other style, which dominates his writing, Faulkner constructs his legend of the South. It is here that all his famous traits are found: the rhetoric, the difficult, involved sentences, gratuitous and exaggerated, the tangle of meanings and motives. So little is left of the touching simplicity and openness, it is hard to believe that the same man writes in both styles. But neither is long present without the other, and even in his most thickly overgrown passages there is always, eventually, a clear space where the artist has been at work, with a skill perhaps more of woodcraft than of words, hacking, draining, clearing the ground. But again the forest closes in, and there are times when even Faulkner is a baffled guide.

This is not good writing; it is unfortunate that it takes up such a large and necessary part of his work. It seems to me necessary as a kind of concealment—this is the only probable motive for such bad writing in so good a writer. (Occasionally—as in *Absalom, Absalom!*—Faulkner's obscurity offers so exact a structural paraphrase of the human relationships in the narrative, it is no longer a defect but a literary necessity.) Faulkner writes poorly of the South (not of the people, the objects, the activities, the countryside, but of his own legend), his sentences like the paths of a maze, to wind and cross and stop dead —because he has to. Clarity about the legend of the South, as in *Intruder in the Dust,* is more than he can afford.

Strictly speaking, there is no legend of the South, not even in Faulkner, because the South is too much a part of the United States. It is just not different enough. The attempt to create a special legend always leads to an overexploitation of the differences in history, race, and culture betwen South and outland (Faulkner's term). Left to itself, this exploitation would die of a lack of resources. Sooner or later it must appear even to the most stubborn Southerner that these differences are not so great as he supposes, and nowhere nearly so significant; and if this is too optimistic an assumption, there is a limit, by way of natural death, which even these falsehoods must face. Say what you will about the deficiency of the liberal imagination, you cannot go on forever making an issue of homogeneous cultures and alleged differences between Negro and white, when none of these issues is real. Consequently, *legend*: a mode of belief that is supposed to exempt the believer from true and false.

But this is only the outer defense, thrown up merely at logic. There is no case for the legend even in imagination. It serves Faulkner only the purpose of defying the outland, and, within the South, the depthless Snopeses who have taken over and spoiled the old tradition; he seldom celebrates the tradition directly. The death of the old tradition is all that matters—one could not be a "Southerner" without it. The tradition is a convenient invention; it need never have been alive. And as a matter of fact, Faulkner believes only in its death: a Crucifixion without Nativity or Resurrection. The South becomes a state of mind with him, proud, anarchic, willfully archaic, a condition of virtue by default of the world. But he does not carry off this theme. For one thing, lacking almost entirely an intellectual culture, he has no way of enriching his theme, of making it sound necessary or convincing—and the reactionary impulse is lost without culture. Besides, his own gifts are more suited to destroy the legend than to perpetuate it. His vision is too violent to sustain the genteel dreams of an agrarian aristocracy. He does not hesitate to call the land accursed; the blood stain of slavery is still deep on it. This limits the romantic possibilities of the Southern past. Its present, even for Faulkner, is immediately in the world. He admits all the weaknesses of the South, its susceptibility to coke and chrome, nor does he pretend that the legend has in any way made it proof against the cheapness of modern life. This honesty, though admirable, is fatal to the legend. It is, like Quentin Compson's outcry, "I don't hate it! I don't hate it! I don't hate it!" an admission from which it is impossible to recover.

In the stories of this collection, the legend is only scantily developed, and while the simpler style has a better opportunity to speak for itself, something is lost without the desperate struggle between his two themes and his gigantic effort of will does not appear. But in a few of the stories he attains so high an art, one can hardly imagine the level his art might have reached had it not been forced to wear itself down in the hopeless inner struggle of most of the novels. By far the greatest story in the collection—it is also one of the greatest in our language—is "Red Leaves," which deals with the death of the Chickasaw chief Issetibbeha. Faulkner's deepest feeling for life is here engaged, and never dissipated, and following one another, with a compression unique for him, appear all the themes of doom and submission, which usually have a questionable ring within the context of his "South." But there is no false legend here. In the prehistory of his Indian narratives, his episodes have an extraordinary self-sufficiency, and his subjects an undiminished power, born without the trauma of the Civil War. His imagination, for once, is set free, it works out its own drama, without the need to plead or prove a superimposed case, and cover with impenetrable rhetoric the traces of a false argument. It is not too much to say that this story, like all his best writing, succeeds precisely because it is something Faulkner has written not about the South, but *over* it, over its dead body, in a moment of complete triumph. In these brief victories over the South he wins his greatness.

David Levinsky: The Jew
as American Millionaire

I HAD LONG AVOIDED *The Rise of David Levinsky* because I imagined it was a badly written account of
immigrants and sweatshops in a genre which—though
this novel had practically established it—was intolerably
stale by now. It is nothing of the kind. To be sure, it
is a genre piece, and excellence of diction and sentence
structure are not among its strong points; but it is one
of the best fictional studies of Jewish character available
in English, and at the same time an intimate and sophisticated account of American business culture, and it ought
to be celebrated as such.

The story is a simple one and fundamentally Jewish
in conception, as it consists of an extended commentary
on a single text, somewhat in the manner of Talmud.
This text is presented in the opening paragraph:

> Sometimes, when I think of my past . . . the meta-
> morphosis I have gone through strikes me as nothing
> short of a miracle. I was born and reared in the lowest
> depths of poverty and I arrived in America—in 1885—
> with four cents in my pocket. I am now worth more
> than two million dollars and recognized as one of the
> two or three leading men in the cloak-and-suit trade in
> the United States. *And yet . . . my inner identity . . .
> impresses me as being precisely the same as it was
> thirty or forty years ago. My present station, power,
> the amount of worldly happiness at my command, and
> the rest of it, seem to be devoid of significance.*

I have set in italics what I take to be the key sentences.
These express Levinsky's uniquely Jewish character, as

they refer to the poor days of his childhood and early youth ("my inner identity") when, supported by his mother, he devoted himself to the study of the Jewish Law. Nothing in a man's life could be more purely Jewish, and his constant longing, through all his later years, for the conditions of his past confirms him in an unchanging spirit. But the remarkable thing about this theme, as the late Abraham Cahan developed it, is that it is, at the same time, an exemplary treatment of one of the dominant myths of American capitalism—that the millionaire finds nothing but emptiness at the top of the heap. It is not by accident that Cahan, for forty years and until his death the editor of the *Jewish Daily Forward*, and identified all his life with Jewish affairs and the Yiddish language, wrote this novel in English (it has only recently been translated into Yiddish). He was writing an American novel par excellence in the very center of the Jewish genre.

It seems to me that certain conclusions about the relation between Jewish and American character should be implicit in the fact that so singularly Jewish a theme can so readily be assimilated to an American one. I am not suggesting that Jewish and American character are identical, for the Levinsky who arrived in New York with four cents in his pocket was as unlike an American as anyone could possibly be; but there is a complementary relation between the two which, so far as I know, no other novel has brought out so clearly.

David Levinsky was born in the Russian town of Antomir in 1865. His father died when David was three, and he lived with his mother in one corner of a basement room that was occupied by three other families. "The bulk of the population [of Antomir]," writes Cahan, "lived on less than . . . twenty-five cents . . . a day, and that was difficult to earn. A hunk of rye bread and a bit of herring or cheese constituted a meal. [With] a quarter of a copeck (an eighth of a cent) . . . one purchased a few crumbs of pot cheese or some boiled water for tea. . . . Children had to nag their mothers for

a piece of bread." But Levinsky's mother, who "peddled
pea mush [and did] odds and ends of jobs," was kind
to him and indulgent, "because God has punished you
hard enough as it is, poor orphan mine."

At the usual early eage, Levinsky was sent to *cheder,*
where he was made to feel very keenly the disadvantages
of poverty, as his teachers risked nothing in punishing a
poor boy. His mother would intervene for him (this impulse was to prove fatal) and fought with many a
melamed for laying hands on her David. In spite of the
humiliations and hardships, she maintained him in
cheder, and after his Bar Mitzvah sent him to Yeshiva
(Talmudic seminary) at an even greater sacrifice, as it
meant he would not be in a position to relieve her dis-
tress by learning a trade. She was determined that he
devote his life to God, and he showed great aptitude for
holy study. He soon distinguished himself as a student,
but his sexual instincts began to distract his mind. His
contacts with women, as was the case with all Yeshiva
students, were extremely limited. It was considered "an
offense to good Judaism" for a pious man to seek feminine company, attend dances, dress in worldly fashion,
or in any other way to behave as a "Gentile." Naturally,
these restraints only multiplied Levinsky's temptations.
He would do penance, undergo a period of religious
exaltation, and again fall into sin (in his mind).

The next great event in his life was the death of his
mother. Levinsky, in earlocks and black caftan, was at-
tacked by Gentile boys on his way from the Yeshiva.
When he came home bruised and bleeding, his mother,
against his entreaties and those of their friends and
neighbors, ran to the Gentile quarter to avenge him. This
was the last time he saw her alive. She was brought
back with a broken head.

It is a credit to Cahan's economy as a writer and to
his grasp of character that at this point, in the sixty-odd
pages which I have summarized, he has already drawn
so convincing a picture of Levinsky, including all essential details, that Levinsky's subsequent adventures in
the old country and America, his further encounters with

poverty and with women, the rest of his intellectual development, and his ultimate transformation into a millionaire, have all been fully prepared. I will therefore cut off the exposition and attempt some generalizations which may serve the understanding of the whole of Levinsky's character and perhaps help explain how the old-world Yeshiva student is essentially an American in ethos.

Levinsky's character was formed by hunger. The individual experiences of his life—poverty, squalor, orphanage, years of religious study and sexual restraint, the self-sacrificing love of his mother and her violent death— all these experiences contain, as their common element, a core of permanent dissatisfaction. This dissatisfaction expresses itself in two ways: first, as a yearning for fulfillment, where it operates to win for him all the goods and values he has been deprived of—wealth, dignity, a "father principle" as well as a substitute for his father (as shown in his passionate attachment to Red Sender, with whom he studied at the Yeshiva), the pleasures of intellectual liberty that attend his break with Orthodoxy, the pleasures of sex, and unrestrained access to the society of women, though he goes among them mainly to find a substitute for his mother. (These are the positive "Americanizing" tendencies of his discontent.) At the same time, dissatisfaction has become an organic habit, a form which determines his apprehension of experience in general, and actually directs the flow of experience his way, so that he is not merely the result of what has happened to him, but on the contrary, the events in his life are predetermined, in large measure, by what he has already become. In the second sense, dissatisfaction is unending; instead of providing the urge to overcome privation, it returns every fulfillment, by a way no matter how roundabout, to the original tension, so that no satisfaction is possible.

Thus Levinsky is a man who cannot feel at home with his desires. Because hunger is strong in him, he must always strive to relieve it; but precisely because it is strong, it has to be preserved. It owes its strength to the fact that for so many years everything that influenced Levinsky most deeply—say, piety and mother love— was inseparable from it. For hunger, in this broader, rather metaphysical sense of the term that I have been using, is not only the state of tension out of which the desires for relief and betterment spring; precisely because the desires are formed under its sign, they become assimilated to it, and convert it into the prime source of all value, so that the man, in his pursuit of whatever he considers pleasurable and good, seeks to return to his yearning as much as he does to escape it.

Levinsky's entire behavior is characterized by this duality. In love, he is drawn to women he cannot have. They are either hopelessly above his rank in wealth, sophistication, and culture, or married and faithful mother-surrogates, or simply not interested. The women who do find him attractive fail to move him. He goes to prostitutes, one frustration feeding the other.

His accumulation of wealth, which he wins through perseverance, ingenuity, and luck, is also of this pattern —it, too, represents a loss, a virtual impoverishment. Before he turned to business enterprise, Levinsky had entertained serious academic ambitions. Though he had broken away from Orthodoxy, shaved his beard, adopted American dress, and gone to night school to learn English, he had retained his Talmudic intellectuality and love of scholarship. He took a job in the garment industry only as a means of sending himself through college. The event to which he attributes his becoming a businessman fell on a day when he was having his lunch in the factory. A bottle of milk slipped out of his hands as he was trying to open it and spilled on some silks. His employer, Jeff Manheimer, who witnessed the accident, broadly made fun of his clumsiness and called him a lobster. The humiliation festered, and that very day Levinsky decided to steal the boss's designer and go into business for himself. This is the reason he gives, but it is a rationalization. He would never have entered business and gone on to wealth had it not been necessary to sacrifice something—in this case his desire for learning. And when he obtains great wealth, it makes a circle, joining the pattern of his love life by condemning him to loneliness, as he suspects all women who smile on him want only his money.

So with everything. All things in Levinsky's life are divided, alienated from themselves, and simplicity is impossible. But no matter how many transformations it undergoes, his hunger remains constant. He longs for his wretched boyhood (which appeals to him "as a sick child does to its mother") from which, were he able to reenter it, he would again be driven in an endless yearning after yearning.

Now this is a profoundly Jewish trait, our whole history is marked by this twist. The significant thing about the structure I have been describing is that it is not confined to single personalities like Levinsky, but is exactly repeated on an impersonal and much larger scale in Jewish history, religion, culture—wherever our tradition and its spirit find expression. Consider *Galut,* the Diaspora, through the centuries in which it has dominated Jewish life: the theme of the Return, of yearning for Eretz Israel, to which are linked Cabala and Messianism, modes of prayer and worship as well as modern political and social movements, so that the whole becomes a compendium of Jewish activity per se—the yearning for Israel runs through the Diaspora in no simple sense, as of a fixed desire for a fixed object. It is a reflexive desire, turning on itself and becoming its own object. This is the meaning of the passage: "If I forget Thee O Jerusalem. . . ." The yearning is itself Jerusalem, as in the words ". . . if I prefer not Jerusalem above my chief joy," and it is to this yearning that the good Jew remains faithful. Otherwise, why the proscription of temporizing in *Galut,* of making any compromise with desire, no matter how small, even down to the obdurate and seemingly ridiculous prohibition of shaving the beard? The hunger must be preserved at all cost. This theme is taken up and elaborated all through

Yiddish literature, receiving its ultimate ironic sanctifica-
tion in the work of Sholom Aleichem, where squalor,
suffering, and persecution become the "blessings of
poverty," signs and stigmata of the condition of being
Chosen, "for which the whole world envies us." The
character of David Levinsky, therefore, does not stand
alone, nor does he come, with his four cents, unattended
to the American shore. He drags the whole past after
him, being himself the Diaspora Man.

But what is so American about this? Nothing directly,
especially if I am right in calling Levinsky the essential
Jewish type of the Dispersion. And yet in the character
of the American businessman and in the surrounding
culture that his figure dominates, there is also such a
twist, a similar play on striving and fulfillment. We
worship success; all the same it is on process and origin
that we place the emphasis of gratification, seldom on
the attainment as such. The value of the successful man's
career lies in "rags to riches," it is defined in our saying,
"He worked himself up." Of those who are born to
wealth we say, "Poor little rich boy." Now this, I am
aware, is folklore, and there is a great deal of irony in it,
too. Nevertheless, our favorite representation of the rich
is of a class that doesn't know what to do with its money.
It has brought them no real accretion of happiness, and
the process of accumulation, on which the emphasis
falls, is manifestly a self-destructive one, as it never can
be stopped in time: the successful man faces the futility
of retirement. He, too, loves to dream about his boyhood
in an unreal *askesis,* having for the most part been
ashamed of the ascetic impulse (poverty, we protest too
much, is no disgrace) which he has concealed under a
conspicuous acquisition; and yet he is not enough a
materialist to enjoy his goods as they come to him and
welcome the spiritual consolations that worldly pleasures
bestow. "Money isn't everything," he will say, making
more, and he says this to preserve an air of disconsolate-
ness, as though virtue were impossible without a sour
face. He does all this for show, but unconsciously his

affectations hit upon the truth. All his life he is at loose ends, and expert only in ennui, which Tolstoy defined as the desire for desire, cousin to Levinsky's yearning. And even if none of this is true, and there is (as I strongly suspect) a direct gratification in wealth as such, it is still significant that most of us profess it to be true, clinging to a protective disenchantment.

Whatever the case with our much disputed and still, I suppose, amorphous American character, Levinsky, the Diaspora Man, had relatively little to overcome (speaking inwardly) to grow into the typical American of fortune. Only the environment was alien to him, but its inner loneliness was anticipated in his own, for one loneliness is much like another; and the very fact that the American environment was alien, and would remain so, to his Jewishness, enabled him to make good in it on his own peculiar terms—to satisfy everything but hunger. To be sure, his is only a single career, a single example of the Jew as American, but it draws our attention to the considerable structural congruity that must underlie the character and culture of the two peoples. And if Levinsky's career is understood in its essentially Jewish aspect, it may explain why the Jews, as an immigrant group, were among the first to achieve a virtually flawless Americanization.

I have purposely refrained from treating David Levinsky as a fictional character and have spoken of the novel as though it were the actual memoir of an American Jew, in tribute to Cahan's power of characterization. Such immediacy of revelation is the novel's strongest quality, and Levinsky is made to talk about himself not only with an authentic accent, but with a motive in disclosure verging on something sly—precisely as such a man would talk. This well known and widely respected businessman tells the truth about himself, his love affairs, his efforts to outsmart the unions, the way other men tell lies—to see if he can get away with it! But as fiction, Cahan's writing lacks continuity: his transitions from subject to subject tend to be abrupt, with a perseveration in the linking of sex and economics. Thus when he describes Levinsky's broken engagement (the cause was his falling in love with another woman), Cahan devotes less than twenty lines to the scene, and opens his very next paragraph (after a line space, but this may have been the typographer's doing) with the words, "Our rush season had passed. . . ." Often the trains of thought collide within the single paragraph, business plowing into everything else. True, Levinsky's mind would work this way, and the habit would also serve him the purpose of saying, "I may not be doing so well with the girls—but think of the money I'm making." (Though business is meaningless to Levinsky, one of the most touching insights of the novel is provided by Cahan's showing how he succumbs to a businessman's vulgarity of tone and manner, and berates himself for the weakness.) Yet it is not always possible to distinguish character from author, and this failure in detachment, the consequence of an imperfectly developed ear for nuances in language, becomes noticeable and sometimes quite confusing when there is no lucky congruity to justify it, as in the matter of the abrupt transitions from pleasure to business.

But these flaws, as I have already indicated, are of minor account. So much so, that I wonder what the critical reception and, no doubt, misunderstanding, of *The Rise of David Levinsky* must have been, that it should languish in the status of an "undiscovered" book, a standard footnote or paragraph in surveys of American Jewish literature, and not be known for the remarkable novel it is.

Commentary, August, 1952

ᴓ Sartre's Underground

"The underground," since Dostoevsky's *Notes,* has been so familiar a concept to the modern consciousness, that we now take its reality and our thorough knowledge of it for granted, and assume that it is a major source of our literature. That this is not the case, even a cursory examination of the writers most concerned with this theme, first among whom is Sartre, will show. Our acquaintance with the underground owes little to experience (I am speaking as an American) and less to contemporary fiction; we have had to rely on journalism, the reports of political refugees, and occasional sociological studies. The latter, in fact, are far in advance of fiction on almost every ground: observe how abruptly the confidence that our literature is in touch with life gave way, in most circles, to a reflex of astonishment at the Kinsey Report. The proper condition, in which literature leads the social sciences and furnishes their insights, is, for the time being at any rate, a thing of the past.

To some extent flattery deceives us on this topic: we like to imagine ourselves underground, living at a perpetual extreme, and we seize on every aspect of our age, its disorder and violence, amorality and unbelief, which confirms this estimate. We achieve by this means a passive heroism, to which romantic periods are prone, especially when the active modes promise little success. But there is still another way in which we deceive ourselves—this is a fundamental error and its cause lies in our predominant style of perception into human matters.

We are used to seeing a subject through its individual accidents; we call on biography to give the direction and pursue the unique and the aberrant to such an extent that almost all understanding has become a form of psychopathological analysis. This has put a high value on confessions, disclosures of the private life and its feelings, usually revulsions, which earlier ages have found neither interesting nor tolerable. The tone of very much modern writing is, accordingly, one of malaise. But we are so accustomed to it, we are seldom aware of it as such; and when we do take this malaise into direct account, we readily mistake it for what it is not—a report from the underground.

These statements are confirmed both by Sartre's imaginative work and the reception it has had. The greater part of his fiction, nearly all of *Nausea* and most of *Roads to Freedom,* is constructed precisely in a way to allow his characters to proclaim and act out their disgust with life. The symptoms are the standard neurotic ones— contactlessness, the emptiness and superfluity of existence, the sexual miseries and perversions, violence and self-destruction. But because Sartre is an existentialist, and because he himself resorts to existentialism for some of his special effects, we assign to these symptoms a meaning they do not bear in the text, and could not possibly carry in any clinical evaluation. Neurosis becomes the equivalent of life. The ordinary syndromes, which we would otherwise discount to sickness, become on this inflated interpretation synonymous with subjectivity, crisis, anxiety, and other existential categories, and we read as ontology what we should recognize as disease.

And so much that is supposed to represent the underground world comes not from the world at all but from swamps of the soul, in which modern life breeds pestilence in all of us. This distinction is crucial. Without it, it is impossible to develop the literary theme, for the underground, if it is to be represented as a world no less real and objective for underlying the one we inhabit in daily life, must be separated from everything which is merely subjective in feeling. The only way this separation can be made is by the method of residuum. I mean by this that one must discard everything which can be explained by psychology and other individual or social perspectives that stop short of the absolute extreme. Once this removal has been made, the residuum, if any, is what we may properly call underground. (The same must be done with religious belief—religious and underground morality are identical in this respect—to make sure it is genuine and not a mere displacement of anxiety.) Neurosis no more entitles one to call himself an underground man than it does to call himself a saint.

But this caution is seldom observed; and in the present collection of five of Sartre's stories it is never in evidence. Consider the title story, "Intimacy," which is about a frigid woman with a screaming abhorrence of sex, who has replaced her impotent husband with a lover; urged by her girl friend, she leaves her husband and prepares to run off with her lover, but at the last moment, unable to tolerate sexuality, she stands up the healthier man and returns to the impotent one. This story, it seems to me, is simply about a frigid woman. To take it for anything more than this, to suppose that it dramatizes "the crisis of modern marriage," or anything equally ambitious, is to run to that same gratuitous extreme under which malaise appears as moral philosophy. Obviously, the fact that there is sexual disorder in our world is not enough to make it an underworld—unless you establish this story as a norm and argue that the state of affairs shown in "Intimacy" is the constant and inevitable condition of love in our time. Not only would such a conclusion be false for the everyday world (which is not that bad), it would be a pollyanna-like distortion of the underground, which ought to be something much worse (sexual neurosis is remediable). To take such a story as "Intimacy" as a note from the underground is, then, to remove all meaning from the underground, which becomes, on such a misreading, nothing more than a duplication of the world we already have. Who needs *two* such worlds?

The other stories in this collection, "The Room," a study of madness, and "Erostratus," of homicidal mania, fall under the provisions I have been making—they are to be regarded as stories dealing with no more than their several themes. The detachment, the philosophical scope, above all, the objectivity which would justify their being regarded as valid generalizations of modern experience in its most disordered aspect, are either entirely lacking, or present only in minimal degree. Yet if we unpin Sartre's fiction from its metaphysical pretensions and let it go free, it gains enormously. He has exceptional zest for a writer of malaise, and his documentation, taken for what it really is, has moments of fictional density and detail that are worth much more than all the rest. He is at his best in his attachment to ordinary life, when he gives up the exploration of depths which his fiction cannot reach; and in the realm of the ordinary, he is most at home in politics. The two remaining stories, "The Wall," and "The Childhood of a Leader," are based on political experience, the first being the account of a prisoner in the Spanish Civil War awaiting his execution by the Falangists, and the second, the coming to maturity and participation in reactionary politics of a young French anti-Semite. These stories are the most successful in existentialist terms—"The Wall," in spite of a trick ending in which the prisoner wins a reprieve, for its vivid anticipation of death, and the other, after a shaky beginning in a ludicrous Freudianism which Sartre may have meant to be satiric, for its build-up of a dead ego through an accumulation of social roles; but their success, I should say, is not nearly as dependent on philosophical principles as it is on the fact that the objectivity of their reports is never in doubt. Here there is no difficulty in defining the world of which Sartre speaks; he has by-passed the swamp and the definition comes to him on the solid ground of political reality. Now his subject is something more than his own distemper. And so, if I may draw a moral, it may be in every case; one need not strain after the effect, one need only write of political experience, and the writing will sound with the full underground tonality, for politics is the underground of our time.

◄§ Stendhal's Rogues

WHEN STENDHAL set to work on *Lamiel* he was fifty-six years old and serving as French consul in the Italian city of Civita Vecchia, where he was terribly bored, under suspicion, and deprived of the contacts with women and brilliant men which the writer in him required just as much as the lover, the gallant, and the witty conversationalist. He worked at this novel intermittently in the five years of life remaining to him, and left it unfinished. It is a composition undertaken to ward off tedium (by a man who had lost his youth and much of his charm, and had grown wheezy and so corpulent he had trouble handling his dishes at the table), but it does not read like one. There are only a few clues to the state of his last years, but these, far from suggesting a decline of his power, give *Lamiel* a bite of rancor which even the greater novels, *The Red and the Black* and *The Charterhouse of Parma,* do not equal. But it is not fair, and I'm not sure whether it's meaningful, to compare a rough and uncompleted work with masterpieces; and since a strictly literary examination would seem to be ruled out by the nature of the case, I should prefer to treat *Lamiel* as an example of "Beylisme," the unsystematic system with which, under his own guidance, everything essentially Stendhalian has been identified.

The most striking thing about Stendhal is his audacity. He affords us one of the few examples in literature of a mentality genuinely liberal but in no way devoid of the daring and willingness to face extremes, the current lack of which Lionel Trilling has so strongly deplored in his criticism of the "liberal imagination." It is on this quality more than anything else that he won his bet, made with himself in 1836, that he would be read one hundred years later. And the most audacious feature of *Lamiel* is not the criticism which he directs at his period—he thought of calling the novel *The French under King Philippe*—but the stand he takes up with respect to his own principles. His is the one literary ego without a blind spot—Stendhal is thoroughly onto himself, and never deviates from this painful self-knowledge as, say, Goethe did, stuffily condoning his lapses into statesmanship and other brassy attractions by which great men are drawn. The whole nineteenth century is replete with such foolishness; Flaubert was not free of it, and Dostoevsky, James, Tolstoy, all had it—there is hardly a name that must be left off the list. The delusion from which most great writers suffered until our own time, in which Thomas Mann alone has refused to abandon it, was the belief that their statements of principle, whether on art or politics, could slow down the universal descent into philistinism; and they bravely held to the role of the artist's traditional responsibility toward culture in spite of everything society did to knock its props out from under their feet. Stendhal experienced the degradation of culture in his own day and saw more of it coming, but unlike his peers he did not imagine that his raised voice could call a halt. "Writers," he declared, "are the hussars of liberty"; but the most he expected of the skirmish was to be spared for the delectation of the "happy few." Therefore his liberalism is utterly without canard, and in his supreme act of egotism, which is his disavowal of egotism, he gives up all delusion, even about himself, not to be duped. Intelligence is the highest virtue.

Out of this complex attitude he derived the structure of *Lamiel,* as he did of all his work. In the story, which was to trace the rise to notoriety of the young orphan girl after whom the novel is named, the criticism of society is given to two characters: Lamiel, and her mentor and would-be seducer, the fat, aging hunchbacked Doctor Sansfin. Lamiel's career is itself an act of criticism—she discovers that the bourgeois virtues on which she is raised are lies, and under Sansfin's influence, takes over her own moral education. She buys a lover, paying a peasant ten francs to initiate her (and responds with the immemorial "Isn't there anything else?"), goes on to seduce the ineffectual Duke de Moissens, whose mother dominates the Normandy village in which Lamiel lives, gets the Duke to marry her, abandons him with a good deal of his money in her possession, and accomplishes the next stage in her climb by forming a liaison with a dissolute Marquis—at which point the novel breaks off. Lamiel thrives on the puncturing of hypocrisies, in which good work she is the protegée of Sansfin, who supervised her education with the object of making her his mistress, but lost her when she learned her lessons too well. Both Lamiel and Sansfin are rogues. Stendhal does not entrust the criticism of society to the virtuous.

Nor does this exhaust the elaborate precautions Stendhal takes in insuring his liberal sentiments against foolishness, blindness, pomposity, hypocrisy, and unprotected egotism. The figures of Lamiel and Sansfin develop in a further complication: before they can be accredited as the disguised representatives of his own ego, they must be purged of every possible weakness and inanity by being made to endure the animus of his own self-hatred. Otherwise Stendhal may simply be plying himself, or merely projecting his egotism in a flattering image. Off comes Sansfin's skin. He is a caricature of Stendhal himself in his last years, an unsuccessful seducer, ugly and aging, his hump standing for the author's abdomen, and his very name, "Endless," a reference to Stendhal's own endless chase after the pleasures of love. He is introduced in a merciless scene: out horseback riding, Sansfin is insulted by the village washerwomen, and in the course of defending his honor, he loses his mount and falls "plump into the sludge, head first."

Stendhal will prevent his humiliation in the eyes of the world by drawing his own blood first.

That the figure of Lamiel also amounts to a self-flagellation for Stendhal is not so apparent: she is an attractive, amiable girl, and the excellent qualities with which he endowed her, reminiscent of his own mistresses, testify to his generosity. Yet she is also a hateful object to him. She is precisely the sort of demimondaine, pitiless and beautiful, at whose hands Stendhal suffered terribly all his life, drawn by the masochist's infallible instinct; the sort of woman who followed Dr. Sansfin's prescription for curing a lover of the complacency of conquest ("The remedy," he tells Lamiel while chipping away the proprieties that insulate her from sexuality, "is simple and amusing: one should always plunge into despair the man who has served one's pleasure") and whose "first sentiment on being confronted with a virtue was to believe it a hypocrisy" (this, from the writer whose greatest joy and longing, all his life, was a passionate, all consuming love!).

He celebrates Lamiel, applauds her career, but there is bitterness in his generosity, and he never lets himself forget what her kind has cost him. He remains in awe of her, and it is this which gives the final reality to the characterization.

All this complex derivation of structure and character represents, I should say, Stendhal's ultimate audacity—his daring not only in, but *toward*, his principles. Whatever his motives may have been by way of *taking out* his own sufferings on the world and his characters, he was determined not to be *taken in*. Sansfin tells Lamiel:

> The world is not divided, as ninnies think, into rich and poor, the virtuous and the evil, but simply into dupes and rogues; that is the key to the nineteenth century since Napoleon's fall.

Above all, not to be a dupe! To be remorseless, not only to one's enemies, but to one's loves, ultimately, to oneself; never to spare the clearest, hardest, and most brilliant intelligence. It was for reasons such as these that Nietzsche acknowledged him, together with Dostoevsky, as his master in psychology, and the happy few for whom he wrote, in large part, owe their very existence (and survival) to him.

New Republic, August 25, 1952

I. Simone Weil as Saint

THE SIX LETTERS BY Simone Weil which are published in this book [*Waiting for God*], together with her essays, "Reflections on School Studies," "The Love of God and Affliction," "Forms of the Implicit Love of God," and "Concerning the Our Father," do not go as far as one might wish toward revealing the life and thought of this remarkable woman. Her position with regard to the Catholic Church is adequately covered by the letters, in which she makes it clear to her friend, Father Perrin, who tried to persuade her to accept baptism, that she feels she belongs outside the Church as a bridge between believers and nonbelievers, and that "God does not want me to join the Church . . . that I may serve [Him] in the realm of the intelligence." Her further reasons for refusing this step appear to be the desire to leave her mind open to all forms of doctrine, and suspicion of the influence of "social organizations." For fear of offending the priest, she says little about the politics of the Church—an issue that must have carried some weight with her; she speaks of such matters with great reluctance. This gives the impression that she is holding back, and not only in fear of offending her correspondent; she may be withholding from herself full recognition of her antagonism to protect a faith which is already full of perplexity. (The fact that she was Jewish is not mentioned, though this must have been of some

importance.) These letters and essays fail to make clear
why her baptism should have been so ardently pursued.

Since Father Perrin's letters are not included, it is
possible to suggest that she imagined the heat of the
pursuit to be greater than it really was. She seems to
enjoy the contention for its own sake, as though she
wanted to be courted and come after. She is careful not
to terminate the courtship by expressing too firm an
opposition to the Church; the possibility is always left
open that the will of God (which she declares herself
ready to obey, even if it meant damnation) will direct
her to join. This may have been the woman in her, but
God knows she was lonely enough.

The real reason hardly appears: that this woman enjoyed, with some regularity, genuine religious experience,
Christ's coming down to possess her. Her modesty at this
point (unless she has described it in her other writings)
is a typical expression of her nature; she is fearful of
satisfactions, of being touched too deeply, and holds herself far withdrawn, as though the tension of waiting and
hungering were more tolerable than delight. To say
nothing of love, even friendship (it is "the one legitimate
exception to the duty of loving only universally") "is
not really pure unless . . . surrounded by a compact
envelope of indifference which preserves a distance." And
so she says nothing of her experience of the divine, except that it generally comes over her during the Lord's
Prayer. She suffered from migraines and these, raging
during the moment of possession, enabled her to share in
Christ's Passion. But exactly what happens, what the
sensation and the images are, is not revealed. She passes
over the experience and for the rest writes quietly, as
though no crucial issue affecting the validity of mystical
union, not to speak of life and death, salvation and damnation or even sanity, were involved. Even languidly;
she is entirely passive and "waiting" is the essential expression of her faith. Her only striving is to hold herself
in perpetual obedience to the will of God. But it does
not appear to be a heroic struggle. Whatever its undis-
closed fervor may have been, the contradictions and in-

consistencies, the guilt trammeling both sides of the decision, and tormenting her, whose allegiances had ranged over natural science and revolutionary politics— by the time she comes to faith, she seems pale and fatigued, at most, convalescent. This is disappointing. One has a right to expect more of this woman whose credentials for religious struggle were of the most dramatic kind—"the Outsider as Saint in an age of alienation," as Leslie Fiedler says of her in his introduction, and in virtue of which he calls her, "our kind of saint."

Were it not for this, that she stands or is said to stand in a special relation to "our world," Simone Weil's case, and whatever claim to sanctity it may contain, would rest entirely with the Church. What is of concern to our world—at least to myself—is the precise nature of this relationship, and whether it is at all possible. I believe no such relationship is possible, and that it is said to exist only because the half- or quasi-religious would like to make an illegitimate use of Simone Weil's case— its withholding of final commitment to the Church—to create a middle ground on which their own religiosity can be safely supported. It seems to me that an either-or is involved, much more drastic than a good part of our generation would like to recognize, that the relation of "our world" to religion can only be all or none, and that Simone Weil, in any event, does not belong in any compromise "our" side may try to make with "theirs."

To begin with, there is no such thing as "our kind of saint." The fact that Simone Weil comes from our world is not significant, for all saints come from this world, from the world of alienation, despair, and dreadful anguish; they leave it. Once out, they are on their own, and our world knows nothing of their salvation. If the term were to have any meaning, we should need the example of a saint returning to the scene of his renunciation, to the very beliefs he abandoned at the start of his journey. I know of no such example, and it is curious that even fiction is void of it. The great attempt in the Russian novel was to document just such a turning full circle: Chichikov redeemed, Alyosha become the Great

Sinner, Nekhlyudov done wallowing in moral sensualism over the fallen Maslova, discovering purity for himself—but the return home was never more than barely outlined; it was not written. Perhaps for the very good reason that it is impossible. The saint leaves our world for good, as Simone Weil does when she says, "The object of science is the presence of Wisdom in the universe . . . the presence of Christ, expressed through matter which constitutes the world." This bars her return; she is "their" kind of saint.

I don't know how serious Mr. Fiedler was in his use of the term. Probably not very, as the whole tone of his argument derives from the substitution of literary and rhetorical categories for religious ones. The fact that Simone Weil's devotion had its absurd aspects seems to be of greater moment to this argument than its devotional character. "The Holy Fool" (she certainly was one) becomes synonymous with "The Comic Figure" (which she was not); the implied equivalence between the two terms is actually a derogation of religion, which must hold its excesses to be sacred, not comic. The important distinction here, which Mr. Fiedler—he is not alone in this—fails to make, is between literature and faith. (The whole contemporary inflation of "absurd" into a religious term is based on this confusion.) So also when Mr. Fiedler speaks of the other excesses of her life—her gaucheries, her asceticism (she starved herself to death, refusing to eat, while in England, more than the ration in occupied France), her hysterical identification with the working class, which led her to work in factories at jobs she had no business doing—he skips altogether the step necessary to the identification, as though the absurd were *ipso facto* religious. But it is only when a state is already of religious significance—and this is determined by faith—that its absurdity becomes a way to God; *even* if it is absurd, not *because*.

Religion is not the only thing left out of this religious appraisal of Mlle. Weil. One would imagine that a bestowal of sanctity from within our world would at least be made in the appropriate context; so that if Mr. Fiedler is ready to celebrate Simone Weil as a religious figure because of her patent absurdity, he should be prepared to postulate some dialectical relation between *holy* and *neurotic*. I can't blame anyone for not wanting to do this, because the relation between these two terms presents a very difficult problem, and to settle it ultimately one must perhaps also have recourse to faith—in God or in psychology (not both). But *our world!* If our world sees the Comic Figure in the Holy Fool, it must certainly see the Neurotic; and at least it must ask, even if it cannot answer the question, what bearing this category has upon the saintly. Are the terms equivalent? Can one be reduced to the other without residuum? If there is a residuum, how can it be shown to exist in Simone Weil's case? (Perhaps "our kind of saint"—to take the term seriously—would be precisely the case in which every possible discount had been made for sexual frustration and all other neurotic suffering, and still the love of God remained over, a residuum not to be reduced to psychological terms or explained away. If such a case seems to involve belief in miracles or to call for superhuman effort on the part of our saint—none has ever asked himself such questions—what else is saintliness?) In any event, how can our world speak of Simone Weil without using its own language, in which the words, severe and unforgiving though they may be, are, by definition, *hysteria, masochism,* etc.?

No, she was their kind of saint. For all her firsthand knowledge of politics, exile, and universal doubt, she made her way out of our world and ceased to represent it. In her own world, in her own terms, she achieved a certain sanctity, and whatever our world may understand by this, it was, for her, wholehearted, an absolute commitment. For which alone she deserves better of us than to be made into a Patron Saint of symposiums on literature and religion in the little magazines.

II. Uprootedness and Animal Nature

THERE ARE A FEW moments of real daring in Simone Weil's book [*The Need for Roots*] of reflections on the destiny of man (in particular, France) such as the ones in which she takes literally the assignment the Free French Government gave her (in what must have been an act of exasperation; she had been begging them to let her help the Resistance movement, and had proposed that they allow her to parachute into occupied France) to write a work useful to the postwar reconstruction; and in these moments not only is Miss Weil at her best, but her work is, of all things least to be expected of her, *sociology*, and of a superior order. Her daring is of the kind frequently encountered among Utopians: with an absurd practicality she comes right to the point, not even bothering to acknowledge the existence of the so-called reality problems that furnish the hard-headed with an excuse for venturing nothing. Her description of the lot of the proletariat in the large cities and factories, the wretched education they receive, and the miserable entertainments to which they turn in the lack of a genuine culture, constitutes, together with her corresponding description of the condition of the peasantry, one of the most sympathetic and "realistic" accounts of modern life to be found anywhere; and her handful of suggestions for reform are startling in their simplicity, and in the impression they create that they might really work. She has the radical insights for which children and, oddly enough, marginal and "uprooted" people are famous (the latter is a significant point, and I shall want to return to it); enough so, to make T. S. Eliot sound very uncomfortable in his preface and impatient to get away from so free and idiosyncratic a use of the Christian tradition. (Incidentally, the period of Christianity which makes the strongest appeal to her is the earliest, and she retains something like an image of it as a standard for all her evaluations; that is probably one reason why she writes so well of proletarians, seeing them as martyrs to an unconscious protestation of faith—they, the most uprooted, exert the strongest demand for roots, which in itself, in her terms, is a turning of the soul toward faith.) In all the sections of her book that deal directly with the problems that the fall of France set for her philosophy of reconstruction, she has the great advantage of writing from a highly complicated perspective: herself a Jew and an intellectual, she knew something quite naturally of uprootedness; at the same time, deeply French in her culture, she experienced the defeat of France as a tearing out of her being from the traditions and values in which she had grown; she had conscientiously gone after a taste of factory work and labor in the fields, so that she came to know the proletariat better than she might otherwise have done, and learned to check somewhat her masochistic tendency to romanticize toil, which restraint deepened rather than lessening her appreciation of its nature and meaning; and she brings together in most of her observations, and often with a surprising twist, a profound learning in both sacred and secular matters, writing at her best with an almost medieval facility and concreteness in her symbolism for linking the material and spiritual worlds. All these advantages make her, when she uses them, not only the great woman she was in her own right, but an intruder of genius into the world of sociology.

Unfortunately, she makes a rather sparing use of these advantages, and much of her book is tedious reading. It is not a meditation on God, written in the tenderness and excitement of holy expectation, like her previous work, *Waiting for God*, but largely a sermon which gets wound up on irrelevant topics, the Roman Empire, the Greeks, the ancient Hebrews (whom she continues to misrepresent, disconnecting them from all influence on Christianity), and similar subjects; and even when the discussion has a bearing on the problems of reconstruction, as in her consideration of patriotism, she brings on such a wealth of illustrative matter that the point not only gets snowed under, but begins to look, some time before it disappears from sight, like a thing of little interest to her. The startling simplicity and vividness of her words about the uprootedness of modern populations are nowhere recaptured.

It seems to me that these are more than faults of composition. She gets lost in *The Need for Roots* because the trouble is one of conception, having to do with the very idea and image of her book, the notion of roots per se. It may well be that the terms, rootedness-uprootedness are a false dyad, in no way so closely connected as they would seem to be through simple opposition.

Uprooted is an indispensable word; there is little danger of going astray with it, for even its utmost meaning, the most drastic image it brings to mind, of plant life torn out of the soil and threatened with death, is appropriate to its sociological use in describing the contemporary world. It is not so with the word *rooted*, and the question is whether the metaphor derived from a sessile organism is ever adequate to the purpose of describing animal life; though it makes sense to speak of a man as uprooted, I am not sure what it means to use the opposite term. Simone Weil herself furnishes an excellent example of the difficulty of this word. The little I know, and have mentioned in passing, of her background, the diverse sources from which she draws together the complicated perspective of her writing, show her to be an extremely *mobile* intellectual; the very sort of woman, in other words, whom it would not occur to us to speak of as rooted. For what does it mean to be rooted? To spend one's life in the environment of his birth will hardly do as a definition. This is not even a desirable meaning to Miss Weil, since one of her suggestions for improving the life of working people is to make a *tour de France* available to the young; and even if it were desirable, it would be too much to ask, as it was of herself, of populations under the constant threat of the displacement of war. This is only the literal sense of the word, but as it is inapplicable, it begins to cast some doubt on the symbolic meanings.

To be rooted in an intellectual, cultural, or religious tradition? If this is not to mean the surrender of curiosity or the circumscription of intellectual life within a narrow compass, some provision must be made for learning of the world outside one's tradition. If this learning is not to be superficial, there must remain the real possibility of one's never sinking roots. Yet the image of the rooted intellectual presupposes a single tradition: a man rooted in many traditions, if this is not a contradiction in terms, would exhibit all the traits presumably characteristic of the uprooted condition. The problem, how to combine the values of rootedness with those of variety and stimulation necessary for growth, is never squarely faced by Miss Weil who, a good deal of the time, speaks out against the settled condition, as when she expresses the complaint of the peasantry at feeling left out of the life of the cities, and urges that something be done to make the countryside more exciting. She gives her case away on still another point when she discloses her suspicion of collectivities, and reserves the proper uses of intellect and will to the individual. A collectivity, she protests, can have no opinions and ought not to be allowed to exercise will; the danger she wants to avoid is that of dogma and tyranny. That this is a danger well worth avoiding is obvious; but it is precisely the danger that lies in a rooted society. It would appear that every time she speaks of the blessings of rootedness, she really has in mind the values of coming to rest—in valid beliefs, useful occupations, a self-replenishing style of life. But such values presuppose mobility, as one comes to rest out of a state of motion and remains free to resume that state. This, again, has nothing to do with roots.

The one meaning of the term, as she uses it, that may be able to stand inspection is that of rootedness as the condition of religious faith. Here the temporal difficulties are avoided, faith presumably being a clinging to values of an order above and beyond the natural world. (I grant, but only for the sake of argument, that such a combination of words is meaningful.) But here again there are difficulties, waving aside the immediate one, whether we are not talking plain nonsense: to the extent that faith really is an act that lifts us out of nature, we are freed of the obligation to represent rootedness in terms of this life, and are in no better a position to reveal what it means; and even if the consequences of faith can be shown to consist in a harmony between ego and universe—the feeling of being at home in God's world— it does not follow that such harmony will manifest itself in man's world, or it should long ago have done so. Moreover, if our objective is the reconstruction of society, it seems to me a confession of failure to resort to the supernatural, and an admission that the condition of rootedness is not to be achieved on earth.

Now it seems to me that such considerations rule out the sessile metaphor. "The need for roots" is merely an expression of the fact that "uprootedness" is intolerable; beyond this it becomes a mistranslation of the genuine need for restful satisfactions. These occur in animal life, in the intellectual's no less than the peasant's, and the need for them in no way lessens our necessarily mobile character. But if one is to accept Miss Weil's own prin- ciple of reconstructing society to the direct satisfaction of human needs, it should follow that not a rooted society but one which allows its members a maximum of freedom is desirable. Actually, the ideal society, to re- construct a well-known opinion of Mr. Eliot, cannot afford to include many deeply rooted individuals. If the risk of freedom is really worth taking, it must proceed, in human culture and society as it once did in biological evolution, through an increase in mobility. A society of the uprooted does not provide this; it leaves its popula- tions to wither. But a rooted society is no better. The clue, it seems to me, is given by animal nature, to the preservation of whose necessarily restless and unstable life-patterns all societies must adjust themselves. Human beings are known to be the most restless animals, and intellectuals, the most restless of human beings. They require open patterns, the right to follow an erratic course; their intellectual prerogative is merely the animal right, in its extreme form, to move unhindered and enjoy the risks and benefits of the rootless life. A rooted society is a sick one, it is an asylum from the fear of animal freedom. A healthy society, which is neither rooted nor uprooted—its forms are appropriate to animals, not plants—encourages mobility among its traditions, with everyone's right assured to pick and cultivate what he pleases, provided it does no harm. It is full of eccentrics and outsiders, people on the margin between alternative worlds; but the health of a society is not to be measured by a uniformity of type among its members. One measure is its ability to encounter without anxiety, and to learn from the rootless intellectual, who, precisely because he is rootless, is free to move among values in search of the best—as, in the ultimate paradox of her life, was Simone Weil herself.

Partisan Review, September-October, 1952

◄§ *What Should My Child Read?*

WHAT SHALL OUR CHILDREN READ? If anyone would
like to consult a book on this vexatious problem, he might
try *Your Child's Reading Today,* by Josette Frank. Full
of ludicrous mistakes and blemishes, it may be treasured
for its faults which, as I shall show, are extraordinarily
instructive; nevertheless, it contains some excellent material and represents, besides, the outlook of a fairly influ-
ential school of progressive educators. Miss Frank is the
staff consultant to the Children's Book Committee of the
Child Study Association, and in this capacity has been
connected with various campaigns to clean up the comic
strips and abolish the more objectionable ones. Her book,
as one would therefore expect, has a manifestly practical
slant. It consists of a series of carefully chosen reading
lists for children graded from nursery-school age to the
teens, and twenty-four chapters of reflection and advice
on such subjects as the parents' role in guiding their
children's choice of books, and the influence of comic
strips, movies, radio, and television on children's reading
habits and their characters. Miss Frank covers a very
wide range of reading matter and touches on virtually
every conceivable topic, from books about sex and sex
education to the various how-to-make-it manuals for
building model airplanes and sailcraft. Parents, teachers,
educators, and child psychologists will surely find these
reading lists extremely useful.

But Miss Frank's opinions and suggestions are an entirely different question, and the usefulness of her views
is considerably diminished by the difficulty of determin-

ing what they are. She writes in an if-but, on-the-one-hand-on-the-other style, for which not only her rhetoric but her basic assumptions about life and letters are to blame, and becomes so entangled in hedges, qualifications, contradictions, and fears of giving offense that she well nigh cancels out everything she says.

Miss Frank always takes the permissive attitude, but handles it so that she makes a serious dilemma of every case in which the child's preference in reading and television programs comes into conflict with the parent's. If the parent considers the child's book "wrong"—say it is too advanced for his years, or full of sadism and horror—he would like to deny him access to it. But if he were to enforce a strict prohibition, wouldn't the prohibition have just as bad an effect? Since Miss Frank assumes that the alternatives are equally harmful, she approaches all such cases with the conviction that a compromise must be found. Unfortunately, not all conflicts are soluble by compromise (this is in the nature of the case; besides, children, once they get the drift of our tactful circumlocutions, are notoriously un-co-operative in such matters), and the solutions Miss Frank offers are frequently no more than formal. The assumption itself—that the effect of parental denial must be as harmful or nearly as harmful as the effect of the thing denied—she fails to examine; but one can readily think of occasions in which it is much better, and others in which it is much worse, for the parent to deny the child than not to do so—to say nothing of the times in which one cannot tell the difference because the case is too difficult or the difference too small.

In every dispute between parent and child, both cannot be right, but they may be, and usually are, both wrong. It is this situation which gives family life its peculiar hysterical charm. Now since compromise is not always possible, each case must be decided on its merits; but to make the right decisions, and to make them consistently, the parent must have some standard, of justice or taste, to go by. Provision for this is entirely lacking in

Miss Frank's position, and as she makes no statement of principles, it is hard to say what she is advocating except that it is benevolent and without any bite.

Her embarrassment with the problem of standards is illustrated in the following passage, in which she sums up in her discussion of the reading lists:

> In the foregoing pages will be found the titles of many books which may successfully compete for the interest of comics readers. They are not all great literature, but they are good reading, *if we define "good" as appealing to young readers.* (My italics)

This, alas, is just what we mustn't do. If good reading is what appeals to young readers, then comics are the best reading since they are unquestionably the most appealing. On other occasions she defines good reading—correctly, I should say—as that which ensures the continuity of the cultural heritage, and sometimes makes it synonymous with the "classics." The problem then becomes how to interest children in *good* reading (as so defined; an entirely different kettle, there being no such problem with "appealing" reading). Parents must be forbearing, they must not push culture at their children, or force them at good books, lest they provoke a negative reaction. Miss Frank feels it is best to offer unobtrusive encouragement, and to see to it that the environment is stocked with good books and other repositories of the values one should like to inculcate. But of course the modern environment is bound to furnish more movies, radios, television sets, and comic magazines than quiet libraries with fireplaces and shelves of excellent, leather-bound books. So what are the parents to do? They must trust that the child's native good sense will eventually assert itself, they must practice forbearance, they must not push culture at their children . . . and so on.

But what is one to do in those cases where the child's native good sense fails to assert itself, and the preoccupation with bang-bang, vrrrooooom, ack-ack-ack-ack, and eeeeeek shows no sign of relenting? Then, says Miss Frank, it is a psychological problem: the reason the child is glued to the TV set or immersed in the comics for hours at a time, neglecting the other interests a healthy child must have, is that he has some underlying problem. Comics and TV are never the cause of the child's disturbance, they are merely a symptom.

Now this is quite true, children are beset with psychological problems that are not traceable to the horrors. But in the present context, it is passing the buck to say so. Healthy child or neurotic, there is still a *literary* problem and a *cultural* problem, and how does one tell the difference between good books and bad, and how does one make the difference clear to his children without defeating his own purpose? And of course one must be forbearing, but how does one combat the modern environment to the extent that it must be combated—after all discounts have been made and all the requirements of permissiveness have been met? In short, the real problem! Of this, not a word.

If we are to observe some standard in guiding our children through reading and TV (otherwise, why talk of guidance?) and if those standards are to have even a remote relation to the ones we follow in our own life and work, the first principle of judgment must be that by far the greater number of things the child reads in the comics and sees on the screen are absolutely worthless. But wouldn't it disconcert him to be told (gently, tactfully, in terms appropriate to his grasp) that he lives in a box-top culture where he is constantly bombarded by commercialism and kiddie-*Kitsch*? Of course it would disconcert him, it might even make him feel insecure. But shouldn't we *all*—man, woman, *and* child—be disconcerted by the quality of our commercial culture? And honestly now, isn't it far worse to be secure in the love of junk than insecure?

Miss Frank would answer that the "bad" books and programs (in the second sense of the word, since here "bad" can't mean "unappealing") may well lead on to something "good." "For example," she says, their listening and viewing are filled with a good deal of science fiction. When they follow their heroes on cosmic adventures . . . are they learning science? Perhaps [*sic!*] not. But they are whetting their appetites and expanding their imaginations to the possibilities which science offers.

If this is so, how can anything possibly be bad? And if the fake, vicarious science of Buzz Corey and Captain Video whets the appetite for the real thing, why not give them Mickey Spillane to read on the ground that he will expand their imaginations to the possibilities of love?

Miss Frank's position, though short on metaphysico-theologo-cosmolonogology, is pure Pangloss, with the very same dreary, drizzly optimism: all is for the best. Television need not be the death of conversation and shared home life: one can always talk about the programs, and TV can weld the family into a greater unity than ever.

> The ball game is often shared by the whole family and it makes a lively family interest. But it does sometimes happen that the last inning is being played just when the five-year-old is waiting to see her favorite clown.
>
> What to do then? We must call upon the good will of the members of the family to work out a solution which, while it will necessarily deprive someone, will have its compensations in mutual consideration.

Just try it. And what does "mutual consideration" mean in this context, where one, and only one, program can be seen at a time? Miss Frank recognizes that you can't compromise between Channel 4 and Channel 5, and someone will necessarily be hurt. So how can there be *mutual* consideration? This is simply the goody-goody formula for solving problems which cannot be solved. And even if it were possible to work out a solution of such a problem, who would be saintly enough to do it with the bases loaded in the ninth? I, for one, would not.

But *amor vincit omnia*. She quotes with approval a father's letter to a radio or television station:

> I am sorry you changed the time of your program.
> Now when I get home late . . . my children have to
> fill in for me what happened in today's story.

and adds:

> What a pleasant picture one gets of mutual appreci-
> ation and shared enjoyment in these families! Here is
> no frowning down the nose at the children's taste, and
> if perhaps there is no conscious attempt to elevate that
> taste, the warm relationship implied . . . has values
> which no amount of "culture" could replace.

Let Daddy only learn to love Howdy Doody and culture
will take care of itself.

Miss Frank writes such nonsense, not because she
fails to see what is involved in the problem of standards
(if anything, she sees too much, as she always gives both
sides of the argument, even when there is only one side),
but because she trembles in holy fear of giving offense—
to parents, children, teachers, authors, publishers, program directors; she has a reasonable word for everyone.
But the basic problem, how to tell good from bad, and
how to win our children for the good, she ignores, presumably because it might cause dissension. The truth is, we
must often struggle and always be prepared to struggle,
tactfully, gently, with as much kindness as possible—
still, *struggle*—with our childen and the world that surrounds them to keep alive their inherent sense for what
is lively and good in art. How to conduct this battle
joyously, in such a way that we will enlist our children's
love and not alienate them from the life of the mind, is
a problem which it may take genius to solve. But it is a
fact that we have such a battle on our hands, and it will
get us nowhere to pretend that we don't.

Commentary, August, 1954

❧ For God and the Suburbs

THE CAMPAIGN MANAGERS of the New Orthodoxy have run through history, economics, sociology, political theory, psychology, theology, and mysticism, but the only one to come up with a really new idea is Herman Wouk. He bases his case for God and the suburbs on the perfervid struggles of Marjorie Morgenstern, a pretty Jewish girl with a talent for dramatics, to preserve her virginity and bag a husband.

So it seems to me on reading *Marjorie Morningstar*. (This is her stage name.) The only continuous action or principle of suspense in this 565-page work is will she—won't she? This goes on for 417 pages to become the longest tease in the modern novel until Marjorie is spoiled of her treasure during a total eclipse of the moon: "Her age was twenty-one years, four months and seven days." The seducer is Noel Airman (*luftmensh;* he was born Saul Ehrman), an intellectual songwriter from the Borsht Belt and Greenwich Village, some ten years her senior, who told her at the outset that he was not the marrying kind. It takes her a long time—and a long pursuit of him through Europe—to come to her senses about Noel. When she does, she returns to the States to marry a lawyer—decent man and steady provider—raise a family in Mamaroneck and keep a kosher home. Somehow, all of this is supposed to show that psychoanalysis is nonsense and intellectuals are bums, and that the accumulated folk wisdom of the Bronx and Central Park West is superior to sex, Bohemianism, the new pediatrics, and the eating of crustaceans and pork.

This is, as I say, an unusual argument. The book overflows with a *Volkstümlichkeit* which, for some reason, reminds me of *Abie's Irish Rose,* and it has a number of pleasant schmaltzy scenes of a Bar Mitzvah, wedding, and other family gatherings. It has an even greater number of *non sequiturs* which are not nearly so pleasant, especially when they come flying at you from all directions, bent on demolishing Greenwich Village and Broadway by the acre. But there have been deadlier barrages. Wouk tries to keep it all on a more or less friendly basis, and you may enjoy being shot at. For the book is enjoyable and seldom hard to read. It is much like the movies in its entertainment value, full of color and splash, with bits for the character actors. The observations on bourgeois Jewish life, its pretentions and felicities, are accurate and amusing, and the slow-motion studies of Miss Morgenstern's *demi-vierge* days are not without topical interest. *Marjorie Morningstar* is, in short, like any other successful object or product of popular culture; it is a commercial concoction, but a careful one, made not only to withstand but to thrive on disparagement. Over and over again we find ourselves enjoying things which we hold in utter contempt; our repugnance, in some strange way, provides sauce to our pleasure.

All the same, there is an extraordinary amount of faking in this novel. It comes in three varieties: fictional, wherein the two main characters, Marjorie and Noel, are rigged; sociological, in which Mr. Wouk lays down reflections on the position of the Jews in American society without having a thing to say; and ideological, in which the ideas place a greater burden on the reader's imagination than his understanding: the trick is to see what bearing they have on the story. These three aspects of the novel keep colliding with one another and produce a lively, though not always charming, confusion. The confusion is twofold: one part in Wouk's mind, the other in the novel. Still another difficulty is provided by the gamut of tone, which changes with the occasion, and runs from love-in-bloom, to cynicism, con, satire, burlesque, *haute monde*, and pastrami.

Wouk's sociological study is concerned with two generations of a Jewish family on the rise and a hint of the third. When the novel opens, the Morgensterns are living on Central Park West, where they have moved from the Bronx. Setbacks during the Depression—Marjorie's father is in the feather-importing business—force them down a peg and they move to West End Avenue, to a smaller apartment, but close enough to the class standard. They have brought with them from the Bronx a good many of their original values, and these are now undergoing refinement at Mrs. Morgenstern's direction. The latter is ruthlessly parvenu, and opposes Marjorie on every issue that carries the least threat of her daughter's departure from the pattern of rise and respectability. Marjorie wins, but her victories are no cause for exulting; Mom is always right.

The vindication of Mrs. Morgenstern's judgment is the most fundamental operation of the book, everything contributing to this end, but it's hard to understand why Wouk should seek it. He seems to see her for what she is—a shallow, narrow, conventional woman, enemy of spirit, who fears life and uses her convictions not so much for the welfare of her daughter and family as for their defensive value against experience. Yet Mrs. Morgenstern is always right! Much of her credo is exposed to ridicule, but the alternative systems receive even rougher treatment, and the final proof of Mama's pudding is given by Marjorie herself, who is shown eating it in Mamaroneck with a silver spoon. The significance of these reflections on the Jews, as far as I can see, is that we should all head for the suburbs, but be sure to pack along prayer shawls and philacteries. I am sure this cannot be what Wouk meant to say, but he says nothing else because he is faking. He gives the story specious overtones of concern with the Jewish "problem" and takes a position right at Mrs. Morgenstern's side—not because she is right (since we don't know the questions, how can we judge her answers?) but because it is such a cute thing to do. In this day and age, what more startling yet safer way is there to appear unconventional than by upholding the conventions?

The ideological overtones are just as phony. Wouk seems to come out strong for religion, chastity, the sanctity of marriage and the home, and against free thought, free love, and Freudianism. But it is like writing on a window pane—turn your back and it is gone. Religion has no place in the story because no one is interested, though some of his characters go to synagogue. Noel Airman, who is cast as the Atheist, covers the subject, when he is not eating lobster, by trying to talk Marjorie into sleeping with him; and Marjorie has even less thought for God, perhaps because she is kept so busy untwisting her arm. No one shows the least sign of faith, and Mr. Wouk, apparently, is content to let the matter rest as an adjunct of "adjustment" and doing what one's neighbors do.

Chastity, one would think, is a clearer notion, no two ways about it, yet Wouk manages to fog this up, too. Purity, as a concept of soul or action, does not even get honorable mention. Marjorie has to be careful that the boys don't consider her a prude, and so she engages in necking. This seems to meet with Wouk's approval; activities the other side of the line definitely do not. It would seem rather dangerous for him to depend on lines in this case, as he is incapable of drawing anything so drastic as a clear-cut division of any other topic. But he does make it plain that sex is of secondary importance in the relation between the sexes, who are better occupied laying plans for a home.

The fictional conceptions are no better. The main characters, Marjorie and Noel, are rigged up to represent opposite principles, but here as elsewhere, Wouk's confusion and his failure to understand the issues he is pretending to raise leave everything in a heavy mess. Noel Airman, who winds up in the waste basket, is no doubt supposed to be the object lesson: this is the price one must pay for pursuit of the pleasure principle. But Wouk puts him down so rapidly, it is quite probable that he has burned his hand. There is the synthetic name, the rejection of Judaism, the psychoanalytic double talk, the cuteness, narcissism and lint of Village beds, which stigmata are meant to stand in indictment of the man, and the sophomoric philosophizing, intended to take care of his intellectual pretensions, to say nothing of his withered arm which, by special dispensation, may be supposed to have Freudian significance. At the same time he is so dazzling and irresistible to women that he qualifies as an author's own wish fulfillment. Noel is handsome, witty, brilliant in dispute (or is supposed to be; actually he talks like a hairdresser), and endowed with a fair amount of talent and excellent insight into the Jewish middle class from which he springs. All in all, he appears to be worthy of Marjorie's adoration, and sometimes even a little too good for her. On the subject of Marjorie, moreover, he does much better than Wouk himself, for he is the only one within miles to come up with at least a workable definition of the girl. He has her taped for a "Shirley"—the kind who flutters under a false nubility, only to harden into the stone image of her own frustrated mother and prove herself inimical to all sweetness, love, and art. No doubt, Wouk gives this opinion to Airman as a measure of the latter's infantilism, but like many a child's remark, it sticks.

Marjorie is the biggest gyp of all. Let alone the fact that she hasn't an idea in her head (the only way in which Wouk has succeeded in characterizing her as an actress) and that she seems to be constructed of chewing gum, she is made to function in a rather dishonest way. It is up to Marjorie to show the shortcomings of sexuality as a principle of life. For this purpose, Wouk sacrifices her virginity and has her conduct an affair with Airman; but he might have saved the girl's honor because, from all indications, she is not qualified to speak. Wouk is so careful to keep her a good Jewish girl, a "Shirley," that he does not let her enjoy it; and it would be a fair guess to say she is frigid. I am aware that the establishment of such charges does not lie within the province of literary

criticism; but it does lie within fiction to give honest
witness to life, and this Wouk has, deliberately or through
ignorance, prevented Marjorie from doing. Her experience on the night of page 417 consists in pain, shock,
and "incredible humiliation," and her general disposition
toward the subject is summed up in her view that love
affairs give actresses reddish eyes, lead them to drink and
late hours, coarsen their manners and speech, and under-
mine their reluctance "to pose for underwear advertisements and nude pictures."

Needless to say, the opposition of Marjorie and Noel
fails to produce the anticipated clash of philosophies and
values. It is more like one mist absorbing another.

In fairness to Wouk, it must be admitted that a novel
in favor of any set of principles, let alone orthodox and
conservative ones, is a hard thing to write. One must be
careful with the presentation of contrary evidence: too
little, and the argument is loaded; too much, and it tends
to steal the show. In general, the trouble is that virtue is
never as interesting as vice. But even if the odds are 50
to 1, as they are in the present novel, where 417 pages
are put against 8, a case can be made, and a fictional
tension generated to support it, out of the author's conviction, and his deepest need to make his wish take on
reality. But here is where *Marjorie Morningstar* is most
fraudulent; for Wouk has used his principles only for
prestigious purposes, not even bothering to state, define,
or feel them sharply; his object was to sound like a serious
writer and make respectability respectable. Nor does he
write out of serious preoccupation with Jewish life, or its
actual social nature; or out of a genuine religious abhorrence of what he considers evil. He simply chooses white,
like a man who plays chess against himself. Assigning
the worst possible moves to the other side, he stakes fame
and fortune on a game he can't lose.

Partisan Review, Fall, 1955

∽§ Broadway "Meshuggene"

THE LATE RISERS [by Bernard Wolfe] is all about Broadway—show girls, call girls, con men, publicity agents, actors, actresses, marijuana salesmen and consumers, columnists, their ghosts, and other *meshuggene*. There is also a dying professor who makes his home in Greenwich Village (Mr. Wolfe does not say professor of what, but it has something to do with Marxism, voodoo, and linguistics—he probably taught at the New School). These characters are linked together in a fantastic plot that operates for seventeen and one-half hours of a single day, at the end of which their masks are lifted, and true natures established—e.g., Betsy Bugbee, who personifies innocence, turns out to be a whore, and Frana Sherwood, the most notorious call girl in town, a virgin, with a medical certificate to prove it—and a high percentage of the dramatis personae is led off to jail. Whirled about in this tricky rigamarole are a few good laughs, such as the elaborate hoax on Biff Jordan, the Hollywood cowboy star, in which half of New York, including the *Times* sign, gets involved, a compendium of bop talk, and a theme of rather surprising weight, considering the general tone and level of this novel.

The serious theme is carried by Movement, a Negro marijuana salesman, whose life turns on the problem of authenticity, developed here in a series of paradoxes. Like most of his companions, white and Negro, Movement imitates the Negro who, in rebellion against the original stereotype imposed on the Negro by whites, imitates the Negro jazz musician. He is "cool," faceless, ex-

315

pressionless, totally without affect, and to all outward appearances mindless—but is a pressure cooker of rage and resentment within. His life, like his vocabulary, grows out of a set of metaphors based on insanity, violence, and death: *crazy, blow-top, cool, gone,* etc. Movement suffers from hypertension and lives on a diet of pills, and his thought—supplied largely by Melville's *Confidence Man* and Wyndham Lewis's *America and Cosmic Man*—is constantly tortured by the search, known in advance to be futile, for a real identity, an authentic self. This, like everyone else in his world, he is totally devoid of: his self is a function of a consciousness that has no center, but keeps turning back upon itself to find a void. All he can do is assume a number of poses or roles assigned by the people round him: Negroes who, like himself, play the part of the "cool" Negro, as well as those who still play the folksy, drawling role; whites who imitate both varieties of Negro, and white women who seek in him, and oblige him to play, the primitive buck, which also doesn't exist. Since Movement is a man in quest of himself to the exclusion of all roles—his self-doubt, however, suggests that this is but another role—his encounters with the world, particularly with white women, infuriate him and bring him closer and closer to the point of explosion. At the close of the book, he has submitted to a lobotomy and wound up in a Hollywood movie, cast as a young Negro doctor. The part had originally been given to a white actor, but his Southern accent and kinky hair made him seem too Negroid; Movement puts on blackface and looks like a white man made up to look like a Negro.

In spite of the exigencies of an improbable plot, Mr. Wolfe has caught something in Movement which is "authentic" as far as it goes. Movement's preoccupations are highly metaphysical, but his role may be studied in millions of interpretations among the hipsters of Broadway, the Village, San Francisco, Chicago's South Side, or wherever the jazz musician is culture hero.

Much of the same paradox of authenticity and inauthenticity is exhibited in the structure of this novel; it is made up to resemble Existentialist fiction (see the novels of Sartre and his articles and reflections on American life), which fiction, in turn, wears a make-up job derived, in good part, from the equivalent of the same Broadway kit.

Commentary, November, 1955

ᴥ§ Castile Soap Opera

RAQUEL is a gold mine: [Lion] Feuchtwanger wrote it for money, I am now writing about it for money, so are all the other reviewers in the papers and journals, and the men of letters who address the luncheons and the Women's Auxiliaries will have themselves many profitable afternoons on the strength of it. Hollywood is making the book into a movie, and it will no doubt be issued in the large paper editions and in all the tongues; an army of agents, directors, producers, actors, translators, and various publishers' men will take a nice long ride through clover, mounted on *Raquel's* fat back. The only thing I can't see is what the reader will get out of it. Though this is a historical novel, it's as sexy as the *Christian Science Monitor* and not nearly as well written (instead of a bosom, the dust cover bears the pure, limpid face of a young and rather cross-eyed girl, halfway between Hedy Lamar and a Siamese cat). The novel is about intrigue and bloody murder in twelfth-century Spain, with Christians and Moslems cutting one another's throats, and taking out their frustrations on the Jews; but it also reads like an editorial for Brotherhood Week, with three good guys from their respective faiths quoting the Prophet, Abélard, and the RaMBaM at one another in interminable disputation. The drift of it is that Alfonso VIII, King of Castile, falls in love with Dona Raquel, the daughter of his Jewish Escrivano, Don Yehuda ibn Esra, deserts his Christian wife and queen and builds a pleasure

palace for Raquel's sake, has a son by her and loves her
even more than he does his hounds, but lets himself get
dragged off to war against the Infidel, where he loses
abominably; and during his absence, Raquel and her
father are killed by a vengeful mob, at the instigation of
Dona Leonor, the Christian Queen. This is obviously a
Castile soap opera, but having already used the metaphor
of a gold mine, let me change the soap to Gold Dust and
call it quits.

But what's in it for the reader? The only profit a rational being can derive from reading this novel is, possibly, a number of reflections on *War and Peace*. Quite
by accident, *Raquel* is an admirable essay on how a serious
historical novel ought *not* to be written, and in its own
modest way it confirms Tolstoy's theory of history. Tolstoy, you will recall, argued that the will of the individual
human being counts for nothing as the cause of historical
action, which is rather a summation or integration of in-
finitesimal acts of will, supporting, contradicting, cancel-
ing and influencing one another. The higher a man
stands among the apparent causes of an action, the closer
he comes to being taken as the independent agent of
historical change, the more dependent he is on the will
of others, the officials and underlings pyramiding away
beneath him. Hence, Napoleon had practically nothing
to do with the invasion of Russia in 1812. The many contradictions and shortcomings of this theory have made us
overlook the fact that one need only change its field of application, from the writing of history to the writing of
historical fiction, to obtain a perfectly valid account of
historical cause from the point of view of the novel. Any
character seen closely, as from the domestic perspective
of *War and Peace*, will be seen as the result of all the
forces and pressures acting upon him. Pierre, for example, or Natasha are not isolated beings endowed with
an energy which enables them to change their environment in accordance with their wishes—they are, rather,
like molecules in a medium dense with other molecules
that influence the course they take, often against their
wishes, and deflect them from the goals which the illu-

sions of consciousness lead them to call their own. This view of human action, a consequence of Tolstoy's theory of history, is so well confirmed in the characters of *War and Peace*, particularly in Pierre, as to require no further justification. Whatever you may think of it as a theory for the writing of history in general, it is certainly true for the writing of *War and Peace*, since *War and Peace* was written according to this theory and no other.

Along comes *Raquel*, which is not written after anything one should dignify by the name of theory—but let us say there are some gross assumptions in the writing. Fuechtwanger has taken a period in history, done some research in it, and laid out his plot on the basis of the chronicles and legends, the ballads and romances that have already been devoted to the same episode; he makes a few provisions for timeliness, such as the plug for brotherhood already noted, and other topics like the insanity of war and aggression, and man's deplorable tendency toward bigotry, persecution, and superstition, then as now. But he has forgotten the Prince of Denmark; the one thing he did not prepare himself with was a conception of character, all the more necessary for a novel like *Raquel*, which runs on the gross assumption that history is directly affected by individual acts of will. In the course of writing this novel, whenever he comes to the point where an act of will is shown in operation, he constructs the character according to a simple-minded deduction. Thus, the function performed in history by Don Yehuda calls for a man, most likely, of proud and shrewd will; therefore, Don Yehuda is shown acting proudly and shrewdly. Don Alfonso, on the other hand, was most likely of a passionate, contradictory, and barbarous type, for the acts of will assigned to his agency make the deduction of these qualities the most probable; hence we are shown a Don Alfonso who acts in contradictory fashion, passionately and barbarously. And so with all the other characters, except Dona Raquel. The one sure deduction that can be made concerning her is that she was a beautiful woman, but beauty, unfortunately, is not an action, and to show a woman acting beautifully is a different thing from showing her acting as a beautiful woman. Raquel, therefore, has no character, for there is no character to deduce from the structure of the action; but Feuchtwanger patches up the difficulty by making an issue of her Jewishness. She has not been brought up as a Jewess, her culture and conditioning are Moslem, which is also the case with her father, Yehuda. But the latter has maintained an affinity for Judaism in spite of his conversion to Islam, and on a word from him she is ready to go to all extremes to prevent the baptism of her bastard son, and to ensure his being raised as a Jew.

But this is a phony doctrine of character; and of history, besides. It would follow from this view that history is the result of the acts of will of important people; but Feuchtwanger does not develop character in its own right, he merely reconstructs it from the historical outcome. Which is the same as saying that there is no such thing as character. For if action, as we are all agreed, must flow from character, but character is only a deduction from action, the terms pursue one another in a circle, and there is no telling effect from cause. Therefore, there is no such thing as character in *Raquel,* or in any other historical novel written the way this one is—which means, alas, practically all of them.

This is one of my reasons for believing that Tolstoy was right. In spite of the difficulties his theory of history presents to the writing of history, it is necessary, or something much like it is, to the writing of historical fiction. First, character must exist in its own right, and be seen in close perspective, as in the domestic parts of *War and Peace.* Then the postulate that our actions, and consequently history, are not the result of our will (at least not always the result of our will) must be set up, so that both action and character can be rendered in their full complexity. In fact, this may not be true, history may well be the result of particular acts of will, but in fiction it is

necessary to proceed otherwise, lest one land in Feuchtwanger's circular mishmash. His method justifies all the
deductions that have been drawn from the events of history, including the salacious ones that are crowding the
drugstore racks. It is a method of lining the pocket while
impoverishing the understanding.

Midstream, Summer, 1956

⊷ Life in Chicago

ALL FACES, coins, and questions have two sides, there is
concave and convex, and what man isn't a Janus-head?
This being topology, it holds good of all things: so also
of cities with their inside and out. I was born well inside
Chicago, four miles from the Lake. Public transporta-
tion being what it was—I might just as well say *is*, but
in those days no poor man had a car—and since the only
practical measure of distance from the Lake was distance
from a beach, all residents of the Jewish West Side,
around Roosevelt and Kedzie, were dry-docked. To see
water, you had to stand long, sweaty streetcar rides (the
red and buff streetcars, reeking of ozone, with their clang-
ing bells and screeching wheels, the wire-mesh window
guards and the air compressors going *diga-diga-diga-diga*
at each stop, the dust, the confetti of transfer punches,
mashed cigarette butts and soiled newspapers, hot rattan
seats on the sunny side, green shades)—how long those
rides were! You might have been living in the heart of
some central land mass, for all the difference it made,
your proximity to water. Herewith, a theory on the
matter.

All cities hug water, but it's available, accessible, visible, sensible water that counts. You wouldn't have known
it, living inland in Chicago—and you won't, I am sure,
to this day—that the city sprawls for miles along a great
lake that is capable of oceanic moods when the right
weather takes it, of biologic odors when its meadows
bloom and its fauna spawn and crawl; you wouldn't have
known that this lake makes sea waves, and in winter,

323

ice cliffs, under a wild-flying spray. Thales never walked these streets, or he would have held earth to be the source of all creation, the peculiar, cracked, ashy, mineral-gray Chicago earth with its derivative dust, grit, and grime that rise swirling when the wind blows. We had sun-pictures in those days: you held a glass negative to the light, backed by a piece of photo-sensitive paper—images of Tom Mix, Jack Holt, Hoot Gibson straddling their lover-horses, or Rin-Tin-Tin in an earlier incarnation, but never of ships, not even a tub or a barge, let alone ocean liners. Locomotives there were aplenty—the Twentieth Century, which runs to New York.

So we were landlocked, and the mind was parched for moisture. Call it Gobi Desert, we were in Central Asia, and even when the rain poured, as it did, from hoses, the sewers would gurgle, the baked earth would crack open again, and only a little mud remained in the depressions we had pocked out with our heels to play killer-in-the-hole. Such is the source of isolationism in the Midwest: it is an ignorance and fear of water.

It took estrangement to make this clear to me. I had to move away and come back a visitor, and at last, as I am now, a residential stranger, to discover the Lake front and its implications. I had to approach the city from the outside, to throw off the heavy, bitter birth-burden and the natural piety by which I held this place dear, to see it under an aspect external to both my love and hate: to peer down its streets and not see myself at the end of them.

The visitor who approaches Chicago by plane from the East gets the preferential view: granite and white marble skyscrapers and museums, bordered by park, bordered by water. Then more of the same by car for some twenty miles along the Lake, over the Outer Drive. Lake, lake, lake, but not really lake, for there is no opposite shore, only water cribs, tankers, lighthouses, sails—and on the land side, tall apartment buildings, a continuous façade. One way, look as far as you like and let the horizon float you into space. The other way, blind and abrupt, no peeking. Chicago is trying to hide something. Walk about and you will see what—not north and south along the Lake—east, let us say, of Broadway, Clark, and State, for there you will see only that which Chicago wants seen, its Gold Coast and Magnificent Mile of Fifth Avenue and occasionally then-some shop windows, stores, hotels, hospitals, restaurants, cocktail lounges, and fashion centers which furnish the home and the mind. Go west, cross State, proceed out on North Avenue or Division, where the hog butcher lives. Architecture is frozen music, but this is cutthroat screaming. Here are the hidden poor in outhouses with inside plumbing—what did the Great Chicago Fire burn that these hutches and coops should still stand? Not picturesque South Halsted Street with strings of garlic and garlands of fig, an atmosphere burning bright of Mediterranean ports and Polish ghettos, but Stashu-plain West Division Street with the blond, brutal, crew-cut hair, or Germantown North Avenue with the saloons and Deutsches Kino, the hardware stores, bakeries, the shiny furniture stores, the railroad yards, the factories, smokestacks, gas tanks. Mile after mile of vanished Nile culture reconstructed out of archaeological debris, but no people, the crowds in the street rendered invisible through incongruity: an inhuman landscape (does anyone *live* here?)—hence, no inhabitants. These are some species of nomad on the move, fellaheen taking off after the Israelites, they, too, fleeing a smitten Egypt. The pyramids are plainly labeled, Butcher Shop, Auto Parts, Wrecking. It goes on forever, the hidden Chicago, not to be seen from the outside. The point of it all is its pointlessness.

Let me say it by birthright. Natural piety revolts, I would not have it spoken by an outsider, to bray it aloud like A. J. Liebling and publish it in Gath. But if Chicago is one of the Seven Wonders, then the eighth is that a city should be so pointlessly huge. You can take down the statement in a mile or two, you get the drift soon enough, of landscape burdened by industry, but it goes on and on, over and over and over, a Walt Whitman storehouse of democracy come alive, a Sears catalogue of people and occupations endlessly varied in repetitive similitudes cracking Leibniz on the numskull conk, identity of indiscernibles, indeed! Why so much, so many, so indiscernibly all-alike-and-different; who needs all these dry-goods stores, groceries, factories, railroad yards, sidings, lamp posts, funeral parlors? Would the world collapse if there were just one less?

No fiery riddles, this is all very plain. I mean to say, Chicago produces practically nothing that it does not manufacture. Between the work of hand and mind a balance must be kept. This balance was never established in the wonder days when Chicago rose from nothing to the nation's fourth largest city in the first generation of its incorporated existence, and our schools, churches, museums, libraries, universities, art galleries, theaters, and concert halls have not yet righted the balance, though we are second in the land.

Come back to the Lake. We have a saying in Chicago; when we want to dispose of someone we tell him to walk east—till his hat floats. The Lake is the city's eastern boundary, and all along this boundary for some twenty miles but seldom more than a mile deep, the East has, you might say, established a beachhead. Chicago can't keep its eye off New York; not only LaSalle vs. Wall Street, the whole city is shot through and has been over most of its history, with rivalrous attitudes. State and Madison is "the world's busiest corner," the Chicago *Tribune* is "the world's greatest newspaper," the Merchandise Mart is "the world's largest office building," Midway Airport is "the world's busiest," etc., etc.

Some of these boasts are well founded. Chicago does rank first in shipping, packing, railroading, its commercial traffic is second to none; but consider for a moment, not the truth but the *direction* of our claims—they are aimed at New York. One by one Chicago has overtaken its earlier rivals, St. Louis, Boston, Philadelphia, San Francisco; we are ahead of them in size, productivity, and importance (whatever we mean by that). But New York stays stubbornly in first place. All sorts of happy statements float about town; now that the St. Lawrence seaway is opening up and Chicago is building port facilities at Lake Calumet (at the southeastern extremity of the city), it will outstrip New York and become the country's number one port. It is so many miles nearer Liverpool than New York is, it has so many natural advantages, not the least considerable of which is the fact that the city is farther from the peak of its climb than New York. Now we are going to make it!

In five years the Port of Chicago may well become what the city's optimists predict, but it will take more than five years, at least a generation, more likely fifty, for the real issue in Chicago's rivalry with New York to be settled. This will require an elemental transformation. Chicago must move from earth to water. Such are the implications of the narrow strip along the Lake.

Such are the implications of the long narrow strip of Lake culture, and its three points of concentration, off the North Shore at Evanston, where Northwestern stands (not properly in Chicago, but its culture necessarily bound fast to it), off the Near North Side and the Loop in the middle, and to the south, off the Midway which is spanned by the University of Chicago. The water culture as opposed to the land means internationalism, an openness to interchange, a hospitality to ideas. The massive land culture means heavy production, but no city can be truly great that does not reach out to water. It need not be nearby. Paris is no seacoast town, neither is Rome, but the Seine and the Tiber are revered, and there men have at least built lovely embankments. The Chicago River, in the heart of town, runs dirty and neglected. It was a great engineering feat to make it reverse its course (in 1900, to draw sewage and foul odors away), but having done that, we were for years unable to think what else to do. Only in the last two years has a strip of embankment off Randolph Street been planted to grass, but so much remains to be done, this hardly counts as a beginning.

There is the matter of bridges, for one. A bridge must be a beautiful thing to symbolize intercourse, joining, but the Chicago River is spanned by no graceful rise of arch. Heavy, girdered bridges flat as a Dutchman's foot join the Loop to its northern and western environs, and the union between the shores is not even a permanent thing, for the bridges must split open in the middle, stalling the land traffic, when a ship sails by. You can imagine how this will snarl an already congested traffic when enlarged port facilities bring an even greater amount of activity to the Chicago River, as they will inevitably do. Not until stairways, benches, and walks sprout among the still unplanted trees and gardens at the river banks will the Chicago become a proper place for loafing and dreaming, as are the Seine and the Tiber, even the commercial Thames and Hudson (where you dream of different things, all, however, touched by water). Not until then will water become a property of the city as a whole.

Look to fishing for our true progress. It is easy enough to sit and fish along the Lake, and hundreds of fishermen do so daily. But the heart of the city must find a place for them, they must not be required to sit at the edge. Only then will commerce once more come to mean intercourse —when one need not turn his back upon it, but can lean back, at ease among busy things, resting against stone and brick, activity wedded to inactivity, action to contemplation, and natural piety blessing all things—bird call and policeman's whistle—as it has done in Paris for centuries.

The beachhead is in a perilous position: it is so narrow, so precious and *précieux;* and it makes up such a small proportion of the total land mass of Chicago. When there has been a particularly violent crime, or when the chronic racial tension in Chicago flares up, I am sometimes taken with fear and I see this vulnerable area, in which the city's cultural life is concentrated, invaded by the land forces, come to smash the records and the art objects and trample the Swedish-blond or Danish walnut furniture of the style centers under hobnail boots.

Violence, not precisely of this kind, has been going on in Hyde Park for years, where the streets are rude by day and unsafe by night, with robberies, burglaries, and assault quite common. To grasp the full meaning of these events, you must know that Hyde Park, for more than fifty years, has been the city's chief seat of culture— a South Side neighborhood of about two square miles in which the famous Midway, left over from the Exposition of 1893, the University of Chicago, the Museum of Science and Industry, the homes and apartments of University personnel, and fine parks, bathing beaches, shops, and hotels are located.

Hyde Park is bordered, on the west, by the terribly overcrowded Black Belt, which slipped its buckle during the war years; the resulting spill-over, plus migrations, still going on, of Puerto Ricans and of poor whites and Negroes from the South, converted the area into one of the city's worst trouble spots, full of crimes, juvenile and adult, and racial incidents. Some of the violence has been checked by arc lights and increased police patrols, which were granted by the city administration, rather belatedly, after the residents of the area held many protest meetings and circulated endless petitions. Conditions are much better now, but the meaning of these incidents persists; at work here are not racial tension, poverty, the maladjustments of uprooted populations, and resentment of the underprivileged alone, but the revolt of the masses, in Ortega's sense, the execration of quality and of things of the mind. It is hard to say how much damage has been done along these lines to the neighborhood and its institutions, and to what extent a recovery can be marked; but in the nature of the case, such blows to the security and ease of a city's cultural life may cause considerable and even permanent harm.

The University of Chicago, faced by the prospect of complete isolation in a roughneck slum, is at last "doing something about it"—together with the Southeast Chicago Commission, the Chicago Housing Authority, and the Hyde Park-Kenwood Community Conference, it is sponsoring conversion of its immediate environs into a high-cost rental and shopping area, which should eliminate "undesirables" regardless of racial lines and enable the "better class of people" to live at ease. But this is hardly a fundamental solution, and it does not affect all of Hyde Park. Tenements, traps, and slums between the Midway and the south side of 55th Street will be torn down, but the area immediately north of 55th Street and within striking distance of the University and its precincts will only become more congested, and deteriorate all the more rapidly; the same may be expected across the southern boundary line, and one cannot suppose that forced removals will turn the gangs and hoods toward benevolence.

But the psychological aspects of this solution stand a somewhat better chance of working out. The strain on liberal conscience (Hyde Park is highly liberal) of opposing racial prejudice while complaining about "the neighborhood" and supporting block organizations to "keep up the standards," may shortly be removed if the redevelopment of Hyde Park produces an interracial area of relatively equal economic, social, and cultural standards. The way one white liberal put it, "We don't care what color our neighbors are, but when they play their radios too loud, we'd rather hear Vivaldi than pops." But a conversation between two Negroes of the upper class, reported to me by Rolf Meyersohn, a University of Chicago sociologist, and his wife Mary Lea, puts the entire redevelopment project under a different light. "What self-respecting Negro would *want* to live in Hyde Park!" I don't know to what extent this sentiment is general among the colored; but the first may be taken to be universal among liberal whites.

Community life in Hyde Park is dominated by the University, its students, faculty, and administrative personnel. I am willing to risk a few generalizations on the University culture—as anthropologists use the word—with the understanding, of course, that no generalizations are as sound as they are attractive.

Not so long ago, under the chancellorship of Robert M. Hutchins, the students at the University—I shall restrict myself throughout to undergraduates—made up a fairly uniform body. Football was out, and with it went the usual rah-rah accessories of collegiate and fraternity life. Raccoon coat, pennants, beanies, megaphones, and slogan- ized flivvers may have flourished in the twenties; but the thirties and forties, under Hutchins, were lean and studi- ous years, with the students forming a self-conscious intellectual elite, newly introduced to Aristotle, Aquinas, and a revolutionary college program which gave great advantages to the bright and more industrious. In the postwar years, when enrollment dropped and the Uni- versity found itself with a critical shortage of funds, a number of changes began to take place, the influence of which is still being felt. Chief among the changes was the succession to the chancellorship of Lawrence A. Kimpton, who views the return of football as a prime educational necessity, and who, a few years ago, shocked the campus by declaring that the University was no place for "queer" students. By queer, Chancellor Kimpton meant intellectuals—a position there is no reason to suspect him of having abandoned.

Kimpton's policies have gone over with the trustees, improved the University's financial position, and attracted a larger and more apple-cheeked student body. The "queers" to be sure, still persist, and always will, so long as the University retains its present scholastic standards, but among the students may now be found a considerable number of the "yaks"—as they are called in derision— more or less healthy and well-adjusted young men and women of rather inflexible mind, who regard life not as an adventure but an investment. In an argument with one of them—we were debating the relative merits of the Hutchins and Kimpton administrations—I found myself routed by my interlocutor, an Ivy Leaguish graduate in law, who declared, "Do you realize that until I came to the University I did not know how to play golf!" As we say, "*Darf men gehn tsu college?*"

Indirectly and by default, the intellectuals are also promoting the return of football. (I trust that the term "intellectuals" may be applied, without too much stretch, to students who are not "yaks" and who may, conceivably, leave the university without learning how to play golf—

in short the "queers." These equivocations are made in
good faith, and are necessitated by an extraordinary shift
in perspective among the students, which I hope to make
clear in a moment. Let us call them the "serious"
students, with the understanding that here, too, the term
requires qualification.)

The outstanding change in student life, over the last
decade or so, is the disappearance of politics as an active
interest. Chicago, which was once considered a "hot bed
of radicalism" by the *Tribune* and the local Hearst press
and is still held in suspicion by the state legislature, has
gone the way of all other American universities, with
revolutionary groups passing into desuetude. In the old
days (I would call them good; it is my own conviction
that politics furnishes the best of all bases for secular
culture) the political interest colored practically every
student activity on campus, with the major division drawn
between Stalinists (who dominated the American Student
Union) and Trotskyites (who worked through the local
chapter of the Young People's Socialist League).* The
two Marxist groups, with their symps and associates,
spoke bitterly about, but never to, each other and avoided
all contact, except to heckle, and occasionally strong-arm,
each other's meetings. Politics was everywhere, in a
measure, one ate and drank it; and sleep gave no escape,
for it furnished terror to our dreams: Hitler, Mussolini,
the Moscow Trials, the Spanish Civil War, the plaguey
bill of Stalinism, the stopgaps of NRA, WPA, and the
New Deal, and the approach of inevitable war. We lived
in the shadow of annihilation, drawing on the pattern of
Guernica and Ethiopia to imagine what bombings would
be like. Liaisons, marriages, and divorces, let alone friend-
ships, were sometimes contracted on no other basis than
these issues, and dominated, in a way that might seem
incomprehensible to the present generation, by events of
the world order. Even students who were *hors de combat*
were involved, for everyone called upon them to justify
their disinterest, and they had hard work convincing

*I am speaking of an avant-garde, the pace setters and conscious
students, and also the ones who were out of it in a special way.

even themselves. Politics was form and substance, accident and modification, the metaphor of all things.

Now this has vanished like Villon's snows. The metaphor is no longer political; it is not even social, but anti-social, and anti-social in a special sense, for the word, as older generations understand it, carries connotations that have become obsolete. Insofar as there is a metaphor governing the attitudes of life, it seems to be derived from the world of jazz, with the avant-garde leading the way in speech, manners, and dress. A few alliances exist with the pipestem, narrow-shouldered Ivy League tradition, and there is a sprouting of striped and buckled caps, but the University, as a whole, has not plunged. This is due to the fact that the University of Chicago is still dominated by intellectual tradition, and no definite tradition comes along with the suit and extra slacks.

But the dominant intellectual tradition is hardly recognizable as one. Tag ends of Aristotelianism and of Hutchins still stick to it, but they are as confused as they are confusing to the undergraduates, who take quite a rocking in the College, while new administrative policies are under hot debate. For the last several years everyone has been predicting the complete disappearance of the College, as Hutchins organized it, in a year or two; the predictions have not yet come true, but slow changes are in process, hard to make out on the surface, which, everyone supposes, are preparing the way for the University with a strapping enrollment and buzzing with the wholesome athletic activities that Kimpton desires. Meanwhile the students have retreated from the more pressing local issues as they have from international ones, and have taken to calling one another "man." This key word of bop talk is highly significant, expressing, as it does, the least common biological denominator, to which all things are reduced by the universal solvent of jazz.

The South Side is dominated by the University, but the University, in turn, is dominated by the South Side. The neighborhood life of the students, their favorite bars and hangouts (Jimmie's, the Compass Tavern, the University Tavern, Stineway's on 57th Street) have developed an interracial clientele of mixed types. Besides the recognizable students (many are no longer so), there are Bohemians, workers, white-collar men, hangers-on, moochers, delinquents, and near-delinquents. From the last four groups, some require a new category for proper classification; I would call them *retired students*—young men, and some women, who need not actually have attended the University; they are no longer active as students, but still follow the student pattern, by habit or imitation, maintain contact with the students, and have a considerable following and reputation among them as "characters." The retired student, a sort of recently discovered missing link, is but one of the many new forces blurring the distinction between town and gown. One meets types in the varied off-campus dives whom one would mistakenly warrant as students, and students on campus who would seem, by nature, to belong on a motorcycle or behind a counter, tending bar. The shrinking of the distance between extremes has produced a student culture typical, as a particular, and lower, social level, of the amalgamations taking place all over society in our conservative time.

Phenomenologically, the student complex consists in bop talk (with its basic expressions, such as *crazy, cool, gas, stoned*, etc., etc., deriving from insanity, narcosis, and death; very often the vocabulary is dated as, in a larger sense, the practice is—the avant-garde leadership in New York, for example, has begun to drop bop), narcotics mythology (marijuana and main-line drugs, as part of the folkways of jazz musicians; very little indulgence, however), rudeness ("man," "cat," and "chick" being the major human designations, they call for none of the amenities that accompany the recognition of human beings as individual souls), hi-fi, short haircuts, jeans, cotton-twill slacks, zipper jackets, and occasionally fashionable but always dirty or neglected clothes, and sports cars parked along the curb.

The ideal is to lead a passionless, "cool" life, exposed,

but uncommitted, to many worlds and to be *au courant*
in them all: to be able to chatter—actually, drone—of
drama, books, art, jazz, hi-fi, recordings, liquors, mixed
drinks, Aristotle and other philosophers, events about
town, the underworld and its leading characters, as well
as the leading personalities in the entertainment worlds;
to avoid extremes of romanticism in sexuality or love, and
all extremes of feeling, which extremes (actually normal
emotion) are held in bad taste and called "frantic." (It
is of course obvious that this antiromanticism is one of
the most romantic of all cults.) One undergraduate I
know calls the composite *formo-frigidist*, an excellent
description, as it unifies the standards of taste over the
entire range, including furniture and literary criticism.
The whole is a masquerade. Intellectuality is cultivated
as mindlessness, is required to confine itself to the crippling, limited vocabulary noted above, and to endorse
guitars, Calypso, and other folk music; the rich students
act and dress poor, and the poor students, within their
means, rich; racial equality, though often genuinely believed in, sometimes seeks hostile expression, the whites
calling their colored friends *spooks*, and the colored (who
often refer to themselves by the same term) returning
the favor through the use of the word *ofay*, so that it is
more than a little puzzling, at times, to tell the dancer
from the dance. The dead-pan Afro-Cuban mask, though
optional, is worn on all occasions.

The foregoing is not, of course, true of all students,
nor does the entire complex necessarily occur in students
who do fit the pattern, but to a degree almost all of
them are growing on this compost. There remain, of
course, purer types, now as at all times, students without
nonsense whose culture heroes might be some great poet,
novelist, painter, philosopher, or composer, rather than
the jazz musician. Their fate is inseparable from that of
the series throughout Chicago's beachhead—and similar
beachheads all over the world.

I don't know to what extent the phenomena of student
life, and the Hyde Park crime rate, may be attributable

to the invasion of the beachhead by land forces. Surely, some such process is involved, but the process must be an extremely complex one, since very often the predator upon the cultural, as well as the material, wealth of the beachhead is himself of the beachhead. (Nor do I mean to imply that all land forces are vicious; most of them, on the contrary, are associated with the prime middle-class virtues of stability, security, and respect for law and order. But the distinction between the lake and the land still holds true in terms of culture.)

I should judge that we are dealing, in Hyde Park, not so much with an invasion of the beachhead, as with the absence, on the beachhead, of an adequate idea of what the cultural life in and around a university should be. In part, the University is also to blame for this; in recent years it has begun to show that it, too, lacks a clear idea of itself.* Its own unclarity is reflected among the students, not only yaks, but non-yaks. In time, the latter may well become a subspecies of yak, also capable of attribu-

* In one small part, the University has passed undamaged through its own turmoil. I am speaking of the Basic Program of Liberal Education for Adults. Classes are held, most of them, off campus, downtown, at the University's Downtown Center; they are devoted to a four-year seminar and tutorial course in reading the great books from Plato and Aristotle through Dostoevsky and Freud—the original Hutchins-Adler idea, somewhat modified and elaborated, and absolute proof against the educational imperatives of football, folk music, and golf. Sports cars, if any, are parked inconspicuously in the welter of downtown traffic, and *steel-bon* and Calypso do not penetrate to the ears of the adult students. We tie ourselves nightly to the mast (there are also forenoon and early afternoon classes, attended mostly by housewives, and 7:30 A.M. "early-bird" classes, attended, I should imagine, by grackles) and have thus far resisted destruction, though enrollment is sometimes precarious. Staff meetings, which occur almost weekly during the academic year, and several times a week during the summer, take on a salutary violence, and the interchange of ideas and criticism reaches an intensity unequaled since the old political days on questions of curriculum, policy, and interpretation of the various readings. For a reason I have not yet discovered, this program, which is quite severe in its demands of both faculty and students, is unbeatable for sheer serious fun. Everybody loves it, and there is nothing quite like it in Chicago or any other city.

ting their "education" to the University—e.g., "Man, do you realize that until I came to the U, I didn't dig folk songs!" It is in this way that they support their opposite numbers from the frats and football claques: by letting their "queerness" become something other than conspicuous intellectuality.

An entirely different culture is exhibited by the faculty, administrative personnel, and older graduate students—but here, too, the distinction between academic and nonacademic life cannot always be clearly drawn; many professional men, strangers to the University, inhabit the area, and in its broader features life in Hyde Park follows a neighborhood pattern rather than a strictly academic one.

This pattern, which my sociologist friend Meyersohn calls the Hyde Park syndrome, shows some remarkable uniformities. First of all, the members of this group are married; and while marriage and family life predominate in nearly all neighborhoods, in Hyde Park people marry, furnish apartments, and raise children in a unique way. The children are all out of Spock and Gesell, with an assist from Bruno Bettelheim of the University's Orthogenic School. The furniture is from Bordelon's or aspires to be (Bordelon's is a modern furnishings center; it has recently closed out its Hyde Park store and moved to the wealthier Near North Side) and a few modern *objets*, such as chairs or tables with wire legs, are sure to be found in every house. Marriage has a youthful, cheerful, share-and-share-alike tone to it, with the young couples doing their shopping together at the Co-op, drawing on the services of the same (or the same kinds of) baby sitters and pediatricians, encountering the same kinds of problems, and solving them in similar ways. Infidelities are rare—such, at least, is the impression; this is my riskiest generalization—and one of the few differentiae between Hyde Park's academic and nonacademic professionals may be drawn along this line, with the incidence of infidelity and divorce higher among the latter. (I suspect that nearly all differentiae between these highly similar groups are reducible to income, and that as the differences in culture pattern become greater, the higher one climbs the income gradient.)

Other things being equal, one sure way of telling whether you are visiting an academic or nonacademic household is by the behavior of the children, and the extent to which you can make yourself heard above their clatter. If it is still possible to conduct a conversation, you are in a nonacademic household. The men and women form groups of their own for tennis, handball, gymnasium workouts, or buggy pushing, shopping in the neighborhood or downtown, but by and large the couples are always together; pub crawling and other single-handed pursuits are rare (at least when it comes to conducting them in the neighborhood).

The Goths may be sacking this Rome, but many of the Romans go on leading the established life, making the big time in their middle-class villas. I call Romans the ones whom it will take fire or other catastrophe to push out of Hyde Park; they are entrenched in their love of place and firm in their liberal convictions; an interracial atmosphere, if not entirely congenial to them, is still a cheerful price. It is not hard to see what they find lovable in Hyde Park. Nowhere else in a city of comparable size is there quite the same "small town" feeling as in this community. It has a relatively rooted, peaceful look, and in some sections, an aged dignity far beyond its years. The residential streets are all planted to lawns and trees (mostly cottonwoods, elms, and catalpas) with hedges, shrubs, and flowers not uncommon. The University's bell tower booms out quarter-hour intervals in shivery tones and sends the strokes of the hour floating over the neighborhood, never on time; the red-tile roofs and crew-cut Gothic of the University buildings shine through the trees like the City of Oz, and when in the right frame of mind you can convince yourself that the outlying houses and streets are a village snuggling up to a castle. (In its administrative complexities, the castle, I might add, is much like Kafka's, but let's not spoil a pretty picture.)

But the key to the small-townishness of Hyde Park is

provided by bulletin boards. These, of course, are all over the University, and it was but a short step to carry them off campus, yet the bulletin-board culture began on a tree trunk outside a bookstore on 57th Street. Hundreds of signs, slips, chits, and notices hang pinned to this tree, all around the trunk, sometimes overlapping, several layers deep, from as high as a man can reach to sidewalk level, advertising rooms and apartments to rent and sublet, baby buggies and cars for sale, beds, armchairs, scrabble sets, English bicycles for both sexes, baby sitters, potted plants, tropical fish, hi-fi apparatus and repairs, rides to points east and west, recorders from sopranino to bass— and the corresponding notices of goods and services wanted. (Recently the tree offered for sale a pair of ladies' straw sandals, worn only once, and a hermaphroditic hamster.)

Similar notices are to be found on the bulletin board of the Hyde Park Co-op, and lost and found signs are posted on tree trunks all over the neighborhood. Telephone numbers and addresses are freely stated, in spite of the degeneration of the neighborhood, on a patent assumption of cultural homogeneity, as though it were inconceivable for burglars to consult the tree for leads. And yet, in all likelihood, they may never do so; at any rate, the assumption of homogeneity is fully justified, for the notices are often worded in such a way as to be unintelligible to outsiders.

There is a compact, solid, middle-class "what-I-shall-assume-you-shall-assume" feeling about these signs, a sense of shared life and values, we are all friends. I don't know of any studies of the subject, but I am sure they would reveal a striking uniformity in outlook and habits among the people who post and read these advertisements, and I venture to say it would go somewhat as follows. For some reason I imagine that they are solidly for Stevenson (I can't imagine a Republican rubber-necking the tree trunk) and yet for Stevenson in a special sense, by way of Independent Voters of Illinois (a special chapter of the ADA), or out of conviction that he is intellectual and not, say, as the hillbillies in the neighborhood are for him. (Hillbillies are also unimaginable at the tree trunk.) Many of our tree-trunkers (let's call them Druids for convenience) work for the IVI and IVI-endorsed candidates, and give of their time to ring doorbells, circulate petitions, and relieve the watch at headquarters during election campaigns. They read the *New Yorker* and the *Reporter*, and buy the New York Sunday *Times* for the Book Review. On clement days in summer they go out to the Point, a recreation area and rocky projection into the lake off 55th Street; there some of them go skin diving. Though the rocks are slippery, sharp, and often slammed by strong waves, our types prefer them to the sand beach at 57th Street; the Point is town pump and tabernacle for all Hyde Park, and if faculty is not as well represented there as are the students this is not for cultural reasons. (Many of them have children, for whom the rocks and deep water are unsafe; and besides, as many of them as are able to, go to the country in the summer. Besides, the tree is one of the chief points where the faculty and student cultures intersect, and the typology I am developing round the tree is meant to hold good for the University culture as a whole, and not for faculty alone.)

There is a complex pattern here, somewhat mystifiying in its principle of cohesion. It is easy enough to see why there should be a division among the faculty, student, and Bohemian aspects of the University culture, but not why or how each group acquires its own particular pattern, or why the culture as a whole should be composed of such various elements as sports cars, bop talk, gin-and-tonic, Station WFMT, cottage-cheese-and-garlic, paper-bound books, short haircuts, IVI, foreign movies, Bordelon's furniture, copper jewelry and earrings, a painfully ambiguous attitude toward the color question, guitars, folk music, skin diving, Dr. Spock, recorder-playing, hi-fi, open sandals, and hamsters as standard zoological equipment for introducing the children to the facts of life. Just what is the secret affinity between hi-fi and short haircuts, for example, that they should so often be found together, or between Béla Bartók and the IVI, or wall-to-wall carpeting and a subscription to *Harper's*? This, to be sure, is not a question for Hyde Park alone to answer; one might very well ask it of urban culture as a whole. The cohesiveness seems to lie in the cohesion; essence lags scandalously far behind existence—and yet, I am sure it is no hodgepodge, some principle must be present.

There is more of the same on the Near North Side. This is Chicago's "New York" neighborhood—but much cleaner, more concentrated, and in some respects more like New York than the original. It combines Fifth Avenue (a number of Fifth Avenue shops, such as Bonwit's and Saks, have branches on North Michigan) with Central Park West and Riverside Drive, but this is only a manner of speaking. Oddly enough, it is the manner spoken here. Actually, this section has a quality and beauty all its own, with the Lake providing the distinctive atmosphere. Again, there is a complex in evidence, a mixture of elements and types, not so oddly assorted as in Hyde Park, but still of considerable range.

One immediately apparent difference is the concentration of homosexuals, and their attendant culture. Some of the shops and night spots have an exclusively homosexual clientele; others are mixed. Even some of the corner drug stores, whose fountains and lunch counters are patronized by cab drivers and local merchants, give preference, in the magazine racks, to jock-strap and body-beautiful cheesecake; the girlie magazines are often hidden behind several layers of brightly oiled young men.

This neighborhood also has its contrasts, the tracks on North State Street distinguishing the right from the wrong side. East of State, there is considerable elegance; west of State, decline sets in, running rapidly to the squalor that begins at Clark. (The Lake culture also begins to peter out at State.) The sharp division between east and west moderates the clash somewhat, and you don't encounter the startling juxtapositions of hotels and hovels so frequently as you do in New York, but the neighborhood is still pre-eminent in contrast. There are mean pigeon-fouled rooming houses, and flops, missions, employment agencies, pigeon-fouled on the outside and

cluttered with lithos and bric-a-brac within, and sky-
scraper apartments with liveried doormen and snipped
hedges, barber shops that serve coffee and barber shops
where you can place a bet, dinky Spanish groceries for
the Puerto Rican colony and greasy spoons, secondhand
automobile lots and secondhand clothing stores, and some
of the better known night clubs, key clubs, and restaurants
that play progressive jazz—all within a few blocks of one
another.

Rush Street, the cabaret center, is brightly lit and
fairly crowded all hours of the night. (Night crowds are
a rarity in Chicago; of the downtown streets, only Randolph, the amusement center, stays awake after the shops
close, and then mostly on weekends.) Coffee houses, that
double as art galleries, and serve atmosphere and *espresso*
(which most of them spell *expresso*), abound in the
neighborhood, and put some three or four ice cream
tables out of doors, if space permits, for that continental
touch (Ricardo's, one of the largest restaurants, even surrounds you with travel posters). There is a rash of key
clubs, with sedate or moderne façades, where you may
enjoy the dubious privilege of entree by card or key only.
These are unknown on the South Side.

The people round about are of several kinds. In addition to the obvious homosexuals, there are office workers
and stenos from the nearby Loop, advertising executives
and publicity men, students, painters, musicians, con
men, chorus girls, call girls, entertainers, wrigglers,
peelers, transients, Bohemians, creeps, and hardy old
ladies who carry shopping bags. The conspicuous difference between the Near North Side and Hyde Park is
the absence of faculty. The University facilities in or
near the neighborhood are mostly for evening students,
and the staff of the University of Illinois College at Navy
Pier either live on the South Side or the Far North or the
North suburbs. At any rate, professors and their wives
are not in evidence, the young-liberal complex is quite
diluted, and bulletin boards and notices on trees are
virtually unknown.

The Near North Side is not as homogeneous as Hyde

Park; it does not have a large, homogeneous middle-class group that lends its character to the streets and gathering places. It is an anonymous neighborhood, transient and big town. Puerto Ricans and Negroes inhabit the outskirts, but racial tensions are insignificant or very well concealed. Crime in the area a few blocks off the Lake is confined to burglary and traffic violations, and street incidents are uncommon. Bug House Square in Washington Park, facing the Newberry Library, does not draw the crowds of the thirties, and there are fewer *nudniks* and spielers.

Nevertheless the syndrome, with a few modifications, is similar to Hyde Park, and a purer formation of upper-class taste and life patterns is in evidence. Bordelon's has a huge furniture and fashion center on Walton Street, and next door Max Siegel, the bookseller, manages to achieve the same effects with birthday cards and books that Bordelon's does in the slip covers—he carries a fair number of books, but they are so carefully loaded on light, airy shelves as to appear purely decorative. The concentrated, foxed, browsy, and intellectually brown atmosphere of traditional bookstores is gone; with a few minor changes the place would do well as a first-class airline waiting room. All is glass and steel, doors that open electronically, and pastel colorcombos.

There are plenty of sports cars here, but their significance as indices of wealth is much more frankly admitted, and since the drivers are seldom students, they can afford to go all the way in accessories of costume, or feel under no pressure to pretend that they can't. Hi-fi also flourishes more openly in the money culture. There are more dogs on the Near North Side than in Hyde Park, but they cannot as yet touch the pigeons for making a mess. The syndrome, then, is hi-fi, modern furniture, Ivy League fashions, exclusive women's shops, and millineries, with politics, faculty life, and bulletin boards significantly absent.

The Bohemians are much like their counterparts to the south, and also lisp of the drug and jazz mythology in dated bop talk, but there are fewer or none of the retired-student types among them, and the quasi-criminal and delinquent motorcycle characters are scarce. The only pure Bohemian hangout is the College of Complexes (the sign is misspelled, perhaps not deliberately) at the site of the old Dill Pickle Club. It offers a variety of lectures and debates on topics in the news, and on off nights the clientele can pursue edification by reading the slogans scrawled in chalk on the blackboard that makes up one wall: "Bed wetters of the world unite," "2+2=4," etc., etc. Other hangouts, such as the Gate of Horn, feature folk songs, American and foreign.

Many of these streets are a joy for their cleanliness, which persists in spite of choked traffic and a great variety of life and activity, and for the harmony between the rooming houses—once highly fashionable houses—and the apartment buildings and hotels. Bellevue Place, at the foot of which stands the former Mrs. Adlai Stevenson's famous 1020 Club, is downright beautiful: quiet, reserved—it seems miles away from everything—big town, modest, harmonious, with well-kept lawns, hedges, and trees.

The quiet life—pace it as you please—is still possible in Chicago. You can live in neighborhoods which have retained a distinctive character, and among middle-class types who have moved with the time into outer space, acquiring tastes and habits unknown a decade ago, but have retained their traditional integrity. Among some of them, in their homes, say, on East Fullerton of the mid-North Side, or on Hyde Park Boulevard, you encounter an attractive mixture of respectable vocation and artistic avocation (mostly painting and writing), with a laudable bourgeois sense of responsibility toward civic and national issues, and a well-cultivated middle-brow obligation to keep up with the right books and magazines.

Among some of these good people you get the sense that discord and neurosis are mild afflictions, that homes are permanent and children a tie which is not resented. These, to be sure, are land virtues, but they are borne

without too much incongruity by people of the Lake
front. Perhaps they live in the strip for the sake of the
breeze—I am not speaking meteorologically—but it is a
sure thing they will not be blown away by it. An evening
in their homes—they often form "drama circles," in which
plays, but more often magazine articles, are read aloud,
and followed by cake and coffee—gives one assurance
of the abiding virtues, of group solidarity, and the abundance of the good, quiet, effortless things of life. These
are the people who are relatively free of the syndrome.
The appearance of well-being is fully developed. The
principle of cohesion is the traditional one, the home.

My proposition, then, is this. The culture strip along
the Lake is not strong or rich enough to defend itself
against invasion or internal corruption. There are too
few plays for one—theater has long been dead in Chicago
—and the recent attempts to found a local repertory
group, outstanding among which were the excellent
Chicago Playwrights Theater Club, died for lack of support. Another such attempt is being launched in October
(1956) in the long-defunct Studebaker Theater, by Bernard Sahlins and Co. (good luck!). Opera came alive
with the Lyric Theater but—good old Chicago!—administrative squabbles are now threatening the whole
enterprise. The press is disgraceful—not because the individual newspapers are so bad; some of them compare
quite favorably with their counterparts in New York, e.g.,
the *Sun-Times* with the *Post*, but because none is excellent.

Criticism is atrocious, and a worse blight than any
slum. Music, dance, and drama get by, considering what
small call there is for discrimination and close judgment;
but books are butchered like pig meat in the *Tribune* and
Sun-Times—the only papers which run reviews (on Sun-
days). Anyone who wants to read competent reviewing
must consult the *New Yorker* or the *New York Times
Book Review*. The other magazines, with the exception
of mass circulators and the middle-class standbys such as
Harper's and the *Atlantic*, make little impression. No one
seems to read *Partisan Review* any more, and few of the

bookshops carry it. (*Commentary* is virtually by subscription only.) There has been some talk of starting a quality review, fortnightly or monthly, but nothing has as yet come of it. (Interested parties please get in touch with me.) *Poetry Magazine* continues to come out, leaning heavily on local endowment, but it makes rather small difference in the city's life.

The art world is kicking up a stir, locally, with the All-Chicago show at the Art Institute (recently concluded) drawing the usual derision from the press, and house-wives, patrons, and collectors putting in their tuppence: it ran, for some surprising reason, almost exclusively to abstract expressionism. Considerable quantity, mediocre quality.

In addition to the Institute shows, Chicago has two annual spring outdoor shows, one for the South Side painters, and one for the North Side. Here the styles are various, and run the whole range of modern painting but usually by way of clichés. Both shows are vastly superior to the Greenwich Village outdoor exhibit, but only because the better painters do not shun outdoor exhibits as they do in New York. The best painters, however, do; most of them are affiliated with Momentum, which runs its own exhibit. This is better than the outdoor stuff, but not by terribly much and my own feeling is that the paintings benefit from being hung indoors, away from the pitiless sun. The only painter of genuine merit with this group is, I think, Edith Smith.

In the last few years the feeling has been running high in Chicago that the town is waking up and beginning to produce. The clearest evidence, for the city as a whole, is in building. New office buildings and apartment houses are going up, and the newly completed skyscraper of the Prudential Insurance Company, at Randolph off the Lake, whatever its merits as architecture, stands in commitment on this score. It will take a lot more building, cleaning, sweeping, and improving to shake off the lethargy that has dogged Chicago for the last two decades. Chicago's new Mayor, Richard J. Daley, a Democratic machine man, has surprised everyone, and pleased most, by seeming to be wholeheartedly devoted to this task. Plans are being made to rescue the Near North and South Sides from blight and indignity by erecting administrative, civic, and art centers in these areas.

But the big job is not, of course, a work for mayors and city officials to accomplish. It is for the Chicagoans who do not run off, and for the small-towners who are drawn here to stay, to accomplish of their own volition and capacity. Above all, it is a matter of defending, preserving, and extending the precious crust of culture along the Lake; of overcoming its terrible disproportion to the rest of the city, and of watering the desert reaches of our industrial moon. We are forever at rivalry with New York, but our laudable ambition to outstrip New York (I suppose it is laudable) will get nowhere until we discover the principle of New York and of all great cities.

As I see it, this principle is very simple (but then, I am a *luftmensch*: with a thirst for water). It is to give the city something to lose. And this is done by producing without manufacturing, consuming without eating (or wearing or using), enjoying without belching, and finding the everlasting in the ephemeral things: not in iron, stone, brick, concrete, steel, and chrome, but in paper, ink, pigment, sound, voice, gesture, and graceful leaping, for it is of such things that the ultimate realities, of the mind and the heart, are made.

Commentary, June, 1957

THIS BOOK WAS SET IN

FAIRFIELD AND PERPETUA TYPES,

PRINTED, AND BOUND BY THE HADDON CRAFTSMEN.

DESIGN IS BY LARRY KAMP.